SERMONS

Also by Peter J. Gomes

The Good Book: Reading the Bible with Mind and Heart

SERMONS

Biblical Wisdom for Daily Living

❋

PETER J. GOMES

WILLIAM MORROW AND COMPANY, INC.

NEW YORK

Grateful acknowledgment is made for use of the following:

Page 224: Excerpt from "Little Gidding" in FOUR QUARTETS, copyright 1943 by T. S. Eliot and renewed 1971 by Esme Valerie Eliot. Reprinted by permission of Harcourt Brace & Company and Faber and Faber Limited.

Pages 227–228: Excerpt from "Choruses from The Rock" in COLLECTED POEMS 1909–1962, by T. S. Eliot; copyright 1936 by Harcourt Brace & Company; copyright © 1964, 1963 by T. S. Eliot. Reprinted by permission of Harcourt Brace & Company and Faber and Faber Limited.

Page 234: Excerpt from "For the Time Being: A Christmas Oratorio" in W. H. AUDEN: COLLECTED POEMS by W. H. Auden, edited by Edward Mendelson. Copyright © 1944 and renewed 1972 by W. H. Auden. Reprinted by permission of Random House, Inc., and Faber and Faber Limited.

Library of Congress Cataloging-in-Publication Data

Gomes, Peter J.
        Sermons : biblical wisdom for daily living / Peter J. Gomes.—
    1st ed.
            p.   cm.
        ISBN 0-688-15874-9
        1. Sermons, American.   I. Title.
    BV4253.G66   1998
    252'.061—dc21   97-50065   CIP

Printed in the United States of America

First Edition

1   2   3   4   5   6   7   8   9   10

BOOK DESIGN BY JESSICA SHATAN

www.williammorrow.com

TO

THE RIGHT REVEREND
JOHN KINGSMILL CAVELL,
M.A., CANTAB

Sometime Lord Bishop of Southampton
Honorary Fellow of The Pilgrim Society

OLDEST OF FRIENDS

*By his faithful example as Father in God
I have always been inspired and sustained.*

Foreword

For me he is a colleague, a member of the Board of Advisors of the
W. E. B. Du Bois Institute for Afro-American Research at Harvard University, a spiritual advisor, pastor, and trusted, revered friend. Born in
1942 in Boston, Massachusetts, The Reverend Professor Peter John
Gomes is an American Baptist minister ordained to the Christian ministry by the First Baptist Church of Plymouth. Widely regarded as one
of America's most distinguished preachers, since 1974 he has served as
Plummer Professor of Christian Morals and Pusey Minister in The
Memorial Church. He graduated in 1965 from Bates College with an
A.B. degree, and in 1968 from the Harvard Divinity School with the
degree of S.T.B.

Peter Gomes's teaching and research interests include the history of
the ancient Christian church, Elizabethan Puritanism, and homiletics,
three fields that come to bear upon his writings and his sermons. In 1996
he published *The Good Book: Reading the Bible with Mind and Heart*,
which immediately became a national bestseller; and previous to this

book, *Sermons: Biblical Wisdom for Daily Living,* he has published three other volumes of his sermons.

I vividly remember when I first met Peter Gomes, or rather, when I first saw him and heard him preach in his church. The occasion was a memorial service for the late Nathan I. Huggins, Professor and Chair of the Afro-American Studies Department at Harvard during the 1980s, who had died suddenly and much too young, and for this reason the memorial service was more somber and grave than usual. My sadness was assuaged somewhat, however, by my fascination with the minister performing the service. He was dressed in the garb of a High Church Anglican, his wit and his eloquence were sparkling and mellifluous, and all of this was contained in a slight brown frame. He was also, I was told later, a conservative Republican. I did not know exactly what to make of this curious figure, The Reverend Professor Peter J. Gomes, and when later I struggled to relate my impressions to my wife, Sharon Adams, the most apt analogy I could muster was that he was a cross between Cotton Mather and Martin Luther King, Jr. This man, clearly, was a man of words, but a man of words with a difference.

Let me confess that I don't think of church attendance as a regular part of my Sunday routine. Rather, church for me has long been something that my family and I "do" on Christmas Eve with my father at the Episcopal church in the center of Lexington, Massachusetts. I used to attend church regularly—maniacally, I suppose—first as a "saved" twelve-year-old in Piedmont, West Virginia, and then between the ages of fourteen and eighteen as a convert to the Episcopal church that my father had attended all of his life. During my freshman year of college I had burned out on church except to listen to an occasional sermon by William Sloane Coffin at the Battell Chapel during my undergraduate years at Yale. There God took a backseat in his sermons to the political turmoil of our times, such as the repression of the Black Panthers, or genocide in Southeast Asia. My attitude toward church remained the same, with a notable Christmas or Easter exception, until I came to Harvard seven years ago and, on that day of the memorial service, met Professor Gomes.

To my own astonishment I now attend The Memorial Church at Harvard whenever Peter preaches, where each week he delivers witty and urbane sermons to standing-room-only congregations representing the diversity of society itself. I love the timbre of his voice, an uncanny blend of high-toned old New England with the biblical cadence of the King James version of the Bible filtered through the black Baptist tradition. Peter's sermons do not so much address such large and vexed questions as the Virgin birth or an eternal afterlife as they do how thoughtful and intelligent people, determined to be citizens of a multicultural, cosmo-politan, secular world, maintain a sense of deep spirituality and social justice within a highly competitive, often brutally irrational and grossly unfair existence, where fragmentation and the dissociation of sensibility are the *sine qua non*, and where bad people profit and thrive and good people suffer, seemingly capriciously. How does one abide, how keep the faith, without throwing one's reason to the wind and embracing keepers of promises, evangelical zealots, or born-again literalists, for whom every searching query of the Bible is an act of bedeviled, heretical betrayal?

Peter Gomes is a man of conviction. His Christianity is inviting and open, thoughtful and challenging, and probing. It, and he, tend to leave the large imponderable conundrums of existence to God as he seeks to help each of us weary and wounded travelers simply to get on with our everyday lives as decent, feeling, reflective human beings for whom the good and the true, and genuine human compassion, manifest themselves only in the most mundane activities—going to work, falling in and out of love, raising families, maintaining friendships, and, when all is said and done, hoping most ardently that our lives and times will be remem-bered as having been honorable and admirable, and that we will be re-called as having been worthy of all of the rewards that life has given us. His work and his example have challenged both liberal and conservative stereotypes, enabling him to refine and embody a renewed definition of individuality, an individuality both Emersonian and, we might say, Gomesian.

At heart he is a teacher, and every page of Peter's monumental work, *The Good Book*, suggests a desire to teach. In a November 1996 *New Yorker* profile, he confesses that he wrote that book "out of dismay at our culture's wholesale ignorance of the Bible," and his hunger to unveil for a modern public the metaphorical language of the Bible in all of its elegant subtlety struck a deep chord. He argues against political or functional approaches to the sacred interpretation of sacred texts, coining the word *bibliolatry*, the act of using the Bible as a self-serving, political device for this pattern of misuse.

Both *The Good Book* and this book are written for any intelligent reader, and the author manages to speak to the broadest possible array of the reading public. In *Sermons* he has met head-on the challenge of opening the pages of the Bible and offering to contemporary readers a relevant and useful set of texts for their daily lives: in this book, as in *The Good Book*, he is determined to preach and affirm this mission in his speaking and in his writing.

While he represents the diversity and hybridity that characterize the postmodern condition of all human beings at the end of this millennium, what is unique about this author, teacher, writer, and professor is his simultaneous love of God and the ease and comfort with which he navigates among his various identities. This capacity brings to his listeners and readers a certain wisdom and perspective that they probably would not encounter elsewhere.

Peter Gomes continues to serve as the spiritual head of the Harvard community. The forty sermons that he has collected for this volume attest to the unity that words can forge among multifaceted congregations. With a profoundly lyrical sense of the pure rhythm of the ideal blend of language's form and content, with self-deprecating humor, and with a mastery of the telling, contemporary anecdote, all grounded in an astonishingly intimate familiarity with the texts of the Bible, his sermons on Sunday morning make for the very best show in town, which is why even cynical skeptics and agnostics like myself find the lure of his form of Christian religious belief so inviting, so profoundly humane, nurturing, worldly, and humanistic, yet so deeply, deeply spiritual. I would not miss a Sunday if I could help it. Readers of the sermons here collected can enjoy this experience leisurely, repetitively, for the effect produced by the immediacy of his rich voice translates marvelously to the page, in part because his sermons begin and end as well-crafted written texts. Reading them for the first time after having heard them delivered, I was struck by how carefully structured is their seemingly effortless flow.

As he asserted in the *New Yorker* interview, Peter Gomes believes that we are all members of Saint Augustine's City of God, "a reminder that we live in two cities simultaneously—one that is eternal and divine, and one in which we merely have to get along." In the same way he demands that we separate our religious beliefs from our politics, noting that we always live in at least two separate realms of being and of thought. He practices what he preaches. The committed life, according to him, is not about policing the boundaries but about breaking those boundaries down and acknowledging the fluid and interactive nature of all our identities. By word and by example he attests that there is not only one way of being, and that the more strongly one nurtures a sense of the contingent nature of all identities, the less likely it is that one will be harmed by them, or in their name inflict harm upon others. Nowhere is that message rendered more eloquently than in this compelling book of sermons. Peter John Gomes is that rarest sort of preacher: a great orator who writes as compellingly as he speaks.

—HENRY LOUIS GATES, JR.

Contents

Foreword   **vii**

Introduction   **xv**

Part One: Seasons   *1*

Advent I: The Art of Impatient Living   **3**

Advent II: Hail, Mary, Full of Grace   **9**

Advent III: Humbug and the Christian Hope   **16**

Christmas Day: The House of Bread   **22**

New Year's Day: Beginning Where We Left Off   **26**

Epiphany I: Baptism   **30**

Epiphany II: Growing Up   **37**

Martin Luther King, Jr., Day: The Ambiguity of Heroes   **42**

Lent I: An Opportune Time   **50**

Lent II: Riches   **55**

Lent III: When Too Much Is Not Enough   **62**

Palm Sunday: Beyond Tragedy   **68**

Easter: When Life Begins   **73**

Eastertide I: Life on the Other Side   **79**

Eastertide II: Ordinary People   **86**

Ascension: The Absent and the Present Christ   92

Pentecost: The Gift of Understanding   98

Trinity: The Big Picture   102

Part Two: Themes   *107*

Patriotism: The Purpose of Freedom   109

Happiness: The Beatitudes   114

Identity: Identity Crisis   120

Negotiation: Getting to Yes   126

Parables: The Kindness of Strangers   132

Miracles: What's in a Miracle? Feeding the Five Thousand   139

Friendships: Friendships and Relationships   143

Sisters: Mary and Martha   148

Frustration: The View from Pisgah   154

Depression: The Question at the Mouth of the Cave   159

Opportunity: Redeeming the Time   164

Communion: Acts of Reconciliation   170

Love: Acts of God   175

Perfection: The Trouble with Perfection   180

Wisdom: Wisdom and the Wise   185

Death: In the Midst of Life . . .   192

Stewardship: Time, Talent, and Treasure   198

The Bible: The Bible and the Believer   205

Behavior: Get Out of the Way   211

Mystery: The Mystery of Our Religion   217

Remembrance: The Fellowship of the Incomplete   225

Thanksgiving: Redeeming the Familiar   231

Introduction

The sermons in this collection represent the harvest of many years of preaching to congregations in The Memorial Church of Harvard University. Framed by the seasons of the liturgical year and the themes for the practical, daily living of the spiritual life, they are all drawn from the wisdom of the Bible.

While the Bible continues to hold an honored, even a ubiquitous, place in the life of busy, modern believers, it is at the same time an elusive and demanding book, and preachers no longer may assume that the Bible is as familiar a part of our common cultural discourse as it once was. Thus, responsible biblical preaching begins with the assumption that the listeners are hearing a message for the first time, and that while they are willing to listen they must be equipped by the preacher in the course of the preaching experience to find the text where it is, and to be taken by the text to where they are. The great paradox of biblical preaching is that while we do not live in a biblical world, and in fact we dwell in a culture far removed from many of its assumptions, the essential word and wisdom of the biblical experience both survives and transcends our world. It is the preacher's task and the function of the sermon to make this clear. When we discover this for ourselves we have what preachers call an "Aha!" experience, and we discover also to our great joy and delight that the Bible lives, and that it not only "spoke" then but that it "speaks" now.

In order for this to happen, however, a transaction must take place, and the preacher and the listener must together enter into the text in order that the text may enter into their hearts, their minds, and their world. The preacher cannot manage this alone or on his or her own, for no matter how able, articulate, or charismatic the preacher may be, preaching works only if the listener together with the preacher enters into the process of the sermon. It is thus a cooperative venture rather than one of performer and observer. For this reason many preachers decline to have their sermons presented in the cold form of print, arguing quite convincingly that preaching as an oral experience depends upon the physical chemistry between speaking and listening. If sermons are to be written at all, they say, they should be written in order that they may be better heard, and they argue that preaching is an exercise for the ear and not for the eye, and a sermon not a well-crafted essay designed for the eye alone but closer in style to the oral tradition of the ancients. I accept this, and insist upon "ear" rather than "eye" preaching for my students, many of whom think that a sermon is merely a well-read composition.

The sermons in this collection, then, were intended to be heard, and were written with the ear and the heart in mind rather than with an ultimate destination of publication. Readers of the sermons will therefore have a somewhat different experience from those who heard them initially from the pulpit: a different experience, that is, but neither better nor worse. The reader, for example, can read at his or her own pace and not necessarily at that of the preacher, and can pause and ponder, peruse the biblical text at leisure, and integrate the reading with other current intellectual and spiritual exercises. The reader of a sermon, in a strange reversal of conventional wisdom, actually enjoys the possibility of a more intimate relationship with the preacher than the listener in the congregation present at the sermon's preaching, largely because it is the reader and not the preacher who controls the interaction with the discourse. Perhaps a comparison could be made between a viewer's relationship with a movie seen in a theater and a videotape of that same movie seen within the privacy of his home. No one would substitute the one for the other but would agree that each is a distinctive and useful aesthetic experience. What the videotape lacks of the immediacy of the big screen experience is more than compensated for by the opportunity it affords the home viewer for further review and contemplation.

Thus, while not apologizing for the oral nature of these sermons, I invite the reader to receive them as words that take on a new form of life in the intimacy of the reader's own world, rather than simply as a reprise of things once said in church. I invite the thoughtful reader to take up the sermons in connection with a reading of the given biblical lessons so that the sermon's context might be better understood; and the adventurous reader might wish to read the biblical materials in several English translations rather than rely exclusively on the translation familiar and cherished in his own tradition. The variety of English translations available today is both astonishing and stimulating, and all to the reader's gain.

A word should be said about this collection comprised of forty sermons. In addition to the fact that Harvard University's academic year consists of nearly forty Sundays, in the Bible "forty" is a number with powerful significance. For forty days the children of Israel wandered in the wilderness; for forty days it rained in the great flood; Jesus spent forty days fasting in the wilderness before he began his public ministry; and in Hebrew usage, forty as a round number was used often to express maturity and fullness of time. Forty is a comprehensive sum, and these forty sermons are selected with that numerical sensibility in mind. Given over a number of years, they represent a significant period in which both preacher and listener have come to some maturity. I offer these words from a long ministry in one church in the sincere hope that through them, in ways unknown and unimagined by me, a wider audience may know, as Saint John wrote, "the word become flesh, dwelling among us, full of grace and truth."

I dedicate this collection not to a member of my congregation or to one who has heard much of my preaching, but to one whose life, example, and friendship have had an enormous impact upon my own life and work. I first met John Cavell and his late wife, Mary, when as a young man I welcomed them in 1970 to Plymouth, Massachusetts, as part of the Mayflower celebrations of that year. John Cavell was then Vicar of St. Andrew's Church in Plymouth, Devon, the church whose members had shown the Pilgrims their last bit of English hospitality in that port city from which those willing exiles had departed for the New World. In the years following 1970, John Cavell and I have maintained a splendid friendship through his translation to Winchester Diocese as Suffragan Bishop of Southampton and his retirement to Salisbury, where he continues to serve as a very lively Assistant Bishop of that great diocese. I associate all that is great and good in the traditions of the Church of England with John Cavell; he honors me by allowing me to honor him in this small way.

In the preparation of this work, as in every written word of mine, I acknowledge with affectionate gratitude the extraordinarily skilled editorial services of Cynthia Wight Rossano, who has both an eye and an ear for the text, of which I have taken shameless and happy advantage. The volume has its origins in a suggestion made many years ago by my parishioner, colleague, and friend Professor Derrick A. Bell, Jr. I hope that it will give him some pleasure to see that at last I have taken his advice. I should also express a retrospective word of gratitude to those countless members and friends of Harvard University who over many years have been the first hearers of these words. No preacher could ask for more conscientious, critical, or committed congregations, and I thank them; and I thank God, to whom be all the glory.

—PETER J. GOMES
Sparks House
Cambridge, Massachusetts
All Saints' Day, November 1, 1997

Part One

SEASONS

❀

The Art of Impatient Living

❖

Text: Be patient, therefore, brethren, until the coming of the
Lord. *James 5:7*

I am going to ask you to do a very difficult thing, and that is to forget
all the seasonal trappings that surround you and seduce you into thinking
that Advent has anything at all to do with Christmas as you and I understand it; I wish that there was a way that I could make this all disappear. I want you to clear away all of the "let's get ready for Christmas"
stuff, all of this manufactured cheer and happy expectation of something
that once happened; clear the decks, rather, and get ready for something
that has not yet happened, for that is the agenda of the entire season of
Advent.

Having asked you to do that, now I ask you to think about an extraordinary set of verses from the Epistle of James: "Be patient, therefore,
brethren, until the coming of the Lord. . . ." The Lord is coming, not in
retrospect, not in a rehearsal of things that happened once long ago. The

Lord is coming in a way and in a form that we have not yet experienced. We wait for that which we have not yet seen. We work for that which has not yet been accomplished. That is the Advent agenda, and it is so often thrown off course by Christmas as simply a recollection of something that happened long ago and far away. The world is welcome to Christmas; we Christians hardly have any claim on it at all anymore; but Advent and its expectations, its call for patience, its earnest waiting— that belongs to us, and how we reconcile the patience of Advent with the impatience of human, modern living is the problem and the opportunity of the moment.

Now one of the reasons that the Bible and the Christian faith lack credibility to most of us, one of the reasons that they are both unbelievable and uncompelling, is that they ask us to do things that are manifestly undoable. They ask us to believe things that, if not believable or true, are at least unlikely. One of the reasons that the Advent season is manifestly an unsatisfactory season for Christians is that it, too, is based on assumptions too difficult to accept, expectations too unreal to contemplate, a phantom of truths that do not conform with the facts.

We know what we are meant to believe; the lessons tell us, the prayers tell us, the hymns are full of it. Light over darkness, hope over despair, gentleness and meekness over might and power—these are all the clichés of Advent. We know that Advent is not meant to be merely a retrospective of things past but an anticipation of things to come. Advent is not Christmas but judgment, not cheap synthetic joy but divine and ultimate justice, and we know that as well.

Somehow we hope that the church will be that place where our impossible expectations and our manifest needs are met and reconciled. That is presumably why we keep coming week after week and year after year. We *know* that Jesus says that the meek shall inherit the earth but we do not believe that that is likely, or likely in any reasonable time. We know that we are to forgive those who have hurt us, but we also know that except in rare and wonderful circumstances it is very difficult to bring ourselves to do it. Today in James's epistle we hear that we are to be patient unto the coming of the Lord—yet one more case of a faith that is too good to be true, of human aspirations flying in the face of human nature.

It is not our nature to be patient. I know this, for I am among the most impatient of people. Patience, some would say, like modesty, belongs to those who need it, and most people who need patience are people who have not yet succeeded in their ambition or their enterprise, people who have not yet achieved, either by their own standards or by our standards. In other words, patience is for failures, for losers, for wimps, for those who have to take the long view because they cannot succeed in the short run. Notice that it is always the achiever who tells the less-than-achieved to be patient, and how patronizing and silly it sounds. First it sounds patronizing and silly to the one who wants to succeed and who has not, and to whom the counsel of patience is discouraging. All piano students, for example, and all beginning athletes know this. Someone who is wonderfully adept at the piano says, "Oh, be patient. It will come." You don't believe it, and it is not a counsel of encouragement, it is a counsel of discouragement; and to the one who is not interested in achieving the skills in the first place, a counsel of patience is a further irritant and hardly a stimulus. All bad students of mathematics and arithmetic, for example, and all bad students in Hebrew, in Greek, in Latin, and in French know this. If you don't care, and you're not good, and someone tells you to be patient, that is an insult and an irritant.

Patience implies passivity, and we wish not to be passive, we wish not merely to be spectators at somebody else's spectacle of achievement. We want to do what it takes to get things done. We want the more agreeable counsel of James earlier in his epistle where he says, "Be ye doers of the word and not hearers only." That we can understand, for practical, sensible, questioning Christians like ourselves want always to know what we can *do*. We don't want to hear what we must endure or bear or suffer through. We don't want to be told to wait. We want to get on with it, whether it is worth getting on with or not.

We are not given to waiting. We are not willing to accept the principle that James offers: "Behold, we call those happy who were steadfast." We know that no one gets anywhere by being patient. "Be patient, therefore, brethren, until the coming of the Lord. Behold, the farmer waits for the precious fruit of the earth, being patient over it until it receives the early and the late rain. You also be patient." Rural, bucolic advice for others but not for sensible urbanites such as ourselves.

My father was a farmer, and he raised that most rare and exotic crop peculiar to New England, cranberries, a tough and exotic piece of fruit not given to easy entreaty or easy growth. Cultivation of the cranberry is a very delicate and demanding art, for it is as difficult to raise as it is tart to taste, which moral tale was early implanted upon me, this son of a cranberry grower. I watched my father at work all of his life, indeed, to nearly the very day of his death, working the ground; and whenever I think of my father I think of this text from James about the farmer patiently waiting for the early and the late rains, and when I read that text in James, I invariably think of my father. Whenever I do this remembering I am reminded that while patience is the essence of farming, the farmer is anything but a passive participant in the process. The farmer is not passive. To farm is to live all of one's hours in and for one's work. Bankers, lawyers, teachers, generals, engineers, and academics know nothing of what real vocational commitment is, but the farmer eats, sleeps, and drinks every day that process of activity and of patience.

One day when we were in the garden and I a young fellow, I told my father that I thought I wanted to go into the ministry. He looked at me, and he said, without changing any one of his attitudes toward his hoeing, "I always hoped that my son would do honest work." I knew what he meant. The farmer lives in proximity to two ultimate truths, which are held in balance by the authority of his own experience. Ultimate truth number one is that the harvest is the result of incredible patience; and ultimate truth number two is that the harvest is the result of incredible work. Yes, he waits and hopes for the autumn and the spring rains, and there is nothing that he can do to induce them. That is where patience comes in. That is where relying on forces beyond one's control comes in. In that season of waiting, however, he is hardly idle, for the farmer does all the work that can and must be done, knowing that time and God alone will bring to fruition what he expects and assists. I have never known an idle farmer who was a good farmer. It is constant work, but the work is full of expectation and fueled by labor and experience. The farmer knows that what is expected is worth waiting for. The farmer also knows that what is worth waiting for is also worth working for, and that is why the farmer is commended by James in this most practical of epistles. James is not writing to farmers, he is writing to a fairly sophisticated audience of people like ourselves who, in having lost the use of their hands in the fields, are now held hostage to the fantasies and disappointments of their minds.

Now, aside from the useful counsel of patience in the face of our natural and reasonable impatience, what is it for which we are encouraged to wait? What is the harvest toward which we promise the incredible energy of our impatience? Well, hold on to your seats, for it is nothing less than the coming again in glory of Jesus Christ! That is what we wait for, the return of the Lord, and not as a tiny baby or as an idea mugged by a gang of angry facts and circumstances, but as the fruition of the divine plan and human hope; and in the second time round it will be got right. The second coming of Jesus is rarely phrased in terms of births and babies and attendant angels; it is almost invariably phrased in terms of ideas that have been translated into ideals, and ideals that are translated into reality. The second coming of Jesus is accompanied by truth triumphant over mere fact, by justice and righteousness and mercy triumphant over a mere accommodation with present circumstances, of joy triumphant over mere pleasure, of peace triumphant over the mere absence of overt hostility.

There is no point in waiting for a return of something that never was. There is no hope in history, no age, no season to which we could return when everything would be fine. There is no place where it works. In essence, there is no place better than where we are right now, and where we are right now doesn't work. So the only place where we can invest, where there is a harvest worth aspiring to, is in the future, and it is given flesh and blood and bone and purpose in the form of Jesus Christ. We look forward to a new heaven and a new earth in which the promise of the creation is to be fulfilled.

This is the language of Advent, and you can understand in some measure why the world is quite content to leave it to us. It is ours without claim or competition, for one cannot make a growth industry out of Advent expectations. This is not merely a "waiting around for something interesting to happen," but, as with the farmer, a working for that for which we wait. That is what, for Christians, the art of impatient living is all about: working well for that for which we wait. Waiting alone will not do. Working for the sake of keeping out of mischief and keeping busy will not do. Working well for that for which we wait, that is the essence of our peculiar Advent hope.

If you want an example of the pattern of which I speak, look not to yourselves nor even to your neighbors, but look to God. Look at God, who is the personification of patience itself; God, who does not give up on the creation although there is plenty of opportunity and reason to do so; God, who does not give up on his creatures; God, who will not throw away the opportunity for redemption until you and I are in fact ready to be the harvest of God. The patience of God, not of Job, is what it takes to turn our impatience from action in the absence of hope to hopeful, hope-filled action in anticipation of hope. Advent hope is not an invitation to easy, silly optimism, nor an invitation to mindless despair or hope held hostage to experience. The only hope worth having and the only harvest worth waiting for is the ultimate confidence which translates the energy of impatience into the art of expectant living in the here and now, of which the farmer is the model.

> Be patient, therefore . . . until the coming of the Lord. Behold, the farmer waits for the precious fruit of the earth, being patient over it until it receives the early and the late rain. You also be patient . . . for the coming of the Lord is at hand.

Hail, Mary, Full of Grace

❖

Text: And Mary said, "Behold, I am the handmaid of the Lord; let it
   be to me according to your word."   *Luke 1:38*

You will doubtless recognize the title of my sermon as the opening words
of the most famous and widely used form of Roman Catholic devotion,
the "Hail, Mary" or "Ave Maria." "Hail Mary, full of grace, the Lord is
with Thee. Blessed art thou among women, and blessed is the fruit of
thy womb, Jesus." We have heard it on the radio at the noon hour; we
hear it as the last words of faithful Catholics before their deaths; we
know it as the inspiration of music and poetry; and we doubtless never
expected to hear a sermon on it in The Memorial Church, for familiar
as the words are, and as universal as is our respect and even affection
for Mary, we children of the Reformation simply do not know what to
do with Mary.

   The story is told that when Dean William Ralph Inge, the late
"gloomy dean" of St. Paul's Cathedral in London, died and was ushered

into the presence of God, Jesus came down from God's right hand and said, "Ah, Mr. Dean, welcome to heaven; I know you have met my Father, but I don't believe you have met my Mother." Who is this woman, we might ask, and why are they making such a fuss over her? Part of our problem with Mary is, I suspect, that we know her to be a woman, and we believe her to be a Catholic, and even in these enlightened days far removed from the intolerance of an earlier time, such an identity creates a problem for us Protestants. Yet it is impossible to consider the advent of our Lord and the will of God in that advent without considering this woman who becomes for us the means of the new creation. We are not certain what to do with her but the question is wrongly put, for it is not so much what we are to do with Mary as it is what God does with Mary. How is she used as an instrument of his purpose?

Someone has said that the angel Gabriel has a lot to answer for, for it is he who interrupts what we might imagine to be the ordinary routine of the life of this young woman about to be married to a carpenter of Nazareth. It is clear that his visit to her was neither anticipated nor particularly welcomed: "But she was greatly troubled at the saying, and considered in her mind what sort of greeting this might be." So much troubled was she that reassurances were needed, and the angel said to her, "Be not afraid, Mary, for you have found favor with God."

It is not an easy thing to be confronted with a message from God. We pray that God will hear our prayers and draw near to us; we pray with ease, and some of us with frequency, but perhaps we pray with such ease and relative frequency because we do not expect any response. Good and faithful people have got along quite well enough with God where he ought to be; the trouble begins when God begins to have more than his usual distant commerce with us. The summons to Mary, for that is what it was, was no different from the summons to Moses, Abraham, Isaiah, and Jeremiah. They all found themselves surprised by the call of God; they all found themselves annoyed, not so much at their own unworthiness for such a high calling, for that would came later, but annoyed at the more practical level of inconvenience. Moses, Abraham, Isaiah, Jeremiah, and Mary, especially Mary, all had other things to do, important, urgent things, the fulfillment of their own destinies, the carrying forth of their own lives, choices, options, and challenges. Mary joins the line of unwilling and troubled prophets for whom God's call is an unsolicited interruption of the routine: "She was greatly troubled at the saying, and considered in her mind what sort of greeting this might be."

"Why me?" "Why now?" "Why Mary?" What had she done to deserve this distinction? Is there some particular virtue or worthy quality in her life that commends her to the attention of God? The angel says simply, "Hail, O favored one" or, as the Authorized Version has it, "Hail, thou that art highly favored." The salutation tells the tale: "Hail, Mary, full of grace," for the angel means to say to her that she is chosen not because of her special grace and quality but rather that she is full of grace and filled with favor because she is chosen by the will of God. God does not choose us to fulfill his purposes because we are worthy of such a choice, or because we are good enough to do what he wishes; we have not won some prize competition, or passed a Rhodes scholarship final interview, as it were. No. God chooses for reasons known only to him, and it is the choice that confers the favor. When God chooses you, you are chosen. Just as there was no particular reason for God to choose Israel as his peculiar people, there was no reason, at least known to us, to choose Mary as the mother of Jesus.

We waste our time in seeking out the special hidden, secret qualities that commend God's choices to him; to be God means never having to explain why. It is the exercise of the power, what the theologians call the sovereignty of God, that allows God to choose what is lowly, ordinary, and of no apparent account to be used for his purposes. Any god can make something good out of the exceptional and the extraordinary. It is our God who makes out of nothing, something; who takes nowhere and makes it somewhere; who takes nobody and makes him somebody, and it is this power of transformation that made prophets of the ordinary men of Israel. It is this power of transformation that made apostles and martyrs of the ordinary followers of Jesus; it is this power of God that makes things that are out of things that are not; and it is this power of God, moving in ways unknown yet not unseen, that confers upon the simple woman of Nazareth the grace sufficient to her new task as the mother of a new creation. God does not choose for grace, but when God chooses, grace surely follows. Thus, when the angel greeted Mary, he greeted her not simply as who she was but rather as one whom she herself did not yet fully recognize: the favored me, the chosen one, she who is to be full of grace. The salutation is one not simply of recognition, "Mary," but of anticipation as well, "full of grace."

If Winston Churchill didn't say it, he should have: "Modesty is for those who need it." Mary was modest in the face of this greeting, for she knew herself unlikely in her own right to be worthy of telegrams from God. Was this strange new role to be some sort of punishment for something she had or hadn't done, a virginal sacrifice not unknown in the pagan world? If it was to be a reward, then, for what? She knew that she seemed insufficient for the ordinary demands of her modest life, so how could it be that heavenly things were in store for her? It is the angel who says simply to her, "You have found favor with God." *Favor* in this sense means not simply "notice" or "positive attention," but "enablement." God will enable you, he will make it possible for you to fulfill what he desires, for that is what grace is: the capacity to will and to do what God will have us do. To be "full of grace" is to be both disposed to the will of God and enabled to perform that will. Such a grace is never earned, never prepared for, it is always the gift—the unmerited and frequently unexpected gift—of God: "Hail, Mary," gifted and enabled one.

In the course of this interview in Saint Luke we have three clues to Mary's reaction. Her first reaction is one of puzzlement and annoyance at the strange salutation of the angel: "What can this mean?" Her words are not recorded but her reaction is. The second time she reacts to the angel's news that she will bear a son, she asks, "How can this be, since I have no husband?" She is a practical, respectable girl, and while probably still troubled and anxious about the speech she hears from the angel, she has, in addition to her consternation, time for a practical question. She knows her own limitations, she knows what can and cannot be done, she is not unaware of the realities of life. Even in Nazareth the stork did not deliver babies, and so how was all of this to be accomplished? There is, I suspect, as much irony as naïveté in that question,

and it always seems to be the women of the Bible who put lofty promises into human perspective. After all, was it not Sarah who laughed
when God told her that she was to be the mother of nations? The angel
replies to Mary that the God who could call her out of all the women
of the earth, the God who could give fruit to Sarah's barren womb, and
the God who could do the same for her own cousin Elizabeth, this same
God could be trusted to fulfill what he has promised, for God can do
what God wills to do. To doubt self is one thing, to doubt God is quite
another. Mary is reminded in this little colloquy that her limitations
must not be imposed upon God, for with God all things are possible.

So, she concludes the interview with the words of our text, "Behold,
I am the handmaiden of the Lord; let it be to me according to your
word." On these lines rest so much of our understanding of and our
difficulty with Mary. Indeed, she submits to the will of God, she offers
herself to fulfill a purpose that is not her own; and there are many more
now than in former times who see in this the resignation of Mary and
the subjugation of all womanhood. She does not struggle, she does not
argue; she does as she is told. Eve's adventurous and dangerous spirit in
Eden is overcome by Mary's quiet and obedient spirit in Galilee. What
Eve lost, Mary won; and that has been the historic teaching of the church
from the patristic age onward. There is a strong set of feminine symbols
in the Bible and in Christian history, but the more interesting ones are
overcome by the less interesting ones, with, we are told, disastrous consequences for both women and men. The medieval cult of Mary has
been replaced in the affections of many by the modern cult of Eve.
Modern feminists criticize the church's exaltation of Mary, for they believe that it exalts those qualities of quiet submission and obedience
that they themselves see as so negative and destructive of the spirit of
women and the true teachings of the church. Strange to say, I am sympathetic to this criticism, for it does indeed suggest that a mindless
obedience and submission to a powerful will is all that it takes for faithfulness in the church, and it would appear to make of passivity a virtue.

I am not persuaded, however, that Mary's obedience to the will of
God is any more demeaning than Christ's obedience to the will of God
in the Garden, when he says, "Not my will, but thine be done." Is it too

paradoxical to say in this case that there is strength in submission? We cannot pretend to know Mary's thoughts, which are, in fact, irrelevant. What is of importance here is Mary's action, and of even more importance, God's action. The power that God has now given her she takes to do and to be what God would have her do and become. She affirms the promise that is within her, and that is no more "submissive," in the pejorative sense, than it is for Bach to write the music that he was given to write, for Rembrandt to paint with the gift that was given to him, or for Mother Teresa to do the work she was called to do. Most of us, especially young people nearing the end of their college days, yearn for a sign of what our gift is, what our destiny is to be: "What are you going to do next year?" is that familiar and dangerous question that we all know. "I wish I knew," is more and more the sad answer. Oh, what we would give for a clue as to what God's will is for us, and what we would do if we knew clearly what our gift was and how we would use it. It is not resignation, not dumb, blind submission to fulfill your destiny; it is the grace of God that allows you to do so, the wonderful gift of knowing your place in the universe, and of fulfilling it. Mary was a free woman because in the source of that strange and cosmic conversation with God's ambassador she discovered who she was, what her destiny was to be, and how she would fulfill it. It was the triumph of the divine vocation within her, not defeat but victory, not submission and resignation but willingness to discover how God could and would use her life in fulfillment of the divine plan of which she was so vital a part. Mary did more than sit there! She did something. She became what she was meant to be: the gifted one of God.

Her story goes on from there. Art Historian Dr. Julia Phelps once described the three statues of Mary in Harvard's Busch Reisinger Museum, which represent the medieval church's view of Mary. The first shows her as the young child-mother of a bouncing baby boy, she still with braids, the sign of youthful virginity; then she is shown as the grieving old woman with the broken body of her son across her knees beneath the cross, the famous *Pietà*; and third, she stands in regal splendor as *Regina Coeli*, the Queen of Heaven and the embodiment of the church. The one who first received the grace of God becomes the means whereby the grace of God is made flesh in the world. She is for us the means of the incarnation, not an accident of history but the human expression of God's willing choice of our race. So this woman, this gifted one, this bearer of God's grace, belongs not alone to medieval adoration, not simply to the Roman Church or to orthodoxy. We dare not confine her to a passive role in the annual Christmas display, nor leave her to the curious gaze of the secular in the Busch Reisinger Museum, for in her call from God and her response to that call, she becomes the mother not only of Jesus but of our vocation, and of our calling as well. She shows us that it is possible for us to be gifted ones with her, the bearers of Christ in our world, and that in us as in her, God's will is made manifest. Such an opportunity and so great a gift we dare not deny. She deserves her titles, her monuments, and her place not because of what we do with her and because of what she does for us, but because of what God has done in her for us.

Hail, Mary, full of grace, the Lord is with thee; blessed art thou among women, and blessed is the fruit of thy womb, Jesus.

Humbug and the Christian Hope

❖

Text: But, since we belong to the day, let us be sober, and put on the breastplate of faith and love, and for a helmet the hope of salvation.   *I Thessalonians 5:8*

There are many people of my acquaintance who take a particular Pickwickian delight in the use of that wonderfully expressive Pickwickian word *humbug*, at this particular season of the year. The word has no precise meaning, no artful etymology from an ancient and respectable language, but it is clear, concise, and forceful when put to hard use. Humbug. Little children like the sound of it; it is expressive, image-making, producing a picture of Ebenezer Scrooge, who to most right-thinking children is a far more attractive and even persuasive character than the insipid little Tiny Tim, and perhaps he is so because of his use of that wonderfully evocative word *humbug*.

We thrive on definitions in this scholarly community. What is humbug? Charles Dickens, who spends pages on descriptions, doesn't waste

time with definitions; he lets his pictures do the talking. Perhaps humbug is to be defined as the late Justice Potter Stewart once defined
obscenity. He couldn't define it, he said, but he knew it when he saw it.
In our heart of hearts I think this is so of humbug and of us particularly
at this season of the year, and that is why we so often find ourselves
trapped in an emotional pressure cooker. We are, for example, surrounded by the signs of good cheer. Lights twinkle overhead, the shops
are filled with the apparatus of happiness and commercial joy. Last week
overflowed and the week to come will overflow with all sorts of organized
effort to make us feel good, do good, and spend money. There are more
concerts, more dinners, more parties, especially of that particularly odi-
ous kind known as the office or staff Christmas party, more efforts to
extend ourselves and be extended, more motion and energy expended
than at any other point in the whole year. Eventually even the most
cynical of us will be caught up in it all if only for a moment, and we
will have a twinge of guilt, also perhaps only for a moment, when in the
midst of it our feelings are not those of comfort and joy but of a dutiful
sense that it must be done in order to be done with.

    How easy it is under such circumstances, normal for this season of
the year, simply to say "humbug," and get on with it, knowing that we
are most unlikely to be rescued by the spirits of Christmas past, present,
or future, from our despair and guilt. We are made to feel that we ought
to be happy, that anyone who isn't happy at this time of year is truly
miserable, and that the signs of cheer and good fellowship are signs that
things are better than they are. We know better, however, and the conflict between what we know and what we feel we ought to feel is that
deadliest of conditions which we then confront with a combination of
nostalgia, cynicism, and alcohol. We compound our problem by mixing
this all up with the church of Jesus Christ and the Christian faith, thinking somehow that a whiff of incense on Christmas Eve or the invocation
of the manger scene with its pious simplicities will somehow make it all
right. Of all the humbugs about, this one is the most grievous. The
Christian faith is *not* the sugar-coated pill we swallow at Christmas to
make us feel better and the world look better. Indeed, the church has a
medicine for this condition, a cure and corrective for this acute case of

humbug; it comes in the form of this Holy Season of Advent and in the substance of what is called the Christian Hope.

Saint Paul, in his famous thirteenth chapter of the first letter to the Corinthians, gives us that wonderful trinity of virtues, faith, hope, and love, of which he says the greatest of these is love. In his earlier letter to the Thessalonians, however, the one from which our text is taken on this Third Sunday of Advent, he places those qualities in a different order, giving the place of honor to hope. Faith, love, and hope, faith, hope, and charity; they are always seen together, the trinity of the Christian graces, but if we were to divide them up according to the emphasis of the church year, while we would assign love to Lent and faith to the great season of Pentecost, hope remains as the imperishable theme of Advent, the season of waiting and anticipation, for it is hope and hope alone that gives meaning and purpose to waiting; it is hope that rises above the seemingly insurmountable claims of reality; it is hope that rescues us from despair, even from fear.

Such is the hope of Abraham, of whom it is said in Romans that against hope he believed in hope that he might become the father of many nations. We are given an even more vivid picture with which to contend when in the prophecy of Zechariah we are told, "Turn you to the strong hold, ye prisoners of hope," and that is what we are, we Advent Christians, "prisoners of hope," captured and captivated by it. Without hope our freedom and our power are useless. Without hope such faith as we have is in vain. Without hope our love has no meaning and no purpose. For Zechariah, to be a "prisoner of hope" suggests a passivity which Saint Paul corrects when he, in typical confrontational imagery, sees hope as a helmet of salvation, a protection in the war against sin, the flesh, and the devil. Hope for Paul is not passive, it is militant. Hope energizes us for the conflict not only with those evil forces of darkness but for the conflict with and within ourselves.

What is this hope all about? What do we hope for? Paul, in another passage, reminds us that we do not hope for that which we see, for what we see is not to be imagined or anticipated. We see it, it is here, we know it, and we know that it is not good enough, no matter how good it may be. The Christian hope is not simply wishful thinking, nor is it simply the hope for peace, for justice, or for joy. Hope moves between the illusions of our own present stability and the reality of things that are not yet come. For Paul hope is not a passive enterprise fit only for the very young and the very old; it is, rather, an attitude and an activity, one that sustains and animates at the same time. Hope such as this for the Advent Christian is found only in Jesus Christ. Our hope is not that reason will overcome silliness, or that somehow good things will come out of bad; our hope is not in our own capacity to do right in the face of wrong and neither is it grounded in the wish to escape the consequences of our own folly.

The Christian hope is not grounded in the ultimate conquest of one philosophical or even theological system over another. The Christian hope, expressed most vividly at Advent, is grounded in the reality that the Jesus who came once in weakness and in meekness will come again in great glory, in judgment, justice, and power, to redeem the world, to save it from itself. The Christian hope is an exercise in what we call "eschatology" in the Divinity School, a word that is translated for the purposes of our work today as confidence in God's future; that's what the Christian hope is, confidence in God's future. Note that it is not confidence in our future, but rather confidence in God's future; and that is the glorious paradox of Advent, that as we look forward to the return of the past, the rekindling of the lights that lead to Bethlehem, we look forward also to that which has not yet been, the lights that lead to the eternal victory we shall share in Jesus Christ.

Paul's hearers always have a hard time with his view of the future. The church to which he wrote in Thessalonica was filled with anxiety and speculation about the day when the Lord would come again and set everything to rights. Would it be soon or late? How would we know? Would it be in our time? Was it really going to happen? If it hadn't happened yet, could it happen at all? We know those questions not from textual study but from our own experience and anxiety. We know, you and I, that we are supposed to believe in the future as the place of God's work. We doubt that God is any more available "there" than he is "here." The future is reduced to some Woody Allen–like aphorism: "I have seen the future and it is very much like the present, only longer."

For some that is a comfort, for most it is a curse, for it is not sufficient to say that there is a future, courageous as that might be in the face of our capacity to destroy ourselves at one fell swoop. The courageous thing, the faithful, indeed the hopeful, thing, is to say that there is a future worth waiting for, worth living and working for, worth praying and dying for, and worth hoping for, for in that future is not more of the same but that of which we have not had enough—God.

At Advent we celebrate the basis of our hope in the future, our con-fidence in the utter reality of what is to be, by giving focus to the reality that was and is, the presence in our flesh and in our world of God in Christ, the divine made human, the God who becomes man in the form of Jesus Christ, that all creation might be made holy. The truth of Ad-vent is not simply that what once was might be again; the truth of Advent is that what was is and is to be, and is to be in such a way that we are able now to live and flourish and contend in the anticipated light of its coming. We are able to bear this present darkness because we believe in the coming dawn, a dawn that is not simply like the night, only longer, but a dawn in which the shadows and shades of night are seen for what they are and are not, and we will be able to tell the difference between hope and humbug.

Who of us is content to settle for anything less than that? How tire-some and tedious is the world of shame and fashion; how hard it is to go on day after day pretending that we are having a good time, that what we see is what there really is, that what we are is what we hope to be. If we believe our own press clippings, we would believe ourselves to be always in control, on top of every situation, confident in our capacity to cope, indifferent to any claims other than those of self-satisfaction and indulgence. We speak so glibly of freedom, our liberation, we call it, from all of the taboos, claims, and demands of an earlier, perhaps less agreeable and more demanding time, and truly we are more free than ever before. There is freedom where oppression once reigned, as men and women know in their hearts, and more freedom remains to be had. What, though, is freedom when we are simply enabled to pursue with everybody equally free the already discredited and ephemeral playthings of our time? Is it true freedom for blacks now to be able to indulge at will in all of the anxieties and inanities of whites? Is it freedom for women to enjoy the self-indulgent and destructive liabilities of men? In our freedom from the ignorance of an earlier age, are we now happy in the freedom we have to end life as we know it or to prolong it into a meaningless medical experiment?

Freedom is not enough, especially freedom as simply the absence of restraint. The paradox of the Christian hope is that it is truly a freedom, a freedom for the things that are to be, a freedom that binds us in confidence to the future of God wherein God's will will truly become our own. This is a freedom not of action but of being, the freedom to fulfill our destiny as an essential, holy, complete part of God's creation.

The Christian hope, then, is the confidence in the future of God that is the basis for all our activity in the present. Eschatology is the basis of ethics, for the Christian models himself not upon the discredited models of past human experience but rather upon things that have not yet been. That is what faith is all about, the evidence of things not seen. The Christian does not live by experience alone but by experience tempered by great expectation, and this is the activity of the Christian hope: to contend with the world as it is in light of the world as it is to be. When in the Nicene Creed all of the teachings and doctrine of the Church are summed up in the last phrase, ". . . and I look for the resurrection of the dead, and the life of the world to come," we affirm our confidence in the belief that the work of redemption, the making of broken things whole, was not only for times past nor a hidden thing of times present, but is in fact the work that is before us. In other words, we have neither been nor are we now where we are going but we have some idea of where we are because of where we are going, and that is why we work for peace, labor for justice, and struggle for love. That is why we do not despair in the face of all the hypocrisy and humbug around us. We have some idea of where we are because we have some idea of where we are going, and that is into the fullness and presence of God's time. The Christian hope is based upon the assurance that the God who formed us out of his love and came among us as one of us will not abandon us in that future into which he calls us.

The House of Bread

*

Text: But thou, Bethlehem Ephratah, though thou be little among the thousands of Judah, yet out of thee shall he come forth unto me that is to be ruler in Israel; whose goings forth have been from of old, from everlasting.   *Micah 5:2 (KJV)*

Bethlehem means "house of bread," and the name refers to the fact that the village was situated in a fruitful and fertile place, where with work its soil would yield food and harvest to the faithful. Grain and fruit could be grown there and there was an abundance of fresh water in the wells. It was not a flourishing place in the sense of a great market town or trading center, but it was a special place where favorable circumstances stimulated by effort could produce refreshment and sustenance for its people. It was not the holy city, it was not Jerusalem, the great capital, the center of worship and ritual and influence. It was a modest village favored not so much in riches as in opportunity, and dear to the heart of the Jews; a village with a history, not simply with a past.

In Bethlehem was to be found the monument to Rachel, for it was here that this wife of the patriarch Jacob died and was buried; and this was the city of Ruth, who lived here with her husband, Boaz, and became the great-grandmother of Bethlehem's most distinguished son, David; and it was here that David himself was born, and thus "the City of David," as the evangelists describe the place, is rich with associations for the Jew—a history, an association that speaks of the future as well. The prophet Micah, distressed with the worldly splendors of Jerusalem and the corruptions that surround him on every side, points to this modest city of Bethlehem, least among the princes of Judah, as the place out of whose past will come Israel's future hope. The text is a promise that in the midst of bad things great things shall come from small things. He warns that in extraordinary times it is in some measure to the ordinary that we must look. It is as the unknown poet said:

> Small things are best;
> grief and unrest
> to rank and wealth are given;
> but little things
> on little wings
> Bear little souls to heaven.

Where you least expect to see the power of God demonstrated in a corrupt and demonic world, there you will find God working out his purpose by the ordinary means of flesh and blood. Though thou art small, little Bethlehem, our hopes reside in thee.

So, on this Christmas day when our hearts are stilled by the magnitude of God's great love toward us, we are reminded that the greatness of God is seen in the wonder both of the ordinary and of the small; the miracle of God, his divine economy, is that he can make much of nothing and something of almost anything. A little town becomes the focus of the world's last best hope; a little baby comes to oppose the forces of Caesar and fear; and human flesh and human life are dignified and made whole as never before. The test of God's power is not in his capacity to move mountains and outmaneuver the phenomena of nature, or in his power to perform tricks or rebuke nature; God's power is in his capacity to make much of little, for that is what he does in creation, that is what he does at Christmas, and that is what he does with us, if only we will let him.

I have never been to the Holy Land. I hope someday to go, and of all the things I would like to see, I would most like to see the oldest church in Christendom, which stands on what is believed to be the site of the nativity in Bethlehem, the Church of the Holy Nativity. It was considered old in Constantine's time, and in its cavelike crypt beneath the high altar where the seven lamps burn eternally is found the place where it is believed that Mary bore her son. It is the most sacred spot of our faith, and both the sacredness and the space are important, for they remind us of the tangible quality of the Incarnation.

Christmas lends itself so easily to metaphor and sentiment. We need our metaphors, and sentiment is the grease without which our human machinery would break down and wear out, but Christmas does not represent a sentiment, an idea, or even a feeling about God. Christmas belongs to those who recognize not the sense of the holidays but the real presence of God in their lives and in their world, not simply once upon a time long ago and far away but here and now, inhabiting our hearts and struggling with us against the tangible realities that surround us. The world of little Bethlehem was real, Caesar Augustus was real, Herod was real, taxation was real, death and slaughter were real, despair was real and normal; and in the midst of all of this God had to be made real, and was made real not in an ideal but in the flesh, for that is what the Incarnation was and is, and that is why we bow before its presence. "God with us," for that is what *Emmanuel* means, is not just a translation of a Hebrew name but a translation of the living, loving purpose of God to be present in and among his creation. God does not abandon that which he makes; he becomes one with us that we may become one with him.

So we join with him and with one another in this feast of feasts on this day of days, for the gift of the Incarnation continues in the fellowship that we have with Christ around his Holy Table. In these most ordinary, these most tangible creatures of bread and wine, flesh and blood, we become at one with him who for us became one of us. Every time a baby is born, the old legend says, God endorses his world; and every time we celebrate the Holy Communion we experience once again his Incarnation. The miracle of Christmas: What is it? Is it the star, the singing angels, the wondering shepherds, the lovely mother, the exotic kings? Is it the cold night, the hopes and fears? Not really. The miracle of Christmas is that God cared enough to send the very best, and that he continues to do so in the gifts now given to us in one another.

Beginning Where We Left Off

❊

Text: And the shepherds returned . . .   *Luke 2:20*

Beginning where we left off is important, for what, for example, would have happened to the sheep and to the livelihood of the shepherds had they not returned but had gone on as the vanguard of some new movement? What indeed would have happened to those sages of the east had they not "returned to their country by another way"? What would have happened to Elijah and to Israel had Elijah chosen to remain at the mouth of the cave in mystic splendor, nursing his wounds and wondering at the strange events that had befallen him? There is a time to lay down one's cares and duties and to run with excited spirits to Bethlehem and the manger, "to see this thing that has come to pass"; there is a time to follow the eastern star and take the road not taken; there is a time to flee for refuge from the troubles of the world and seek the safety of the mountaintop. There is also a time to return—to the hillside, the laboratory, the scene of one's labors, to begin again where we left off. The church in its rhythm knows this, and that is why the seasons are planned as they are. It is a lesson we might well learn, and there is no better day than New Year's Day on which to consider it.

It is a hard lesson, for once persuaded that we should in mind and heart go even unto Bethlehem, it is very difficult to tear ourselves away. The view that the manger and all that it means is apart from rather than a part of life has given rise to the problem of great expectations and greater disappointments. It is no accident that the prisons, mental hospitals, and places of refuge know no greater season of agitation and stress than at Christmas. Somehow it promises so much and delivers so little. Christ is born, but wars persist, marriages continue to decay, the job is no better on the twenty-sixth of December than it was on the twenty-fourth. Joy, cheer, peace, and goodwill—these are guaranteed minimums for this season, and when we are denied them, things are worse than before.

Is the world any different out there because we employ all the symbols to suggest that it is? Is the newness, the novelty that we seek going to make it and us better than it and we were?

The expectation of the New Year is that somehow circumstances will be adapted in a new and happier way, and that with them we too shall be brought along. In the bleak midwinter, though, how can this be? The circumstances are all against us. The headlines read the same, the earth is cold and barren, "water like a stone." What can come out of this? In the ancient Western calendar, before the great reforms adopted in the English world only in the eighteenth century, the New Year came not in January but in March, and somehow, for our purposes, that makes sense. There is in the earth a natural cycle, a sense of new life that one can see in the fields, feel in the air; and in harmony with the natural elements of spring and resurrection one can affirm that there is a new thing afoot, there is a new and renewed chance, things need not necessarily be as they have been.

Thus the genius of Easter is that it occurs when all nature can affirm it, and not in the face of overwhelming evidence that refutes life in the face of death. It is harder in January than it is in April to go back from the altar to our work feeling that something has happened to us and that we, not circumstances, are redeemed and born anew, yet that is precisely what we are called upon to do. Of course the world has not changed and the duties that we have avoided or put off await us with grim determination on Monday morning; the magic of this season is too great to play with so trivial a set of things as that. What is transformed, what is capable of transformation so that where we left off is not the same place as where we now begin, is of course ourselves, for we have come from an encounter with the world of the possible in the midst of the impossible. We, like Moses and the shepherds and Jacob have seen God face-to-face and have prevailed, that is to say, have survived to tell the tale, moving about not knowing that our faces shine with the encounter, bearing the mark of our encounter forever, and marveling in the darkest nights of our soul at that wondrous star-filled night.

So here we are, called to begin where we left off and yet to make a new beginning. It is an old choice and a new chance for us and for the world. Christmas and creation are part of the same process of God; they have everything to do with one another, they each speak of loving purpose and renewed hopes, and is it not cause for joy that our gospel, the good news for which we seek, is a gospel of second chances, new opportunities to claim the love of the Father, new opportunities to share and express that love in the world, new opportunities to discover who we are and what we can become in Christ? The routine beckons, the familar haunts require our attention and our presence, and before too long the memory of this holy time will disappear and be packed away with the paraphernalia of the season; and yet by God's grace we will be open to his most remarkable grace and surprise in the world.

The world will not change until and unless we change; the spirit of Christmas cannot be borne out into the cold January air unless we are borne out by it and indeed born again by it. We may, we must, return from whence we came, but we need not return as the same tired creatures, care-worn and spirit-lost, for we have seen wonderful things that have come to pass, strange and mighty sights that will never let us look at the skies in quite the same manner as before. Every baby that comes into the world, every man and woman born of woman is no longer of the same old flesh but a promise and token of Christ, and to deny them is to once again deny him room, while to love and cherish them is to receive a new Christ in each of our lives and worlds.

Christ's presence has hallowed all that we are and every place that we are, and by his grace the world and we can never be quite the same again. Therefore we begin again, that in leaving the manger we may embrace the world for his sake and for ours.

Baptism

❈

Text: "Then to the Gentiles also God has granted repentance unto life." *Acts 11:18*

The baptism of Jesus, the church has always taught us, is an epiphany story, and we are in the season of Epiphany. This is the season in which the identity of Jesus, his real identity, is made clear and clearer to all who will look and see. What began with the very private annunciation of the angel to Mary and then to Joseph, what was then made manifest to the shepherds and to the animals in the manger is now made increasingly clear to an ever-expanding audience of witnesses. The circle gets bigger and bigger and bigger, more and more people are included in these manifestations, and from this Sunday to Easter day everything that we read and hear in Holy Scripture is an epiphany of Jesus. These epiphanies just get larger and larger and more vivid and bigger until we are included in every one of them, the manifestation of who and whose we really are. This is the most important season in the church's year because this is the season in which we come to see who Jesus is, where he is to be found, and where we begin to understand what he is about. This epiphany business is like a stone that is dropped in the water, which sets off a series of concentric ripples that get bigger and bigger and bigger until the entire surface imperceptibly is witness to the initial movement of that stone. That is what the Epiphany is all about and that is where we begin to find ourselves with our fellow believers in all places and at all times, drawn in relationship to those circles that emanate from the Incarnation of Jesus Christ.

The Epiphany is that manifestation of God in the world where the message is greater than the manger and goes well beyond it. To leave the story of Jesus Christ in the manger, to pack it up as we have done with our crèche and put it away for another year, is to fail to understand what the Epiphany is all about. So we are giving increasing visibility to the story of the coming of Jesus, which goes beyond the manger. Everything we say, everything we do in church in these coming weeks is part of this growing process of discovery of who Jesus is and where he is to be found. That's why this season is known as the season of light. On this Sunday of the Epiphany, the Church and its scriptures provide us with three splendid lenses, three wonderful stories, three glorious accounts with which and through which we can see the Christ.

The first of these lenses you all know about. The first is the most vivid, the most familiar, the most engaging, introducing to us the great characters of the Epiphany: the magi or the wise men or the three kings. January 6 is their great holy day. In the Eastern church, the church of the Greeks and the Russians and of Armenia, the arrival of the magi on January 6 is celebrated with tremendous festivity, pomp, and circumstance. They arrive as representatives of the exotic, the secular, and the scientific world beyond that provincial little burgh of Bethlehem, and their arrival is a sign for, and in behalf of, us all. You know who they are, you know these kings better than anyone else in the manger scene except perhaps for Mary and the baby Jesus himself.

They are our Epiphany witnesses; we understand them and their hectic, exotic journey and we love to see them at the manger for if we understand rightly who they are, they are very much like ourselves. They opened their treasures and presented to him gifts, though it was the gift given to them that brought them to their knees. They saw God made manifest for us.

So that's the first lens through which we look at this Epiphany activity, and we know something of it and appreciate something of it. The second Epiphany story, the second lens through which we look, we also know and love. It is the account, appointed for some years on this Sunday and found in Saint John's gospel, of Jesus' first miracle at that famous wedding in Cana of Galilee, where, once again, it was Jesus who gifted the occasion. He rescued the wedding from certain disaster by replenishing the supply of wine; he turned the water into wine, and not just wine equal to what had been previously served, a sort of *vin ordinaire*, but wine much better, thus reversing all the rules of practical, sensible catering and hospitality.

It was in this manifestation, this display, that the disciples saw the work of the Savior, and they believed in him. Here, in this wonderful tale, we're often tempted to think that it is a story about a great bit of alchemy, a great trick about wine, and water turned into wine, but the story is not about water nor is it about wine; it is about being a witness to who Jesus is. It is a story about seeing Jesus. As the magi are not the subject of their own visit but modify the Savior in order to amplify him so that we can see him, so, too, neither the bridal party nor the wine is the subject of the marriage at Cana. They modify the Savior to amplify him in order that he might be seen as he is and that we might see him as the one upon whom God has shown extraordinary favor, and by whose presence we are gifted.

So there are those wonderfully exotic figures from the East at the manger, and then there is that extraordinary sleight of hand in Cana of Galilee. The third lens of the Epiphany is one about which we have already begun to speak. This is the lens of the baptism of the Lord, and this is the least public, the most profound, and the most accessible to us.

We will not be able to mount camels and go to the Far East and see the babe lying in the manger, nor will most of us be fortunate enough to attend a wedding reception in which Jesus again performs his miracle, but many of us by our baptism have already been present at this manifestation, and it is this epiphany that is the most immediate one for us. Saint Matthew has the baptism of Jesus as a dialogue between Jesus and John the Baptist. John, who has been the forerunner of Jesus, realizes that the main act is about to begin, that Jesus, long awaited and long foretold, is now finally here, and we know it must be the real thing because John is not at all backward about coming forward. John is not famous as a modest or retiring fellow who wants to give way to anyone who comes to town. John yields because John has no choice. John yields because he realizes that the one to whom he must yield, Jesus, is now here. John protests that he is not worthy to baptize Jesus—we know of all of his protestations in the gospel—but Matthew makes the point that it is not a question of merit but of the fulfillment of God's will.

John then consented to do the deed. Jesus is baptized not to repent of sins, for he is without sin, but to establish and give witness to a relationship that shows that he belongs to God and is called to do God's work in the world. He is baptized as a witness to God's claim upon him. He is baptized, and by that action says, in effect, "I belong no longer to myself or to my parents or to my work, or even to the world; I belong to God." God is simply reclaiming that which he created at the beginning. Baptism is the renewal of a relationship with God that began at creation. He is baptized to manifest both to heaven and to earth that he, Jesus Christ, is the means by which God will accomplish his will and work on earth.

If this is about manifestation and display and witnesses, we may very well ask, "Who saw all of this? Was there a great throng along the shore watching John and Jesus do their thing in the water?" Many years ago an undergraduate couple came to me and asked whether I would baptize them. I thought about it and prayed about it, and talked with them, and agreed after much prayer and discussion that, yes, this is what we do and we are privileged to do it. It became more complicated, however, because they said, "We would like you to baptize us by immersion." Well, I should be pleased with that, I'm a Baptist, that's what we do, but we're not well equipped here in The Memorial Church to baptize people by immersion, so we had a problem. We had to consider how, simply, to accomplish this. All the water and all the bowls in the world would not do the job. So we considered where we might go. Unfortunately, it was October, but one of their fondest associations was with Walden Pond, so, to make a very long story short, we picked a decent afternoon in October, we took ourselves to Walden Pond, the three of us, with blankets, a flask of a suitable liquid to warm us after the experience, a Bible, and a will to witness for Christ, fortunately privately, because who on earth would there be at Walden Pond on a late October afternoon?

We came to the shore and we found a fording place. I walked in and the man and woman came in and we had a few words of testimony. Then I performed the deed as I was taught: down and up and down and up. As soon as I brought the woman up from the water, she being the second, there was a great burst of applause. We were not alone. We looked and we found that the shore was full of people who had come out of the woods and were absolutely fascinated at this bizarre activity going on at Walden Pond. Many strange things have been seen at Walden Pond but nothing, I'm sure, quite as strange as this, and clearly some word of explanation was in order lest they call the police. I explained that this was what Christians did when they wanted to make a profession of their faith, and I quoted a little scripture. One of the fellows on the shore asked, "Do you do a lot of this sort of thing?" I replied, "Not as much as I would like, but, yes, I do." He and his friends on the shore scratched their heads and said, "Well, it looks like fun," and off they went into the woods and we came back into Cambridge. What was meant to be a very private affair suddenly became an opportunity for witness, a manifestation.

Jesus' baptism wasn't quite like this. His was private, so we read. Who were the witnesses? Who saw it? The kings were at the manger, the disciples at the wedding, but who was at the baptism? Saint Matthew says:

Behold the heavens were opened and he saw the spirit of God descending like a dove, and alighting on him; and lo, a voice from heaven saying, "This is my beloved son with whom I am well pleased."

Who was there? Martin Luther in his commentary says it was the angels in heaven and all the company of heaven, those cherubim and seraphim who are continually crying. All of the angels of God were there, the Holy Spirit was there in the dove, and God himself was there. What was implied by the worship of the kings at the manger, what was revealed by the miracle at Cana to the disciples, is proclaimed by God in the baptism of Jesus. God is the witness: Here is the one upon whom my spirit rests. Here we know completely and fully who Jesus is. He is not some child pretender to King Herod's throne. He is not some miracle worker in the wilderness. He is the man upon whom God's spirit rests, in whom God is well pleased, and to whom the heavens are opened up with everlasting praise and glory. "This is my beloved son with whom I am well pleased." Medieval paintings of the baptism show an empty shore, Jesus alone in the water, and the heavens filled with the company of all sorts of people looking down with approval. God himself is witness to God's work in man. It is not unlike the account in Genesis which, after the creation, says, "And God saw all that he had made, and it was good."

This is where we come in. As it says in Acts, in Peter's great sermon to the Gentiles:

"And I remembered the word of the Lord, how he said, 'John baptized with water, but you shall be baptized with the Holy Spirit.' If then God gave the same gift to them as He gave to us when we believed in the Lord Jesus Christ, who was I that I could withstand God?"

The "them" in that passage are the Gentiles, the non-Jews, those who would not be present at the manger or at the miracle at Cana, but who like the magi would come from afar and come from out of time. In other words, ourselves. The gift that God has given Jesus in baptism, the gift of his Holy Spirit, he now freely gives to all, even to us Gentiles. God is no respecter of persons, God is not partial. Peter is making the point, incredible as it may seem, that God's love and spirit extend beyond the chosen particular circle of time and place. The apostles believed at first that you had to be a Jew, you had to have been there, you had to be in the right place at the right time, you had to be the right person to be a witness to the wonderful events of the Lord, but Peter says no: The true miracle, the true gift, the true Epiphany is that God gives himself in Christ by the witness of the Spirit to all people in all places and at all times. We need not be bound by the parochial division of time, space, or circumstance. The expansion of work of the good news, the growing and widening recognition of who Jesus is, extends now to include us, even you and me and even here: "And they glorified God, saying, 'Then to the Gentiles also God has granted repentance unto life.'" Then to those beyond this particular place and beyond this particular time God has granted repentance unto life, which means even to students and professors, even to townspeople and suburbanites, humanists, scientists, the bright and the dim, yuppies and street people, the old and the young, the rich and the poor. Even to all of us removed so long, so far from Bethlehem and the manger. Even to us God has granted repentance unto life.

We can't get on camels and we aren't invited to the best weddings but we share in the baptism of Jesus and by that we are renewed, re-generated, called back to the life we were meant to live when we first were created, for when God had done with us the first time he said that it and we were good, and he doesn't rest until he gets us back. The miracle of the baptism of the Lord is not what he gives up but rather what he takes on: *us*. By the light of the glory of his countenance he shows us that we are the subject of his work, and that we are his work; and finally, in us will his glory be made manifest, for ultimately and truly and finally we are meant to be not simply witnesses to the epiphany of our Lord in the world: We *are* his epiphany.

EPIPHANY II

Growing Up

❃

Text: And Jesus increased in wisdom and in stature, and in favor with God and man. *Luke 2:52*

We know very little about those years of Jesus' life between infancy and adulthood. Only in Luke's gospel do we come across Jesus uttering a word before the time of his baptism, yet surely he must have said something in the idle chatter of childhood and in response to the formal instruction he would have received as a young Jew in the local synagogue, and at the hands of his father and elders. Those words and instructions of his early years evidently took well, for Luke tells us that he astonished the learned doctors in the temple with both his questions and his answers. Some people have tended to envision in this scene or confrontation a precocious, bratlike child who battered the old graybeards with the incessant "Why? Why not?" of childhood, and others have seen a little old man in the body of a twelve-year-old child disputing in sagelike fashion the philosophical elders. It simply is unknown what the substance of that exchange was, but we can assume that it dealt with the questions that a bright young Jewish boy might have after studying for years the Torah and the history of Israel. At age twelve he would have been at the point of what Jews now call bar mitzvah, and such questions and answers would be normal fare for a boy of his age. The temple doctors, the rabbis, and the learned men might well have been attracted to such a little boy who lingered after the High Holy Days to listen and to talk with them.

The portion of the story that generally gets the attention, however, is not so much what Jesus said to the doctors and they to him, but rather what his parents and he said to one another. The anxious, fretting parents hasten back to find their son talking, obviously not at all aware that he has caused great difficulty; perhaps there was that maternal edge in Mary's voice when she asked him where he had been, but the scripture tells us that his cool answer confused his parents: "Did you not know that I must be about my father's business?"

Lest we think that this exchange represents youthful rebellion, the New English version of the Bible tells us, "Then he went back with them to Nazareth, and continued to be under their authority. . . . As Jesus grew up, he advanced in wisdom and in favor with God and man."

Jesus did not simply grow older, he grew wiser. It is the quality of mature development that concerns us, of the growth that Christians both experience and need—the growth in our personal development, the growth in our religious personalities, the spiritual growth that makes it possible for us to cope with the world in which we live.

In other words, it is growing up as Christians that concerns us. For us as for Jesus these are often the hidden years, but for us as well as for Jesus the process of spiritual maturity is the most important one in which we can engage, for it prepares us to accept his call and to serve in the world Jesus both served and saved. This, then, is a sermon about the growth of the soul.

What do we need to grow as Christians? Wealth, prestige, a powerful experience? The new poverty? No! We need only those opportunities that time itself presents.

I know two maiden ladies, twins in fact, in Plymouth, who recently celebrated their ninety-third birthday with all their relatives and their wits about them, and when they were asked the usual newspaper question, "To what do you attribute your longevity?" the laconic answer from Miss Minnie was "Time."

So too it is with the Christian, for time presents the opportunity for growth and too many people waste too much time waiting for epochal "mountaintop" experiences as a stimulus to growth when there is so much work to be done in the valleys, where we spend most of that time anyway.

Christian growth is not simply a matter of time, however, but the quality of that time, and it is quality time that we call maturity. The text suggests that Jesus grew up not only in terms of years and physical development, but that he grew in wisdom and stature, that he matured as he grew. Christians too need to grow and mature in their experiences. I can remember in the prayer meetings of my boyhood hearing the ancients give testimony as to where and when and under what dire circumstances they met the Lord, and after some years I became aware that the same people always told the same story, and it seemed to me that it was the same old experience over and over and over again. "Why haven't they any new stories?" I would ask. "Haven't they ever again met Jesus since that time?" was another naive question. People talked the same way about when they "joined the church," or when they "were saved," or, in Christian-speak, when they were "born again."

This childhood incredulity has left me with the conclusion that there must be not only a religious experience simply in the past tense, but religious experiences in the present tense as well. One is always being lost and found, one is always leaving and joining the church, for if one is alive one is growing in the experiences of God as perceptions develop and grow. To store up the past religious experience like a bit of preserved ginger to sniff on in emergencies seems to me to be a sorry parody of living faith. The matter of Christian growth, then, seems to be a willingness to expose oneself to new ideas, to widening opportunities, to new awareness of what's happening in the world around, and a new cordiality toward time itself.

Christian growth also involves knowledge, and an ever-increasing supply of it. True, God delights in the simple and chooses the wisdom of the wise to foul them up, but that is no excuse for the appalling lack of knowledge today about things of the spirit that lead to Christian maturity. When you consider that most religious people operate on a second-rate second-grade Sunday school education, it is no wonder that a sharp young man could say how much he liked that "story of Jesus and the bullrushes" or how "Saint James dictated the Authorized Version of the Bible." One of the greatest curses of a religious people is the shallowness of their knowledge concerning the very foundation of the faith. The great radical movement in the Christian church is not going to come when and if churches ever get their liturgies in the currently fashionable argot, nor will it come when they finally organize their bureaucracies into efficient corporate structures. It will come only when children and adults begin to learn about Jesus Christ and the church and world he served and saved, with the blinders off. Only then is there even the possibility for growth which takes Jesus and us beyond the happy obscurity of the manger. Growth requires knowledge.

Paul tells us, in that famous chapter in Corinthians: "When I was a child I spoke as a child, I thought as a child, I reasoned as a child; but when I became a man, I put away childish things." This is growth that pulls and stretches us, the "growing pains" about which all of our aunts speak, but these are necessary changes: stimuli for maturity.

For many of us, the Women's Movement has been just such a stimulus for growth, for it has raised in our hearts and in our minds the deepest questions concerning our churchly and manly repression of the expectations of women from the very top to the very bottom of our society. It is a disturbing stimulus for growth because we cannot profit from it without indicting ourselves by it; but such liberation, while some of its style may offend and divide us, is true liberation in the sense that it forces us to look at ourselves both as we are and as we ought to be. This is difficult, painful, embarrassing, and hard, but no one ever said that growing up was easy.

Who knows, perhaps in the process of change that the movement for human justice has forced upon us over the last twenty years, we will grow to the point where we will be free enough to "speak the truth in love," as Paul has said. Perhaps we will be able to drop our carefully constructed and maintained facades of cool disinvolvement and give vent to our feelings. We must learn to grow in dependence, that is, to speak our needs to each other in whatever way we best can. In my time here both as a student in the Divinity School and now in The Memorial Church, I have found the bulk of most interpersonal problems to be those of communication. Why can't we say, "I love you," "I need you," "I fear you," yes, even "I can't stand you"? These are the hardest words, and because we know so many words, we use all but the right ones and nobody understands anybody. If we are to grow, we must learn to grow together, to lean not only on Jesus, as the old gospel hymn goes, but to lean on each other. Here is where our love is put together, here is where we are liberated to grow in relationship to one another; here, as Paul says, "Speaking the truth in love, we are to grow up in every way into him who is the head, unto Christ, from which the whole body joined and knit together by every joint with which it is supplied, when each part is working properly, makes bodily growth and upbuilds itself in love."

When all has been said and done we are speaking about an interior process, an inner growth that tampers and tinkers with the most delicate parts of our machinery: the heart, the soul, the mind. We are talking about attitudes and opportunities, a power that is not generated by our will but by God's spirit, and it is this last kind of growing, the growing in grace, which makes all of the other growth possible. It is that unexplainable gift of God himself, the gift of grace, that gives us the capacity to cope, to understand, to hope, and to help; so let us grow up and grow together toward the light like the plants that we are.

The Ambiguity of Heroes

❀

Text: And thou shalt remember all the way which the Lord thy God
led thee these forty years in the wilderness. . . .

Deuteronomy 8:2 *(KJV)*

It was Harvard's fourth president, the not-so-famous Urian Oakes (1675–
1681), who, in speaking of the theological necessity of history, reminded
us that "we are to be the Lord's remembrancers." By that felicitous
phrase he meant to remind his New England hearers that it was their
duty to remember those mighty men and mightier deeds that God had
raised up among them that his providence and purpose would not be
forgotten by the generations rising in aftertimes. Such an injunction was
not new with Oakes, nor was it peculiar to New England. As the Puritans
read the Bible they found it a veritable warrant for such a view, and if
it was nothing else, the Bible, from Genesis to Revelation, contained
the stories of men and women whose lives were used to instruct man
in the ways of God. The patriarchs, judges, kings, and prophets of Israel,

the apostles, martyrs, and saints of the New Testament community, that "great cloud of witnesses" of which the book of Hebrews speaks with such passionate eloquence—these were living testimonies, designed to reveal not human heroics, though they frequently did, but rather God's continuing grace.

> Now praise we great and famous men,
> The fathers named in story;
> And praise the Lord, who now as then
> Reveals in man his glory.

So wrote William Tarrant in his 1812 paraphrase of the famous verse in Ecclesiasticus, "Let us now praise famous men . . ." What Plutarch did for the pagans of the ancient classical world, Christians were to do for the worthy faithful, and for them both biography was the means to accomplish this end.

"Read no history," proclaimed Disraeli, "nothing but biography, for that is life without theory"; and Emerson, writing somewhat earlier in the last century, observed, "There is properly no history, only biography." Carlyle, not to be outdone, and indeed the first of these, cited, "No great man lives in vain. The history of the world is but the biography of great men." The lesson preached by Urian Oakes was well remembered in America, and such an assiduous apostle of the biographer's art as Cotton Mather saw himself as the American Plutarch, the official "Lord's Remembrancer" for the new world. What was begun in the seventeenth century continued well on into the nineteenth century, where it could be said that the chief form of literature was biography. People kept company with the great and the near-great through the reading of biography, and in a nation destitute of and desperate for a sense of the worth of its own past, biography was the means to greatness. Parson Weems's famous biography of George Washington was a bestseller, and Jared Sparks became America's first professional and profitable historian because of his popular biographies of the founding fathers.

Biography is a two-edged sword, however, for what can be exalted can also be brought low. While biography continues to be a reasonably popular form of literature even in our day, aided and abetted by its less modest sister the autobiography, and its distant cousin the memoir, its nature and purpose seem quite different from that of its ancestor. We would rather have human than heroic types, and we tend to prefer exposés to the exalted portraits of ideal types. Rather than read of the qualities that separate us from the hero we would prefer to read that the hero is really no better than we are, and in some cases, quite a bit worse. Gossip and scandal help, and qualities that level rather than elevate are the stuff of which our expectations frequently are made. There is a shortage of heroes for our day, and those few who remain stand on very tenuous pedestals. To fill our need, however, we have created a substitute, a synthetic—the celebrity, of whom we expect little and who usually delivers less. Celebrities are a part of our consumer throwaway culture; they are here today and gone tomorrow, and that is why we must create so many of them. Energies we no longer dare invest in the immortality of heroes who may fail us, we may place for an instant in the riotous procession of the newly famous and the quickly-forgotten. When we lose them nothing is lost, for their successors have already taken over their moment in the sun.

Our romance with heroes and the heroic is not so quickly settled, though it is now tempered with a heavier dose of reality than in the past. Indeed, perhaps because of rather than despite the disappointments and deceptions we have shared as a culture, we continue to be, in the words of Judge Charles Wyzanski, a people "in search of sages": anxious and eager to find people worthy of our loyalty and love. Such a search is accentuated in times of crisis and uncertainty, and the hero whom we seek is one who, unlike ourselves, can transcend those times and move them and us by the sheer power of virtue. Emerson, in his essay "Heroism," writes:

> The characteristic of heroism is its persistency. All men have wandering impulses, fits and starts of generosity. But when you have chosen your part, abide by it, and do not weakly try to reconcile yourself with the world . . . always do what you are afraid to do . . . whoso is heroic will always find crises to try his edge.

The purpose of biography is to identify such people as these and to share them with a future in which they would be in short supply: the Lord's remembrancers.

Now the Greeks, as usual, had a saying for it, several in fact, and the old tag went something like this: "A people are known by the heroes they crown." "Tell me whom you admire and I will tell you who you are" is a simple translation of that text. The choosing of heroes, therefore, is a very important thing, for by that choice the character of a people may often be determined. To deprive people of heroes, or of the opportunity to choose them, is the ultimate form of conquest. The Romans in their conquest of the barbarians, the Christians in their conquest of the mission field, and the Communists in their conquest of Eastern Europe all recognized this ancient axiom; and so, we may ask, how are heroes chosen? What qualities are there that define heroism and commend it to us?

The term itself provokes a fundamental ambiguity, for in the Greek it referred to a being half-divine and half-human. Do we identify with the qualities most like our own, or do we seek to invest in something so much different from ourselves as to represent all those things that we wish we were but are not? Can we take to ourselves someone who is larger than life, and is someone of less than that stature worth the taking? Perhaps this is best expressed in Groucho Marx's quip about exclusive clubs: "I wouldn't join any club that would admit me." Perhaps there is a clue to this dilemma in the history of Israel's heroes. Every one of the heroes, in addition to the particular qualities that commend him to man and to God, has about him as well the participation in struggle, failure, and apparent defeat. Outward circumstances or inner turmoils similar to our own stake their claim on our attention, such as Adam's hiding from God, Jacob's foxy nature, Jonah's anger, Peter's denial, Paul's thorn in the flesh, Jesus' cry of dereliction. These are the human believables that make the divine bearable, and as it was with these, so it was with Joseph.

We all dream dreams, the daydreams of castles in Spain, dreams of conquest and power, dreams of success and glory. Dream theory is a popular portion of the psychologist's work, and since Freud no dream is devoid of the most telling analysis. How silly this boy Joseph was to share so arrogant a dream with his brothers who, while he dreamed away, found themselves doing the work. Perhaps for a moment our sympathy or our identification shifts to the angry brothers and their irrational and indignant response: "Let us slay this dreamer, and then we shall see what will become of his dreams." He is not slain and moreover succeeds in having the last word, albeit a gracious and generous one, with his churlish brethren, and he is gathered in honor and glory to his ancestors. There are aspects of this story with which we can identify, but on balance, the story, and Joseph too, are beyond us—this hero of the house of Israel.

Joseph and his dream illustrate for us the ambiguity of the heroic: that given the chance we will destroy the very means to our own salvation in order to preserve the shreds of our dignity. Heroes we may have and in fact need, but the very qualities that make them heroic, visions larger than our own, set them apart from us at their own peril and ours. Therefore, as Emerson says:

Just and wise men take umbrage at his act, until after some little time be past, then they see it to be in unison with their acts . . . for every heroic act measures itself by its contempt of some external good. But it finds its own success at last, and then the prudent also extol.

"The prudent also extol"; and so they and we do, and why? Perhaps it is, as William Morris puts it, "Dreamer of dreams, born out of my due time, why should I strive to set the crooked straight?"

With the death of Martin Luther King, Jr., at the hands of an assassin, we learned once again the reality of those words of Joseph's brothers: "Here comes this dreamer: let us slay him, and then we shall see what will become of his dreams." With Dr. King's birthday, which we celebrate today and tomorrow, as the Lord's remembrancers we seek to remember, in the words of our text, "All the ways wherein the Lord hath led us in the wilderness." As you remember, Dr. King was slain in Passion Week, 1968, and the first Sunday after his death was Palm Sunday. How rich were the associations with his death and the death of that other dreamer who too in times out of joint came to set the crooked straight.

There could be no more vivid lesson in proximity than this one that reminded us of our ambiguous relationship to those who would save us: "Jerusalem, thou that killest the prophets and stonest them that are sent unto thee." The association was too great, and in recent years we have moved our commemorations of this man from the tragedy-laden time of his death to the more hopeful season of his birth. With this we have managed, I fear, to translate this man, always difficult to live with, into a myth with which we are more comfortable and at ease. This too is the risk of the heroic.

Unlike many of the preachers and orators who speak his name these days, I did not know Martin Luther King. I never heard him speak nor did I ever see him. Some of you may well remember his visits to this pulpit in the ministry of my predecessor, and we have all heard him on the radio and the television, but I am not among those who can claim a relationship. I think he would have made me uncomfortable, for moral power, spiritual rigor, intellectual acuteness, and physical courage are all qualities that we admire in the abstract, but when we confront them face-to-face, especially if we doubt our own supply of them—well, it is difficult to be anything but awkward. Even within his lifetime, to many he appeared aloof and preoccupied, and many blacks resisted his natural ascendancy and single-mindedness. At the time of his death his vision called him to the basic needs of the garbage workers of Memphis, Tennessee, and to the immoral enormity of our war in Southeast Asia. In so many ways larger than us all, his ministry was concerned with the least of our brethren. The wave of guilt that swept the nation at his death was equal perhaps only to that at the deaths of Lincoln and Kennedy, and we all blamed ourselves for creating the climate of violence and indifference in which he could be slain for seeking to do good. In death he was able to claim the loyalty denied him in life, for it is far easier to honor the dead than to follow the living, and so we take the dead to our bosoms, for there they can no longer do any harm; and we can translate a living, breathing, both noble and fallible human being into a heroic impotence, satisfying our need to both admire and be protected from something larger than ourselves.

We cannot long afford such heroes as these, restricted to the moral archives, but these are all that we will have if we concern ourselves only with their personalities and their heroics insofar as they differ from our own. The purpose of biography, the task of the Lord's remembrancers, is not to create a cult, a personality that fed upon public guilt and culpability, but rather it was to see revealed in the life commemorated the provident plan of God. The art of Christian biography is to see in the human the hint of the divine, and to see the divine in terms of flesh and blood that we could understand. If we fail in this delicate translation, we will be left with either just one more matinee idol or one more victim.

We are led to remember Martin Luther King, Jr., not because the liberal press says we should, or self-serving organizations and individuals hold us moral hostage to do so. We hold him in remembrance because he was in our time a part of that great company of witnesses from before our time whom God has raised up to raise us up from our bondage to the things that are, to the liberty of the things that can and ought to be. If we look for human perfection in him we will not find it, for he was a man born of woman and shared in the sins and weaknesses of our human flesh. If we look for him to be the burden-bearer of our times, our race, or our nation, we will find that he is unable to bear that burden, for he was in the struggle fully as much as we. If we look for him to serve as our moral substitute and to "cash in" on his virtue, we will find the supply insufficient, for in that each must bear his own price; but if we look to see in him what God is trying to do and to say, if we look beyond the cult and the deeds, if in fact we look where he was looking, we may begin to see just what it was that sustained him that is freely available to sustain us as well, pilgrims and saints, people always in process, always moving.

When the Jews spoke of righteous Abel, faithful Abraham, successful Joseph, and mighty Moses, they saw those great heroes as the mirrors of faith in which God could be found and through which God could do his work with us. Such lives were not testimonies unto themselves but unto God, and the recital of such lives reminded the faithful hearers that God has always taken frail flesh and made of it something of his own for his own. What is more, such a recital reminds us that what God has done with our foreparents he can and will do with us, if only we will let him. He has told us this so many times. We are the heirs of the promise, all of us, male and female, white and black, red and brown, rich and poor, bonded and free; we are the heirs of those fruits of the spirit of which Saint Paul writes: love, joy, peace, patience, kindness, goodness, faithfulness, gentleness, and self-control, for against them there is no law.

Urian Oakes would remind us that heroes serve as beacons of virtue. No real hero is so unless the attention that he attracts is directed beyond himself and reflects what we must do and what God can do. He stands, the hero, as a means and not as an end. The difference between the celebrity and the authentic hero consists in this: The celebrity can attract only curiosity and imitation of himself, whereas the hero sends us to the source and end of his virtue. Insofar as any hero is worthy of praise, it is to the degree that he at once reveals what we could be and what God is.

We have learned much in the perilous years since this last dreamer was taken from us, and yet his dream, the dream of the ages, remains deferred to haunt us in its incompleteness. How could we mortals be expected to handle it? He and we should have known that it was too much for us, and yet the grace of his life and ours is that God continues to inject himself into this world where he is both needed and not wanted. Such is his love toward us that he sends us himself and gives us dreams to disturb our slumber and dreamers to disturb our waking. God grant that in our pilgrimage it may ever be so.

An Opportune Time

❋

Text: **And when the devil had ended every temptation, he departed from him until an opportune time.**   *Luke 4:13*

At its most obvious this is a lesson about temptation, temptation in the context of an extraordinary contest of wit and will between Jesus and the devil. For many centuries this portion of Saint Luke's gospel has been read in the churches of Christendom on the first Sunday in Lent, as a not-too-subtle reminder of our own struggle in the spiritual wilderness during these forty days between the mortality of Ash Wednesday and the victory of Easter Sunday.

In our lesson Jesus is tempted three times by Satan, and the first temptation concerns itself with the physical facts of hunger, the basic need for survival and nourishment. Jesus was hungry. "All that time," says the New English translation, "he had nothing to eat, and at the end of it, he was famished." Real hunger, not just the premature craving for a meal which is on the way, is nature's most devastating device.

It can alter the personality, it can warp the judgment, it can reduce the rational human being to abject bestiality; hunger can drive a person to desperate lengths. So we find that Jesus was hungry, "famished," as the text reads, and the devil, always clever at marketing, offered him bread. "If you are the son of God, turn this stone to bread." Jesus, not willing to buy survival at any price, declines the challenge and the offer.

The second temptation is in many ways far more subtle than the first. The first dealt with basic survival, but the second deals with almost as basic a human desire, if not need: power. The devil took Jesus up onto a mountain, showed him all the kingdoms of the world, and offered them to him if he would but pay homage to the devil. The commentaries tell us that the so-called Mountain of Temptation sits in a wasteland hundreds of feet below sea level, and that the view it affords is not of large kingdoms but of tiny, impoverished hamlets and sheepfolds, and that the only town nearby is the famous but humble Jericho. The devil, however, wasn't offering real estate so much as he was appealing to that human need for the temporal power of authority, sovereignty, and a sense of territory. Now the devil can't really offer what he doesn't have, and it is clear that he does have what he offers here, for the world is the devil's. Next to hell it is where he is most at home. To have had Jesus accept it would have saved both Jesus and me a lot of preaching and you a lot of listening, but this Jesus, of whom it would be said, "His power was made perfect in weakness," was once again not so easily bought.

The third and final temptation in Saint Luke's account is fully as ingenious as the others. This one appeals to the sense of identity and the need to prove who we are. "If you are really who you think you are," says the devil, "prove it by casting yourself down to the ground. Surely those angels will come and pick you up before you crash. God can suspend gravity if it's all in the family. Try it and see." No one likes to have his identity challenged or threatened; we are insecure enough without someone always demanding proof that we are who we say we are, but once again Jesus is able to transcend the question, "Thou shalt not tempt the Lord thy God."

Jesus has been tested at the most vulnerable human points of survival, power, and identity. His will and endurance have been tried by the most artful of tempters and the devil's knowledge of human psychology and human nature would do justice to a Social Relations conference. The lesson is thus a lesson about temptation and the resistance thereto. If the devil had known my grandmother he probably would have quoted her words with pleasure when, in response to her doctor's admonition that she avoid temptation when it came in the form of her diet, she said, "Better to die from havin' it than wantin' it." Surely this seems like a lesson about avoidance: Jesus gets credit for not doing anything—and perhaps that is where some of the negative ideas of Lent-keeping come from, such as the giving up of candy, sex, or gin. The text has far more to offer us than that, however, and for that matter, so does Lent.

Not only is this a lesson about temptation and the avoidance thereof, but at its more basic level it is a lesson about confrontation. Jesus confronts the devil, Jesus confronts his temptations, Jesus confronts his vulnerable points and his spiritual conflicts. The devil is able to cloak himself in that guise which is most appealing to our weakest points. To the student he might come as an easy grade, to the professor perhaps as tenure or scholarly acclaim, to the Christian he comes in that soothing voice of the Pharisee that says, "I bless God that I am not as other men." While the confrontation with the devil is most attractive, the confrontation with one's self is more necessary, and that means looking at ourselves behind the elaborate social cosmetic we create in order to protect ourselves from our own vanities. The confrontation the lesson suggests—confrontation with our ego and ambition and fear—is the ultimate confrontation with the devil and the evil he incarnates. It would be pleasant for us to deny the reality of such inner vexation but to do that contributes to the problem rather than resolves it, and such bedevilments will not go away simply because we refuse to acknowledge their presence. If life were meant to be a process of perfection by avoidance, the monastery and the nunnery would be oversubscribed. Jesus did not avoid the devil nor did he dismiss nor underestimate him, but rather he contended with him, wrestling with him in an agony of spiritual sweat.

As Thou with Satan didst contend,
And did the victory win,
O give us strength in Thee to fight,
In Thee to conquer sin.

So, the lesson is about temptation, and it is about confrontation as well. Ultimately, it is a parable about perseverance, and that in two kinds. It would be satisfying to us if this account of Jesus' temptation ended with the triumphant defeat of Satan after the third trial, but it doesn't, and the story ends on a rather ominous note. "And when the devil had ended every temptation, he departed from him until an opportune time," or, as the New English version puts it, "So having come to the end of all his temptations, the devil departed, biding his time." The devil left, but not because he was defeated. Rather than a defeat, it was a strategic retreat, a retreat until an opportune time when Jesus would once again be both vulnerable and susceptible to Satan's blandishments. Lurking in the shadows of the agony in Gethsemane, hovering about the passion of Calvary, Satan had not by any means quit the contest. Jesus' temptation was not over. The frightening import of the text is that in reality it was just beginning.

The devil awaits that opportune time with us, that time when he can appeal to our injured pride, our wounded ego, our fear of not being appreciated, our anger at being ignored. These are those opportune times when the devil's persistence reaps great benefits.

The devil's perseverance must be matched, however, by our own, and such perseverance in the spiritual wilderness is what the Lenten discipline is all about. The struggle with evil in the world begins with the struggle with evil within ourselves, and that struggle depends upon self-knowledge: knowing and acknowledging our limitations and our capacities. Such introspection should take place at all times with us, but Lent is that particular time in the church year when we pay attention to that process. As Jesus prepared himself for the discipline of his ministry by his time in the wilderness, we prepare ourselves once again for that ultimate renewal that comes to us and to the earth in Easter. There are many routes to Easter, but none of them escapes the shadow of the cross, that point where our time and God's eternity converge; and at the center point where time and eternity meet is the Christ who makes it all possible. In the shadow of that cross we make our way, acknowledging who and what we are, sinners who stand in need of God's forgiveness and the forgiveness of our brothers and sisters. All this we know. We need to be reminded to remember it, all the same; and Lent is an opportune time for that.

Riches

❊

Text: The disciples were astonished when they heard this, and exclaimed: "Then who can be saved?" Jesus looked at them and said, "For men this is impossible; but everything is possible for God." *Matthew 19:25–26 (REB)*

I am going to offer this text in two translations. First, the Revised English Bible:

> The disciples were astonished when they heard this, and exclaimed: "Then who can be saved?" Jesus looked at them and said, "For men this is impossible; but everything is possible for God."

Now here is how J. B. Phillips puts it, in his *New Testament in Modern English:*

> The disciples were simply amazed to hear this, and said: "Then who can possibly be saved?" Jesus looked steadily at them and replied,

"Humanly speaking it is impossible; but with God anything is possible."

There is a wonderful nuance of difference between the phrases "everything is possible for God" and "with God anything is possible." It is on the "anything" that I want to focus this morning because I think it is the "anything" that is the hinge of this story.

Think of the story of the rich young ruler as you tend to remember it: conveniently and inaccurately. In the "Shrinklit" version of the story—that is, in the version with all of the details, narratives, transitions, and important points left out—the story goes something like this: "A young Jewish yuppie has everything; he wants, as most yuppies want, more. He wants to be perfect. Jesus says he can't be. The yuppie finds one thing that money cannot buy. Jesus gives him his moral comeuppance, and more than this, Jesus says that all yuppies, or all Jewish yuppies in this context, will have a hard time getting into heaven." End of story, moral clear, you can take that home to lunch.

There is great personal satisfaction for most of us in this version of the story, inaccurate as it may be, because despite our American fascination with success stories—and we love success stories, Horatio Alger and all that sort of thing—we generally don't like successful people. We like their stories, but we don't like them. Their stories are interesting, but they are not. These are the people who have it all, who know it all, and who tell us all about it in endless, endless prose. Who, I ask you, really likes Donald Trump? Who is not annoyed by Martha Stewart?

This version of the story, which goes by the Tale of the Rich Young Ruler, gives us an even more vivid set of synoptic reasons to dislike this young man intensely. Consider the characteristics of this young man who comes to Jesus. First, he is rich, and that is reason enough to dislike him. Most of us, fond as we may be of riches of our own, are not fond of those who have more riches than we have, and therefore it is not that we don't like the rich in general, we just don't like those who are richer than we are. It is probably inherited wealth anyway, in the case of this rich young man, generational theft, as it is called, and it means or implies that he doesn't have to work, which is another source of envy and discontent to those of us who do have to work. So, he is rich, reason number one to dislike him.

Reason number two: He is young. The older we get, the easier it becomes to despise the young. We know Mencken is right when he says, "Youth is wasted on the young, how fortunate that they won't have it for very long." There they are, these young people; look around at them, these undergraduates, full of potency and potential, and it is wasted in pleasure and diversion.

Our rich young man is rich, he's young, and he's a man, or a ruler, one and the same thing in this setting. He is entitled. He is a member of the establishment. He is a member of an exclusive club. He is a Mason, an Odd Fellow, a Knight of Columbus, he has the key to the executive washroom, and his father or his son, doubtless both, went to Harvard.

So much, then, for the rich young man, easily taken apart, easily ridiculed, easily held up to scornful examination by the daily talk-show hosts. The text and Jesus are considerably less harsh on this fellow than we are, however, and instead of what our perceptions tell us, let us see what the text tells us about this rich young man. We know straightaway that he is a virtuous man. He knows the law and he has kept it. "If you want to enter into life, keep the commandments," says Jesus. "Which ones?" asks the young man. "All of them," says Jesus. Not seven out of ten, or every other one, or some winning combination as you choose, but all of them. That would silence most of us. "I have kept all of these," says the young man. This is no small thing: He knows what is right, he knows the law, and he has kept it. He is good, he has done good, he has done all that can be asked, and, annoying as such manifest virtue may be, we cannot fault the boy with spiritual pride, for remember that this recital of his accomplishments is extracted from him by Jesus, and is prefaced by two very important questions.

The first one is: "Teacher, what good must I do to gain eternal life?" The second one, after this discourse has been concluded, is: "What do I still lack?" What is still missing in my life? These are not insincere questions. These questions do not suggest some kind of spiritual smugness or self-righteousness. They do not imply conceit or pride. Indeed,

they cast this young man as one of the genuine spiritual seekers, genuinely bewildered, genuinely concerned, genuinely interested in his own
salvation. With all that he has, with all that he has done, with all that
he is, he still is not satisfied. He still does not enjoy the satisfaction of
knowing all that there is to know, being all that he could possibly be,
and he knows this. He is not satisfied not because he is greedy but
because he lacks substance in his being. He is incomplete and he knows
it. That knowledge of incompleteness is breaking his heart, and it brings
him to Jesus. What am I lacking, what must I do, what do I need to
fulfill my life? Having done all of those things I was expected to do, all
of the things I am able to do, having virtue and knowledge and wisdom
and opportunity, I still can't make it? I have everything that life has to
offer, and I still lack something. Note the poignancy of that little word
in the question, "What do I *still* lack?"

Those of you who have read the story know that here comes the punch
line, and it should teach you how to ask a question of Jesus, for you are
likely to get an answer that is both surprising and memorable:

"If you wish to be perfect, go, sell your possessions, and give to
the poor, and you will have treasures in heaven; then come and follow me."

A footnote to which I am going to return is that the hard part here
is not in selling your possessions, though that is difficult. The hard part
here is in "come and follow me"; but more on that point later. "And
when the young man heard this he went away with a heavy heart for he
was a man of great wealth." "Aha," we say. When it came to doing
something of practical worth and use, not just keeping the law and mem-
orizing all that mumbo-jumbo and having abstract virtue, but when it
came to giving his money away to the poor, he refused. Thus, we say,
this is a story of greed, materialism, and misplaced values. End of story.
That is where the rich young man exits, never to be heard from again
in the pages of scripture or in the pages of history. Yet it is exactly at
that point where the story begins and where you and I enter into it.

Who of us willingly and easily and without a very heavy heart would give up that which is most dear to us in order to pursue some vague and aimless destiny with Jesus? The problem of the rich young man is not that he is not good; he is just not good enough. Or more to the point, goodness is not good enough.

His position is ours exactly. We are virtuous, you and I. You and I strive after ever more virtue. We may not always achieve it, we may not always have the right definition of what it is, but I am convinced that more often than not more of us than not are striving after the good. I am convinced that most people still pursue the good insofar as they can discern it. They keep the laws, even stupid laws, as best they can. They do good works in the face of overwhelming ingratitude and inefficiency, and God help us all if those who do good works ceased to do them. We prize virtue, you and I, and we prize wisdom and knowledge. We are neither venial nor stupid. We may not be rich, but we all have things that enrich us and with which we would be unwilling to part. So that rich young man is not so far removed from our own particular place in time and in circumstance.

To make sure that we understand that this is not simply about money and therefore applies only to those who have more than we have, translate the text "sell all your possessions and give to the poor" in this way:

"...give away your talent, your time, your brains, your looks, your board scores, your tenure, your partnership, your pension plan, your children, your spouse, your dreams, your ambitions. Give up all of that and come follow me."

That makes it painfully clear that it is not just about money and it's not just about those who have enough disposable income to dispose of it. It is about us. Since this is the case, you and I also would go away sorrowful with heavy hearts for we too have many possessions. We, too, are very wealthy, and our sadness, like his, is that now that we know what it takes to achieve that ultimate peace and perfection for which we so dearly long, we also know that we are unwilling to pay the price. We know what it takes, and we are still unwilling to pay the price. There is not one of us here who is willing to do that.

Sorrow, you see, is not the fruit of ignorance but the fruit of knowledge. We know but we are unwilling to do. We know, but we are unwilling to give up. We will hold on to these treasures like the drowning man in a shipwreck who holds on to his gold rather than let it go in order to grasp a life preserver.

Here, of course, would be the neat little moral: You must lose in order to gain; and that may very well be where you expect this is going, yet another stewardship sermon in disguise. You must give in order to get. You must dispossess yourself in order to possess treasure in heaven—but Jesus is not Kahlil Gibran, given to pious maxims for tea bags. The disciples are amazed—the better translation is "horrified"—at the story. For if this young man of ability, promise, and achievement, who had everything going for him including modesty and spiritual ambition, if this young man cannot be saved, in the words of the text, "Who then can possibly be saved?" "Humanly speaking," says Jesus, "it is impossible." In rational, human, sociological, sensible, psychological, physiological, philosophical terms, nobody is going to do as Jesus directed, and therefore, because nobody is going to do it, nobody is going to be saved. We have no right to expect all of you to become like Mother Teresa. That is unrealistic, and you're not going to do it even if it were realistic. So, in human terms, if that is the criterion, nobody is going to be saved. "Humanly speaking," says Jesus, "it is impossible; but with God anything is possible."

There is a collect that says, "Almighty God, who seest that we have no power of ourselves to help ourselves..." Thank God salvation is God's business and not ours. Unitarians at the turn of this century had as one article of their reformed and liberal creed "Salvation by character." Well, it may have saved Harvard's President Charles William Eliot, but few could depend upon their character for salvation, then or now. The rich young man by all accounts had a fine character, and yet even he knew that it was not enough. "Humanly speaking, it is impossible, but with God anything is possible." Anything, including, perhaps, the salvation of the rich young man himself. Speculate on that in the large economy of God's salvation. Anything, including perhaps your salvation and mine, despite our virtue, despite our wisdom, despite our riches, despite our knowledge, despite our fears. God saves us in spite of ourselves because of himself. If God can make the universe out of nothing, think of what he can do with you and with me. "Humanly speaking, it is impossible, but with God anything is possible . . ." Even this.

LENT III

When Too Much Is Not Enough

Text: One of the multitude said to him, "Teacher, bid my brother divide the inheritance with me." *Luke 12:13*

Here in Saint Luke we begin again with a matter of inheritance not unlike the matter of inheritance at the start of that most famous parable of the Prodigal Son. Here it says, "One of the multitude said [to Jesus], 'Teacher, bid my brother divide the inheritance with me.' " Now what could be more human, sensible, rational, or practical than that? It seems a reasonable request to make. What little we know of the law of property in ancient times suggests that the inheritance in this particular case is a shared one between two heirs. We do not know whether this inheritance is land, cash, or both, but we do know that it is probably greater in one piece than in two divided pieces, and to split an inheritance among sons is in essence to lose the estate, in some sense to lose the power of the whole estate, to have it broken up. So the options were either to give the estate whole to the eldest, in the principle of primogeniture; or to give it whole to the joint heirs to hold in common for the sake of preserving the power of the estate; or to divide it up among the heirs by some formula, a portion here, a portion there.

However you deal with it, it all means trouble, and only the lawyers take any profit from the proceedings because they are the only ones who never lose. Wills and inheritances bring out the worst in people because the stakes seem to be so high when in fact they are so low.

Let me tell you my own experience. As the only heir of my mother, I well remember having to sit before a lawyer's desk. My mother had rejoiced in the cosseting and making of her will; she made it many, many times over in the course of her life, and she rejoiced in not telling me what was in it. Then came the day when I had to confront her aged lawyer downtown in Plymouth; and I went in and he offered me his profound condolences and said what a great and good and godly woman my mother had been and how fortunate I was to have known her, and he was to have known her, and to know me, and we went through a great sort of to-do. Finally he cleared his throat and said, "I expect you're here about the will." I said, "Well, as a matter of fact, I am." He said, "Well, let me see if I can put my hand on it"; and he looked around and it took some time but in a great sheaf of blue papers he found the will and he put his glasses on and looked at it very carefully, and he looked at me, and then he looked at it again, and then he put it down. "Now, was your mother previously married?" he asked. I said, "Not that I am aware of." He then said, "Were there any other issue of the marriage?" I became very nervous and said, "I am not aware of any other issue of the marriage." Then he said, "Did your father have any other children?" "No, no, no, no, what is all this about?" I asked. He looked down at the will very closely and then looked up at me, and he said, "Well, then, I guess it's all yours."

The matter today begins on a legal note about inheritance with that same sense of anxiety and frustration that I as sole heir had encountered in my own experience, and there is in both the sense of grievance and of greed, I confess it, two very human factors. The tone of the question that the man puts to Jesus, "Bid my brother divide the inheritance with me," suggests frustration and failure at perhaps previous efforts to settle this amicably and without resorting to the law. Genteel, fraternal relations, and efforts at conflict resolution—"Come now, let us reason together"—is what this tone suggests has been tried, and we can infer that it has failed; and we all know that there is nothing more divisive in family relationships than an attempt agreeably and informally to divide up property and money. The brother will not give up, he will not give way, and he will not give in. The brother who will not yield to this resolution might fear the loss of the estate, some division, the loss of influence, or the loss of income. Who knows? We don't. We know that he wants to hold on to what he has. The first brother, the one who speaks to Jesus, however, has his own agenda. We don't know exactly what it is, but we do know that whatever it is he wants to achieve it by himself, on his own, with his own share of the inheritance. Who knows, his brother may be a wastrel, a poor manager, the town drunk, for all that. He may be impairing the family fortune, running down the estate. We can only speculate, but we do sense grievance and we do sense some reasonable sense of greed: "I can do more and better with what is mine than with what is mine and his." We know that Jesus imputes greed in this circumstance because in refusing to function as an unpaid lawyer, Jesus says, "Take heed, and beware of all covetousness" (Luke 12:15). Who has evidenced covetousness in this text but the first brother?

First, however, it is a matter of prosperity, for this is the substance of the parable that Jesus tells in order to set the inquiring brother straight. It is a matter of prosperity, for we read, "The land of a rich man brought forth plentifully" (Luke 12:16). Two things we learn very quickly: The man was rich and his land made him richer. He was so rich and he did so well that he had more than he needed. He clearly was a victim of abundance and operated not simply at a profit but at a surplus, and doubtless he had acquired his wealth, we must infer, by hard work and diligence and labor and sobriety and all of those virtues that our mothers and fathers tell us about. He acquired his wealth by not ever spending more than he took in. Prudence led to property, property led to prosperity. He had done very well indeed, and note, please, that Jesus does not condemn the fact that he has done well. Jesus does not condemn the fact that he is rich. Two footnotes to the text.

This rich man who was getting richer by the moment makes two fatal and all too human assumptions, however. In the first case he assumes that his good fortune will continue and indeed that his good fortune will not only continue but that it will increase, and that like Monsieur Coué, every day in every way he will get better and better, and richer and richer and richer to the point where he will need bigger and better warehouses to store his profits. What a wonderful dilemma! "What shall I do," he asks, "for I have nowhere to store my crops?" (Luke 12:17). We should admire his industry, his MBA response to the problems of the surplus— don't give it away, don't plant less, find bigger warehouses in which to keep it—but we should be wary of his second assumption that the good times will continue. He clearly, by that assumption, was not a New England farmer, for our farmers always know that here in this land where the most reliable crop is stone, good fortune is simply a prelude to disaster. A good harvest means a disastrous winter, a good winter means a poor spring, a good spring means a dry summer, a dry summer means a poor harvest, and the whole cycle begins all over again. "Expect little and you will never be disappointed, but sometimes pleasantly surprised" is a basic rule of life not followed by our friend.

Now that second error is compounded when he believes that he himself has done all of the work that produces this prosperity, and thus he can now live off the profits; yesterday's profits yielding tomorrow's ease. "Soul," he says, "you have ample goods laid up for many years; take your ease, eat, drink, be merry" (Luke 12:19). Notice that there is a phrase missing, one that you have heard in that wonderfully secular classical aphorism: "Eat, drink, and be merry, for tomorrow we must die." This is no epicurean enterprise; he doesn't expect to die tomorrow, he expects to live on forever and forever, eating and drinking and being more merry and living off more income compounded daily. What he has he believes he has earned; it belongs to him and is for him to enjoy and to dispose of as he will. He can now afford to relax and to rest for he is what he has accumulated. The work and the worker and the results of the work have all become one and the same. That is where his identity is, that is where his enterprise is, and that is where his reward is, here and now. None of this postponing pleasure until tomorrow, none of this waiting for heaven to be rewarded; no, "I have done it, and here it is."

Here Jesus says, "Fool," and in the Bible "fool" means one who does not acknowledge the existence of God. "Fool!" he says. "This night your soul is required of you . . ." you will be foreclosed upon tonight even though you don't have a mortgage. You will be foreclosed upon tonight, "and the things you have prepared, whose will they be?" (Luke 12:20).

These things that you have accumulated and laid up and invested in, whose will they be? Here is where the silence of the text speaks vividly, because they will not be yours. What will become of those bonds and those surpluses? You are rich in the world but when the world ends and you with it, what will you have if you are not rich toward God?

When she was five years old, the daughter of Christina Onassis, in the midst of childhood innocence and bliss and ignorance, inherited something like five billion dollars upon her mother's untimely death. What was a five-year-old child going to do with a billion dollars for every year of her life? As we know how things work, that amount will grow still bigger and bigger and bigger. This reminds me of a story I heard about her grandfather, Aristotle Onassis, and the vast wealth that was his when he died. After his funeral his rich oil friends were eager to learn the true extent of the fabled wealth of Mr. Onassis, and so they asked the question "How much did he leave?" To which the answer was "Everything." He left it all.

"Fool! This night your soul is required of you; and the things you have prepared, whose will they be?" More to the point, again in the silence of the text, "Whose will you be?" If you are defined by what you have, or by what you do, or by where you are, what happens when you don't have anything, and you are nobody, and you don't do anything anymore? Who are you?

Now, strangely enough, this text is not a story about money or wealth. Jesus neither praises prudence nor condemns prosperity. This is no simpleminded socialist tract, no ethical injunction to give all your goods to charity or even to Harvard. This has nothing to do with philanthropy; it is not an exercise in estate planning. Some try to take it with them; remember the story of the lady who wished to be buried in her Cadillac because she had worked so hard to get it and was not prepared to go on without it? There are others who want to control it after they are gone, their power extending beyond the grave through endless codicils, wills, and testamentary devices.

The one who is rich toward God, Jesus says, is the one who recognizes here and now that treasure is not in what one has, or even in what one leaves or gives away, or even in what one does. Those are not riches. Treasure is in who one is, and ultimately that treasure is defined in terms of the relationship one has with God. Treasure is knowing that one belongs not to self, or to work, or vocation, or ambition, but that one belongs to God. You don't belong to your talent or to your skill or identity in the world. Treasure is knowing that you belong to God; treasure is knowing that therefore you are not alone. You are not isolated, you are not on your own. Treasure is in knowing that you are loved and that you love because you are loved, and that knowledge of self and relationship and purpose is what treasure is all about. Treasure means rich in relationship to God, that which the world cannot give and which therefore the world and all of its adversities and all of its trials and tribulations cannot take away. The one who would then be truly rich is the one who cultivates that treasure, that knowledge, and who does so with all of the effort that other people use to cultivate earthly but perishable goods. So that when you leave "everything," as we all most certainly will leave everything, you can take "it" with you, for it is the only thing you ever truly had, and that is the love of God.

Beyond Tragedy

❖

Text: If thou be Christ, save thyself and us.   *Luke 23:39 (KJV)*

You may be aware that this Sunday has two titles, those of Palm Sunday and the Sunday of the Passion. Today also has two moods. There is that festival frenzy of the palms, that marvelous chaos which we organize every year. We try to capture the mood of that triumphal entry with donkeys and asses and yelling Jews and screaming disciples of which the gospel speaks. The only one who seemed to have any peace or calm or mind about the whole thing is not Jesus but the donkey. The donkey is the only one who knows where he is going.

This is the first mood of Palm Sunday, and it is the mood with which many of us were brought up: a festive dress rehearsal for an Easter triumph. There is a second mood as well, and that is reflected in the traditional reading of the Passion narrative with its account of the betrayal and death of Jesus. This is the solemn side of the day, and it is almost unbearable in its anguish and pathos. Here we confront the dark side of the human experience, and when we are forced to cry "Crucify, crucify" along with the biblical mob, it is painfully close.

Here are these two moods, these two sentiments, these two attitudes that jangle and are out of sync for they violate that law of physics that says two objects cannot occupy the same place at the same time. Ours is an emotional law of physics that says the same thing, and so we move to resolve our "problem" as many of us did when we were in other ages and in other churches and in other styles: by removing the Passion from the palms, by saving the suffering for the faithful few, those moral masochists who will come to church on Maundy Thursday and on Good Friday, and thereby leave today "free" for the triumphalism and the dress rehearsal for Easter. Palm Sunday addicts like the procession, they like the anticipated glory of Jesus, and they love the sense that the Lenten gloom imposed these last six weeks has at least risen if not fully departed.

Now I know that I exaggerate. That is what preachers do and that is what preaching is, exaggeration, the making of small points large so that small people like ourselves can see them. In this caricature, however, perhaps you do recognize yourselves even as I see myself, for like so many of you I was brought up on this "let's have a parade" theory of Palm Sunday, that discreet form of Protestantism that could not bear the embarrassment or the indignity of the cross. So we liked to remember that the palm was the symbol of Roman victory, and to bear your palm was to have achieved and triumphed over your foes.

To bear these palms, however, is to bear the symbol not of victory but of the vanity of human foolishness, the illusion of what passes for victory in this world. The branches of palm, while rotting and getting dry as they do throughout the year, ought to remind us of both vanity and of modesty: the vanity of what we think we can do and the modesty of what we actually can do, or of what we don't do. They are not signs of triumph, moral merit badges—they are not that. They are not signs even of tragedy, a highly developed force of dramatic but unreal enterprise. They are not signs of triumph or of tragedy, they are signs of suffering, the suffering of the Savior, the suffering of his people, the suffering of all creation and of us with it. The palms remind us of what the psychologists have just learned: that victory is just the other side of defeat and failure is just the other side of success.

So in order to resolve our dilemma we will be tempted to assign the victory side of things to our heads, and the Passion, the suffering side of things, to our hearts. Thus can our rational and emotional centers segregate this confusion in which we find ourselves on Palm Sunday, with which it is too difficult to live, even though we know that such emotional segregation is neither possible nor desirable. Those who achieve it we call schizophrenic, or as having split personalities, and we know that that is a disorder and not an ambition. No, the church's call to wholeness is a call to holiness, to an ability to take the ambiguity, even the confusion and conflict of emotion, and see in the whole that the only reconciliation possible between them is the reconciling love of God in Jesus Christ. That is the only thing that stands between rank and utter chaos, insanity, and an attempt to stand whole and full and complete in the middle of ambiguity and beyond tragedy. That is the only reality: that God's love is the only thing that makes sense out of suffering, conflict, and tragedy. God's love does not do away with conflict, or suffering, or tragedy; the cross should teach us that. God's love does not do away with it, God's love is the thing that makes it possible to bear it, to see it, to share in it, to understand it, and to pass through it. That is the truth of the gospel, that is the essence of the Passion.

We will want to interfere, you and I, we will want to make it all come out right, and sooner rather than later. We will want to do what the Victorians did to the tragedies of Shakespeare. I don't know if any of you ever read any of the Victorian editions of Shakespeare, but the Victorians in their optimistic moralism could not allow Shakespeare's corrupted sense of reality to have the last word and influence young and innocent minds, so they changed the grim endings of *Romeo and Juliet*, and *Macbeth*, and *Hamlet*, and so forth. Their version of *Romeo and Juliet* has the lovers suddenly recovering, and not only do they recover but they are reconciled, and not only are they reconciled but their families are reconciled, and they all live happily ever after, and Father Lawrence has a wonderful wedding to perform, and it is a tremendously glorious occasion.

Now our impulse may be more sophisticated than theirs; we may not be tempted to "dress up" the Passion and turn it into something fit for prime time, with an upbeat, happy ending like Mel Brooks's *The Producers*, with that wonderful kick-line about Nazi Germany, "Springtime for Hitler." We will, however, want to interfere and avoid what we know is going to happen. We want to make it all come out right, which usually means doing nothing: no suffering, no Passion, no ambiguity, no pain, and as the jocks say, "no gain."

The church, however, preaches and teaches the truth, and the human condition is one of unresolved ambiguity, and the suffering and death that come from the ambiguity are real. Those critics of Martin Scorsese's *The Last Temptation of Christ* were most upset that Jesus is depicted as vacillating and his last week, indeed his last hours, filled with conflict, ambiguity, and tension resolved only by death itself. When Catholic prelates and Protestant fundamentalists agree I get very, very nervous, and in this case their agreement and their anger come both from misreading the Passion and from not seeing the film. Now I, too, as well as any bishop, can review a film that I haven't seen. I haven't seen the film but I have read the Passion, and you have too, and that is the very point of the Passion: the conflicts of mood, the vacillation of the will, the confusion of sentiments, the crowd that yells "Hosannah" at one minute and cries out "Crucify" the next, and it's the same crowd. The Savior who says, "Let this cup pass from me," also says, "Not my will but thine be done," and is the same Savior. The steadfast disciples who become within minutes deserters and deniers are the same disciples. Indeed, even the impenitent thief, that most cynical commentator on the cross, who asked the question that we all want to ask—"If you're so good, why are you up here?"—points out the irony and ambiguity of that supreme moment in Calvary. In the midst of the crucifixion he says, "If thou be the Christ, save thyself and us." Ambiguity, the name of the Passion is ambiguity. Read it!

Is that not our question? If you are really Jesus, really who you say you are, really who they say you are, really who you want us to believe you are, then spare us the embarrassment of this very tacky scene. Spare us and yourself the humiliation of a public failure. Spare us and yourself the ridicule of unbelievers and intellectuals, spare us the cynically bad and the indifferently good. Spare us, Jesus, if you are who you say you are, the embarrassment of taking our palms to lunch and having people wonder what they are all about. "If thou be the Christ, save thyself and us," now.

He does not, not yet, for we must suffer with him that we may be glorified with him. That is what the Passion is, not simply to see suffering as in a play or a Greek tragedy, but to share in suffering, to weep as Jesus wept at the brokenness of what is meant to be whole, to see a thing as it is meant to be and to experience it broken, fractured, and shattered, not just the Savior's body but the body of the world; to suffer with indignity and inhumanity, to weep at injustice and crime, and violence and deprivation and depravity, to enter into the sorrows of another as if they were our own, because they are our own.

Jesus did not die in order to spare us the indignities of the wounded creation. He died that we might see those wounds as our own. He died that we might live, and live fully and hopefully—please note the correct use of the adverb "hopefully" as "full of hope"—not in some fantastic never-never-land not yet arrived, but in ambiguous reality here and now. Look at the cross and the suffering bleeding Savior. Beyond tragedy is truth redeemed. Look and live!

excellent –

When Life Begins

❀

Text: You have nothing to fear.   *Matthew 28:5 (REB)*

The resurrection is God's way of getting our attention. It is God's way of making us listen up, God's way of getting us to look, to listen, and to live. The first thing to remember, once God gets our attention, is that there is nothing subtle about Easter, nothing vague or ambiguous or vain or clever or cute about it at all. To make that point, God does not begin Easter Day as the slow, gradual triumph of the dawn over the darkness; rather he takes a leaf from the notebook of Cecil B. DeMille himself, and God begins Easter with an earthquake. "Suddenly there was a violent earthquake," says the gospel. "An angel of the Lord had descended from heaven and came and rolled away the stone, and sat down on it. His face shone like lightning; his raiments were white as snow. At the sight of him the Roman guards shook with fear and became like dead men."

God knows how to get our attention. God knows how to begin an epochal new relationship. Easter is not a morning for artful arguments, subtle distinctions, the stuff of seminars. Not a bit; it does not creep up on us on little cat feet like the fog. Easter is confrontational; you are hit in the face by it. Confrontation of the highest order. Nature itself is overwhelmed, nature is contradicted, for an earthquake is not a gentle dawn and Christian faith begins not with a whimper or an argument but with a bang. It is God's intention to get our attention, and he does. The women are placed at the tomb so that they can be confronted by this phenomenon; they are the audience before whom this great attention-getter is to be played. There they are, like you and like me, preoccupied with their own thoughts, worried perhaps about the roast or the guests or both. Their private griefs, their personal agendas, their memories, their expectations, and indeed their fears are interrupted by God in a mighty way, but it is not simply the convulsions of nature to which they are drawn and by which they are compelled. An earthquake is an impressive, terrifying thing indeed, just ask anyone who has lived through one in California or Armenia. Earthquakes are meant to be taken seriously, and the wise do so.

It was not nature that provoked this confrontation but an angel of the Lord, and even the unflappable, unfazable Californians might be impressed with more than nature's temper tantrum if out of the middle of it there appeared an angel of the Lord, an angel so powerful that he could and did roll away the stone unassisted, an angel so audacious—this is not one of your flapping-wing angels—gutsy, and arrogant that he sits on the stone in triumph as if it were a throne, glorious in his apparel, glorious in his enterprise, as if to say, "See what I did. How's that? And if you think that's a great act, wait till you see what's next!" With this God certainly got the attention of all of the relevant parties, and the purpose of all of this extraordinary activity was to get a message through, to deliver a message to thickheaded but goodhearted people such as ourselves.

"He is not here; he is risen as he said; he goes before you; spread the good news; do not be afraid. You have nothing to fear." That is the first, and that is the only message of Easter: Jesus Christ is risen from the dead and is not to be found where the dead are. He told us this, and it is so. He is out there ahead of us, and our job is to spread the good news that he lives; and, by the way, relax, stop worrying, stop thinking that it all depends on you. It has been accomplished. It has been done.

Life begins when God gets our attention, and for many of us it takes an earthquake or two to do just that, and life begins when we can hear what God has to say and we can act upon it and live upon it. Now there are a variety of ways in which God gets our attention. Some of those ways are sudden and dramatic—a brilliant moment of insight, a flash of lightning, one of those lightbulb moments when the light comes on and "Aha!" we say. "I understand. Aha! I see what it all means." An inbreaking of peace or serenity, an inbreaking of understanding where in a moment of revelation we see things as they are and ourselves fully and clearly as we are. Such moments are to be treasured and such moments are hard to anticipate, to evoke or invoke, they are hard to define, they are hard to defend, but we know them when we have them, and we have all had them from time to time.

God gets our attention through tragedy and terror, and Lord knows we have had enough of these; yet in and through them we ask questions, we are more responsive to revelations of truth, we are made more acute, we are placed on edge. God does not send the terror or the tragedy to do this, but he uses the terror and the tragedy and even the death of God himself on the cross even as he uses the sublime and the beautiful, the mysterious and the rational. All of these are used to get our attention, to get through thickheaded but goodhearted people; and life can begin only when God gets our attention and we are in a position to hear what God has to say.

Now life began for those women, those earliest of the witnesses of the Lord, those first apostles, not simply when they heard the message of the angel but when they acted upon it; and to make sure that they would do so, they heard that message again from Jesus himself. They meet Jesus on the way, they fall down before him, and Jesus says, "Do not be afraid. Go and tell my brothers to go to Galilee: there they will see me." They heard the good news, and whether they understood it or not they acted upon it. "So the women hurried away from the tomb, afraid yet filled with joy, and ran to tell his disciples." That is what Saint Matthew wants us to understand: Life begins when we are able to take hold of what has been given to us and to run with it. That's literally what it means. Life begins when fear and joy, that odd couple of human existence, enable us despite the one and because of the other to get on with the serious and glorious business of living and of loving. Life begins for Easter Christians when we realize that we do not have to die to live. You can begin it right now, right here. You don't have to have an after-death experience. You can live life while you're still alive. What a bargain, what an extraordinary thing! Who would believe it? But you can. Life begins when you run with what you have, run with what you have been given; and we have to remember that life in the power and the spirit of the resurrection, the faith of Easter, is not simply quantity time but quality time.

Now I know that that distinction between quantity time and quality time sounds like some sort of adolescent psychobabble, making appointments to have breakfast with your children and that sort of thing, but life really begins not when you realize how much or how little time you have but when you figure out what it is that you can and will and must do with whatever time you have, whether it is your entire life before you or a few moments. Life begins when you figure out how to use your time; that's when life begins.

So it is with the women and the men of Easter. It was not how long they would now live after Easter; it was how they were empowered and transformed by the risen Lord to live their lives in newness of life. Life began for them when they stopped being afraid. Life began for them when they stopped being afraid both of what they did know and afraid of what they did not know. Life began for them when they could dare to believe that the risen Christ, the living, walking, talking Christ, made a difference in their lives; and life began for them when they believed this to be true even if they could neither explain it nor understand it.

Life begins when you see life not simply as an unexpended bit of time, a balance remaining in your savings account with dangers, chances, and fate all taking their part. Life begins when you realize that by removing the fear of death, Christ has given you, for the first time, full possession of your own life. What you have always had, you now own. See the difference: What you have always had, you now own. It is yours, free, full, and clear.

When I talk with some of my psychiatrist friends and some of my psychologist friends and some of my medical and clerical friends, and even with the few legal friends that I have, and we get down to cases, we discover that the basic fundamental thing that appears to hold our professional lives together and define all our relationships with our clients and our parishioners and our colleagues is not sin, which you might expect me to say, but fear. Everybody is fearful, terrified of some public or private demon, some terrible unnamed fear that gnaws away even in the midst of our joy, some cloud that hangs over our head or in the recesses of our spirit. It is fear that not only holds us together but keeps us from being whole. Fear, not sin, is the great curse. Fear that I'll be recognized for the fraud that I am—the great imposter complex. Fear that I will fail in some worthy endeavor or fear that I will succeed in some unworthy enterprise. Fear that I will not have enough time to do what I must. Fear that I will hurt or be hurt. Fear that I will not know love. Fear that my love will be painful and hurtful. Fear that the things that I most believe and trust are not so. Fear that I am untrustworthy. Every one of us is a hostage to fear.

"Be not afraid, you have nothing to fear." These are the empowering words of Easter. Freedom from fear is the achievement of the resurrection—not freedom from death but freedom from fear. We do not fear death; death is the incarnation of our fears. Thus to defeat fear is to defeat death and to defeat death is to defeat fear. It is not death that lurks in the background, it is the fear of death, and to diminish those fears is to gain life everlasting.

Some people we know fear death; they are terrified of it. This we can understand, but the greater curse, I argue, is those who fear life, who dare not embrace the fullness of their opportunities for life, who fear to live because they fear to fail or they fear to succeed or they fear to move anywhere out of even the sustaining circle of fear. Such defensive living is not the stuff of which Easter faith is made. It is not the stuff of Easter Christians, and it is twice made clear in Saint Matthew's gospel; the angel says "Be not afraid," and Jesus says "You have nothing to fear." Having got our attention, that is what God has to say to you and to me.

The women were told not be afraid of the earthquake or of the fearsome angel or even of the resurrected Jesus, and more to the point, Jesus has not simply conquered death, although that he has surely and certainly done, but even more important than Jesus' conquering of death, Jesus has redeemed life so that you and I can live it here and now. Jesus affirms the good news that life is worth living now, here, in all of its fullness, all of its amplitude. You don't have to die to live.

Because Jesus lives we too may live, with as much time as God gives us, free from fear of the past, free from fear of the future. Christ ever goes before us. "He goes before you," says Saint Matthew. He goes before us blazing a path for us to follow, and where Christ has gone we need not fear. Christ went to the cross; we need not fear the cross. Christ went to the grave; we need not fear the grave. Christ has gone into the future; we need not fear the future. Christ inhabits life; we need not fear life. God gets our attention at long last by earthquake or sublime experience or terror. He tells us that he has come in Jesus Christ that we may have life and that we may have it more abundantly. Because he lives, so, too, may we. Life begins, my friends, when you discover this truth for yourselves, and act upon it.

Life on the Other Side

❋

Text: Jesus said to them, "Children, have you any fish?" They answered him, "No." He said to them, "Cast the net on the right side of the boat and you will find some."   *John 21:5–6*

Life on the other side of Easter is a strange thing, a very peculiar thing indeed. Life on the other side of Easter is not easy and we are tempted, and in fact we succumb to our temptation, to go back to where we were, and to what we were, and to what we were doing before Easter came along and interrupted us with its power, its glory, and its transformation. The clergy, quite frankly, rejoice that Easter is over and comes but once a year. Who can sustain that level of energy, that level of labor? The musicians are secretly glad that Easter is over, for they can relax a bit. The only people who lament the passing of Easter and the fact that it isn't every Sunday are the florists and the haberdashers.

On the other side we all get on with it, we all get back to it. That Easter business is gone now, it is too far away, it is too distant from our experience to anticipate again, and it is too foggy in our experience to recall it to mind. In a way, is it not as if it never happened, it never existed? To look at us, to see us, to look at the churches of Christendom today would be as if Easter—three weeks ago, or two thousand years ago—never happened at all but was a dream, a fantasy, a fiction even more incredible than all those others in the New Testament.

We are not alone in this rather strange experience of the other side of Easter. The text from Saint John's gospel, which is commonly called a Commentary on the Resurrection, is about life on the other side of Easter, life on the other side for the disciples; except, for those disciples, remember, their Easter Day was far less impressive than ours. Their Easter was much duller than ours. There were no trumpets on their Easter Day, there were no sermons trying to explain it to log-headed Christians, there was no cultural support, no sort of world prepared to accept for a day the truth of it.

No, their Easter was far less compelling than ours; all they had to show for their Easter were those strange conversations with the risen Lord whom they never seemed to recognize.

"Let's get back to normal, get on with it, get back to business." Is that not the advice that we all give to friends and relations who have just suffered the death of a loved one? We tolerate their mourning eccentricities for a little while, we sympathize with them, we send them casseroles and we write cards, and we call on them for about ten days or so, but then it comes time for us to really give them some serious advice. We say, "Now you really must get on with it. Do something, go back to what it was that you used to do." Or, "Stop doing whatever it was that you used to do, and get on with it. Work it out. Don't just sit around and mourn and grieve." We've all used that as our way of helping people get on with their lives on the other side of a great tragedy, on the other side of a great loss. We know what that is like.

Despite the post-resurrection appearances that the New Testament provides for us, life on the other side for the apostles was as ordinary as it had been before Easter, and their solution was to take the advice they gave themselves, the advice we would give to people in similar situations: "Get on with it." They went back to work. They became who they were before Easter. "I go a-fishing," says Peter. What's so extraordinary about that? That's what he did before Easter. He is by vocation and experience and inclination a fisherman. The others say, "We will go with you," and they do, and they do the only thing they really know how to do. When you think about it, the apostles were not very good at the profession of being apostles. They were not very good disciples in the craft of discipling. They were not very good students of Jesus. They never understood what he was saying, they never recognized him, and they never healed anybody of any substance, and they never really knew what was going on. The only thing they were good at is the thing that Jesus called them from doing, and so they went back to doing it, they went back to fishing, the only thing they knew how to do.

Jesus, Saint John tells us, appears on the beach at daybreak. The disciples don't know it is Jesus and the gospel is clear on this point, but they hear him ask them, "Have you any fish?" Now Jesus is like a very good lawyer who never asks a question to which he doesn't already know the answer. He can see that their labors of the night have been unsuccessful, not by any extraordinary second sight, at least not yet, but from the shore he can see that there is nothing on one side and there's a lot on the other side. That's why they had night spotters for night fishing. I got that out of a commentary; you can check it out if you want to. Jesus can see that their labors of the night, the thing that they are good at, have been unsuccessful. What they are doing is not productive, even though it's all they know how to do. "Children, have you any fish?" he asks them, and they reply, "No."

Now there are varieties of "no" in the world and we know what they are. There is "No, and it's none of your business!" There is "No, and we are sad, and disappointed, and frustrated," and there is "No, can you help?" Which is it here? I don't know. No one knows, and don't trust anyone who tells you that he does know. The text does not tell us the flavor of the "no," but we can suspect that all three of these feelings and emotions are at work: no = anger, no = frustration, and no = can you do anything about it, can you give us a hand? Anger, frustration, and the hope of assistance all are at work here.

"Children, have you any fish?" That's a wonderful question. That's what we call in my business a preaching point. "Children, have you any fish?" It is not the purely rhetorical question that it seems. If we translate that question into the vernacular, our vernacular of living on the other side of Easter, the stranger who looks at us from afar and who sees more of us than we can see of ourselves, and who sees more of what we are doing than we ourselves can see, asks us:

"How are you doing? Are you doing well? How are you getting on in your work? How is it going? Are you happy in your job as a teacher? Are you satisfied in your work as a lawyer? Are you successful in your labors as a housekeeper, as a merchant, as a scholar or an enterpriser? Are you happy as a student? Are you satisfied? Do you get pleasure, satisfaction, utility from what it is that you think you do best?

"Children, have you any fish? Children, do you have anything to show for what it is that you spend most of your time doing, and what it is you think you are good at and best at? Children, have you any fish? Have you anything to show for how you spend your time?"

Now remember, Jesus does not ask the disciples in this case if they are successful evangelists. He doesn't ask, "Are you good preachers for Christ?" He doesn't ask, "Are you witnesses to the risen Lord? Are you finding spiritual comfort and moral perfection?" He doesn't ask those kinds of churchy questions. He asks them the realistic, hard questions, the sensible questions:

"Are you getting satisfaction out of what you do best? You are fishermen; therefore, have you any fish to show for your labor? What do you have to show for all of your efforts, all your investments on the other side of Easter?"

The answer is very simple: nothing. You and I have little to show for all of the energy, labor, imagination, and investment that we put into our lives and our work, nothing; and maturity is the growing consciousness of how little we have to show: nothing, if the truth be known. Nothing to show for it, "We have worked all night, as only we know how to do. Our lives depend upon our labors; there is nothing to show for it and the day is newly breaking when we must cease working," because the kind of work these fishermen do is best done at night. When the sun rises they have to stop, and if there is nothing to show for it, it's all over. They can fish no longer. "Nothing," they replied to the question "Children, have you any fish?" "Cast the net on the right side of the boat and you will find some." Try the other side.

Now I know that one could write many books on the virtues of the left side of the boat as opposed to the right side of the boat. One's political affinities might be based on the left side of the boat as opposed to the right side of the boat, but that's beside the point; it isn't the left side or the right side, it is the *other* side. Whatever side you are laboring on, it is on the other side where Jesus invites you to cast your net. They do so, and *Bingo!* a net full of one hundred fifty-three large fish! One hundred fifty-three—not twelve, not twenty-four, not nine-ninety-nine, but one hundred fifty-three fish.

Now, you will all wonder, you numerists, what does one hundred fifty-three mean? Once again, I don't know, and who cares? That, again, is beside the point. The hundred fifty-three is meant to signify exactly what it does: abundance, fullness, overwhelming success; and these are big fish. The text makes it quite clear that these are not little minnows, these are big fish, so big that they can't haul the net in, but the net miraculously is spared from being broken so that they don't lose any of them. Because, as the text tells us later on, they will have to use some of these fish to have breakfast on the beach with Jesus. They will have to share their abundance with him who made it possible. So, one hundred fifty-three, there's something wonderfully tangible about that number and about those fish. This moves us from the level of spiritualizing and metaphor to something really real, something really tangible.

Here we miss the point if we leave this at the level of just another miracle and conjuring trick that this Jesus does, for Jesus makes the point that life on the other side need not necessarily be the same as it was before. Indeed, the other side is here and now, tangible, and it is full of abundance here, now, in the midst of what we do, in the midst of where we are. These fishermen do not have to wait until the coming of the Lord in glory or until the end of the world, or until heaven itself, to experience the abundance of life in Christ on the other side. In other words, you don't have to go to the other side to experience the power of the other side on this side here and now.

Now I know the danger of talk of the "other side." In our sort of prissy, sanitized language, the other side means death and heaven or some vicinity therein. "We shall all meet on the other side," we used to say in my Baptist church when I was a boy. We say, unconvincingly, at Easter that the other side has some vague connection with resurrection, with heaven, with eternity, and with immortality, whatever those things are. The other side is vaguely acquainted with that place of perfect and boring bliss.

The post-resurrection accounts of Jesus are hardly a spiritualized set of epiphanies, ghost stories, as it were, séances with dim visions into the future or the past. They are told in the most tangible, fleshly fashion possible. They are told around food and drink, breakfast on the beach, supper in the upper room. They are told to remind us that this other side is tangible and real, not a ghostly metaphor but something that lives in living people here and now, and that you do not have to die to know the resurrected life.

"Children, have you any fish?" "Have you satisfaction, have you pleasure, have you success? Have you achieved what it is you spend so much time doing?" You and I know that the answer to that has to be, "No." Then what is the response to that? "Try the other side." Cast your net in some other area, in some other place. Try something else, something new, something different, try responding to the invitation that Jesus Christ gives us. For so many of us, living consists of maintaining unfulfilled lives, doing what we do because we cannot imagine doing anything else. When Jesus says to try the other side, he is offering new life to those of us who are trapped in making a living and not in making a life. He is offering the possibilities of freedom, freedom from our routine and the captivity of what we've always done, and freedom for a new and abundant life that is full to overflowing.

What happens to our fishermen on the other side? They are transformed; and you and I are the result of their transformation. They're not made over instantly, abracadabra, but they grow in awareness of self and of Christ. They develop, they become rehabilitated witnesses of the risen Christ in a fallen world. Peter who denies and lies becomes his preacher, his martyr, his prophet. The rest of them go on not simply to glory but to witnessing Christ in the world. They become the community of the faithful whose heirs you and I are. They live fully before they die gloriously.

Life on the other side is life today for you and for me. It is Easter not just liturgically; it is Easter existentially. If you want to know what that life is like, my friends, "cast your net on the other side," and respond to the invitation that Jesus Christ extends to you. Just as God called his children out of Egypt and led them dry-shod onto the other side, so too are you and I called now. Cast your nets on the other side and let him fill them with such an abundance of joy that your lives cannot begin to contain it. Isn't that what you're looking for? Isn't that what you want? Why not try it? You don't have to die to live. There is life before death. You need only try the other side to experience it fully, joyously, here and now.

Ordinary People

❖

Text: Now when they saw the boldness of Peter and John, and perceived that they were uneducated, common men, they wondered; and they recognized that they had been with Jesus. *Acts 4:13*

A few years ago the Dean of Marsh Chapel at Boston University and I engaged in one of our frequent exchanges of pulpits, and each of us took an old sermon across the river to preach in the other's pulpit. It is probably no secret to you that sermons are recycled. If the great works of Bach can be heard over and over and over again, why cannot the best offerings that we have to make? The only rule is that you don't repeat it to the same congregation. So Dean Thornburg came over here to Memorial Church to preach to Harvard, and I went over to Marsh Chapel to preach to Boston University. In the business of the week when we exchanged the information for our respective bulletins so that the people would know what it was we thought we were saying, we each found out what the other was preaching about. Dean Thornburg chose to give to his sermon the title "God and the Know-it-all." The sermon that I took from my pile without consultation with Bob was titled "Ordinary People." Someone who knew us both wondered if we were trying to insult our respective congregations on that morning, and there were some people at Boston University, sensitive souls, who rather resented the fact that the preacher of Harvard University should preach to them about ordinary people.

Now I know that to be thought of as "ordinary" to many of us is frankly insulting. Many of us have built our lives, our reputations, our careers—our ambitions by-and-large—by being extraordinary. For a teacher to tell the eager parents of a preschooler that their little princess, their little girl of three, is quite an ordinary child, is to risk a lawsuit. For a professor to write in a letter of recommendation that young Johannsen is quite an ordinary young man is to risk physical reprisal, and for a tenure committee to describe a potential colleague as ordinary is to doom the candidacy to outer darkness. Nobody, it seems, wants to be ordinary, and therefore it seems that no one is ordinary.

Yet, for Christians at least, one must confront the fact that our faith is founded upon the experiences and expectations of ordinary people, men and women who do not shake or shape the world on the world's terms. Easter does not come to the philosophically wise or to the intellectually sophisticated or even to the morally perfect, nor does it come to the politically powerful and the wielders of influence and ambition. It comes in the first instance, this new life of Easter, to ordinary and perplexed people much like ourselves who, despite all of our efforts to cover our fears and our anxieties and to hide our ignorance, are really ultimately fearful, anxious, and ignorant. If that does not describe ourselves in our most intimate and honest moments of confrontation, then I do not know what does.

The text reminds us that Peter and John were illiterate persons, untrained in the schools, uneducated, common men, people from whom very little was expected, and more to the point, people who expected very little of themselves. We remember these ordinary people very well indeed. Peter, on whom you would not want to depend if your life depended on it, and John, who loved Jesus and whom Jesus loved, but who

always seemed in those pastel portraits in the gospels to be more needy
than needed. Once again, not a strong reed upon which to lean. There
they are, with their strange and motley company of women and men
who lurch from mourning to rejoicing to confusion. A few weeks ago we
found them frightened, cowed by circumstances, full of the terrors of
the dark. Today, here they are in Acts 3 and 4 causing all kinds of trouble,
all kinds of tumult, getting themselves arrested, curing the lame, preaching long sermons, causing the authorities to confront and to arrest them
and to consider how they might deal with the threat that these ordinary
people now pose to the civilization of which they were so modest and
minor a part. What accounts for this change of circumstance?

In this fourth chapter of the Acts of the Apostles, there are at least
two tempting places to look for the action. We want to know who does
what to whom, and when. If we can summarize it and get a clear picture
of it without having to wade through text, to press fast-forward as it
were, we will do it. So I am helping you fast-forward through this dense
business, the Acts of the Apostles. The first place that you might want
to look for the action here is in the long sermon of Peter.

Peter preaches this sermon about the doings of Jesus Christ in the
world. Here we see in that sermon the great miracle, the miracle that
God himself comes in the form of Jesus Christ. He invades the world,
he transforms the world, he claims it for himself. That is the substance
of the gospel and because it is, those who hear it are transformed, emboldened, and encouraged. It is the word that changes and transforms,
and that is what we find in that sermon of Peter, and that is where the
action is. Who says that words don't make a difference? Who says that
words don't influence people? Who says that mere words do not turn
the world upside down? For good or for evil, words have incredible power,
and to say that that is mere rhetoric is to underestimate the power of
words. When the word is trustworthy and true to experience it transforms night into day and the dead into the living. So that's where the
action is, in Acts 4, in the first instance, in that long and very successful
sermon of Peter.

We know all of that, however, and you've heard these long sermons
all of your days, you've read them, you know that God comes into the

world and that God does great things, and that that's what God is for, to come into the world and do great things. That's how it was imagined and maintained. That's the way it's supposed to be. So we know all of that and therefore we must look to the second part of this lesson to interest us and to find where the action is. The most natural place for us to look for action that makes sense to us beyond words is to the miracle that causes all of the trouble.

Peter and John on their way to the temple are confronted by this man who asks them for spare change. Now we do not know exactly what the exchange is but we do know that Peter says, "Silver and gold have I not." Now remember that when you're passing along the street and somebody asks you for money. You can say, "Silver and gold have I not"; but then Peter goes on, "But I give you what I have: in the name of the Lord Jesus Christ of Nazareth, walk." Now try that yourself. Don't stick around to see what happens, but try it. I suspect that whoever asks you, if he or she recognizes you later, will never again ask you for spare change. "Silver and gold have I not, but I give you what I have; in the name of the Lord Jesus Christ of Nazareth, walk." He did, as the text says, "And immediately his feet and ankles were made strong. And leaping up he stood and walked and entered into the temple with them, walking and leaping and praising God." Now there is a miracle for you. He doesn't limp away to wait for a period of recovery and recuperation, and the translation wants us to know that not only is this a restoration but almost a new creation—he leaps—new power; and in doing all of this he attracts an awful lot of unseemly attention. It would be nice if people who were healed would just go away and write a decent letter of thanks, but here he embarrasses everybody and creates this tremendous firestorm in which Peter and John are caught up. "And all the people saw him walking and leaping and praising God." They knew this fellow, he was a fixture near the temple, always there, lame from birth, "and they were filled with wonder and amazement at what happened to him."

So, if you want to know where the action is, there's that great sermon of Peter's where five thousand are converted and the whole history of salvation is made clear, and then there is this vivid, unambiguous story of healing and leaping for joy; but neither of those two points is *the* point. They are good, but they are not good enough. They are really not the subject of this passage, and therefore neither are they the subject of this sermon. They are decorative and essential details but they are not the subject. The subjects of the story are those scandalously ordinary people, Peter and John, "uneducated and common men, illiterate and uneducated in the schools," who, "because they had been with Jesus," that's the important phrase, were themselves transformed. That is the miracle, not the sermon and not the healing but the transformation of Peter and John. Not so much that they were transformers, but they were transformers because they had been first transformed by the presence of the living Christ in their lives. That's where the boldness came from, that's where the authority came from, that's where the power and the courage, and indeed the joy, came from; and that is the power of the Easter good news, that is the power of the resurrection—that ordinary people are given in Christ a chance to do extraordinary things and to take nothing and make something, to go from nobody to somebody.

Why is it that people respond to the gospel of Jesus Christ? Why is it that the poor, the oppressed, the old, the weak, and the marginal respond to the gospel of Jesus Christ in all ages and at all times? Because they have expectations of transformation. They know that who they are as they are where they are will not do, it is not good enough, and therefore they look to the risen Christ to perform in them that which will transform them and renew them, and that, I suspect, is the ordinary expectation that binds you and me and all of them together in this place at this time. The desire to know the transforming power of the living, risen Christ. Because they, knowing who and what they are, ordinary people, also know that in Christ they—we—become capable of extraordinary things.

What is this transformation? What is this thing that enables and transforms? Are we the ones whom they will see? Is it our cleverness, our skill, our power, our fidelity, our witness? Not really. Note that the text says, "They were uneducated, illiterate common people and they wondered at them; and then they knew that they had been with Jesus." These critics recognized that that power, that boldness, was not in the peculiar gifts and personalities of Peter and John; it had to come from somewhere. They didn't have it to begin with; they're ordinary people just like you and me. They were not born saints, they were not born heroic, so where did it come from? They had been with Jesus, and this was the explanation. They had somehow caught the infection of the resurrection and believed themselves to have the same power as Jesus Christ. How else could they say, "Silver and gold have I not, but what I have I give to you; walk in the name of Jesus Christ"? How else could they make that preposterous claim? How else could they presume, these inarticulate people, to proclaim the gospel so that five thousand people responded? How else could they be emboldened to stand up before the civil authorities of church and of state and say to them, "You may do what you want, but we must preach that of which we are witnesses, the risen Jesus Christ." Where does that stuff come from? Not from a course on personality enhancement; it came from an infection of the risen Christ which they caught and which they spread, and that's what changes ordinary people into extraordinary people.

Paul Tillich once said that the saint is a saint not because he is good, but because he is transparent for something that is more than himself. Being a window of opportunity, being a means of grace, being the place in which the Holy Spirit makes its dwelling, is the vocation of ordinary people. That is why shepherds are summoned to the manger, that is why women are summoned to the tomb on resurrection morning, that is why fisherfolk and the most ordinary of ordinary people around are summoned into the vanguard of Jesus' movement, so that through them, through us, Christ might be seen and known. This is the continuing miracle of Easter. Not so much that Jesus Christ rose from the dead but that you and I may rise from the death in which we now find ourselves, and become in our ordinary lives beings of extraordinary witness to Christ so that in addition to the ample silver and gold that we all have, we may give something that the world needs: power and the love of the risen, living Savior Jesus Christ. That is the vocation of ordinary people, and it happens to people just like ourselves.

The Absent and the Present Christ

❧

Text: "... why stand ye gazing up into heaven? this same Jesus, which is taken up from you into heaven, shall so come in like manner as ye have seen him go. . . . Who shall separate us from the love of Christ? . . ."   *Acts 1:11 and Romans 8:35 (KJV)*

Happily for the preacher and mercifully for the congregation, there are always at least two ways of looking at any text. The texts for Ascension Day and its Sunday are vivid examples of this option. The vividness of the events described in the Acts of the Apostles does not necessarily make any clearer our understanding of them, and yet there is an implicit choice available to us in the text. You may choose between the "upward" and the "downward" visions of the Acts of the Apostles, and your choice, I suspect, depends upon your sociology and astronomy fully as much as it depends upon your theology and your Christology.

    In the upward vision of the text there is that wonderful motion and movement toward the skies, a second Easter with its triumph over the natural order and its promise of great things to come in that other bright and brilliant place. Christ returns to that heavenly splendor from which he has come in the form of a human being, to the heavenly throne and the glories of the divine court to be seated at the right hand of God the Father Almighty, from whence he shall come to judge both the quick and the dead. That is what the creed says, and that is the flavor of the music we sing at Easter: "The head that once was crowned with thorns is crowned with glory now" and "Soar we now where Christ has led, following our exalted head," in that greatest of all Christian hymns, "Christ the Lord Is Risen Today."

The imagination of poets, painters, and preachers has been exhausted in thinking about heaven, what it is like and the glories that await those who enter there where God reigns and Christ is his Viceroy. The direction is clearly "up, up, and away." The cold, dreary earth with its petty reason and its silly pride are "lost in wonder, love, and praise." The Ascension reminds us of that wonderfully enigmatic passage in the Revelation of Saint John, ". . . and lo, in heaven an open door . . ." A glimpse of heaven, a hint of the future, a sense of promise. Despite the clutter of American and Soviet tin cans floating about in the heavens, despite the scientific conquests of the moon and outer space, the idea of the skies still fascinates, and the notion of heaven still demands notice and interest.

I know that heaven is not a place so much as it is an attitude. I know that in some real theological sense speculation about heaven is a foolish and wasteful exercise, and yet, despite the best efforts of the modern scientific age, I continue to be fascinated by the idea of heaven, and I suspect that I am not alone. To go "out there," to think of "up there," to recover an imagination beyond the paltry "realities" of this life—all of that is stimulated when one uses this language of spiritual geography. Is it real? Is it a place?

You may recall the story that circulated upon the death of Professor Paul Tillich. Some of his friends called Karl Barth with the sad news that Paul Tillich had at last died, and Barth's immediate response, we are told, was "Well, now he knows." The knowledge of heaven is not for us, at least not yet, and that is why we have been given the idea and the imagery, and the vivid descriptions, and that is why on Ascension Day we must give some thought to the idea, for that is where we are told Jesus now is. "The heavenly places": What a vast notion, and yet it is not alone for Jesus, for the collect for Ascension Day has us pray that "we may also in heart and mind thither ascend, and with him continually dwell"; and we also pray that we may be exalted "into the same place whither our Savior Christ is gone before."

What an interesting reversal for us who are so used to praying that Christ come down and be with us. "O Christ, come sit with me during this exam." "O Christ, come and worship here in my church this morning." "O Christ, be with me as I drive here, or play in the game, or bet on the lottery." We are so used to asking that Christ be found here in the midst of our reality that we find it odd, peculiar, and even off-putting to think that we might be with Christ anywhere but here. When you think of it, it is rather selfish, and yet the upward view of the Ascension is that we may also in heart and mind thither ascend, and with him continually dwell. I love that word "thither." It is so right, and means more than simply "there." The Christian hope, after all, is not that the Lord will in all good sense and justice come back to dwell on earth, and ultimately in the northeast corner of the United States where he would find a lifestyle to his liking. The Christian hope is that we will be with the Lord, elsewhere.

That's it: elsewhere. Ascension reminds us of that "other place," that "better country," as the book of Hebrews puts it, for which ultimately we are destined. Does it not all stir the imagination and enlarge the capacities to see and feel and hope? On these great feast days I become more and more aware of how necessary the imagination and the heart are to faith. They are the things by which vision is enlarged and life as a consequence made not simply more bearable but even redeemed. In this sense theology is but the maidservant of faith; it is to belief what grammar is to speech, each a means to the glorious end of communication. Once upon a time I would have apologized for the hopelessly archaic language and images of so primitive a feast as the Ascension. Today I celebrate it with its three-decker universe and as one of the few but necessary means of liberating us from the bondage and tyranny of analysis and sensibility.

Modernity has its benefits, but not sufficient to exclude the lively imagination of a pre-modern sensibility. Religion is in some sense insensible, and that is why when all is said and done we do not understand, we do not control, we do not behave, we do not even describe, but we do worship; and he whom we worship is not with us but is gone on before us. So we embrace the mystery of faith, we rejoice in the promises of God, and we would follow Jesus as best we can, not simply in what he tells us to do but also to that place where he has gone. The triumph, the glory, the kingship, and the dominion are all God's and all ours, for we are God's as well.

Yet I suspect that there is more depression than glory at that hilltop of Ascension. Saint Luke's account has the apostles racing to Jerusalem filled with joy after the Ascension, babbling like reformed alcoholics about what they have just discovered. I prefer the starker realities implied in the account in the Acts of the Apostles from whence comes our first text. Standing there watching the ankles of the Lord disappear up into the cloudy heavens, surely there must have been for the apostles at least the thought of being abandoned, neglected, left to cope alone in an alien and hostile universe. The brighter the vision of heaven, they say, the gloomier the perception of earth. For forty days they had enjoyed the intense fellowship of the Lord, knowing who he was and what his will was, and now, with an irony almost crueler than the crucifixion, he is taken away from them. Jesus appears so unreliable, always popping off when you most need him. What kind of a religion is it in which the faithful appear regularly abandoned by their God? In a little book that has given me much comfort in the past few months, in talking about the death of his wife, C. S. Lewis, in A *Grief Obsessed*, writes: "Talk to me about the truth of religion, and I'll listen gladly. Talk to me about the duty of religion and I'll listen submissively. But don't come talking to me about the consolations of religion or I shall suspect that you don't understand." Heaven's all right for those who are there, but what about those left behind?

Ascension Day is not simply an essay about the future. It is not simply *bon voyage* to Jesus. It is not simply upward in focus. It has a downward, an earthly dimension as well, and that is where we come in, just as did the poor old disciples, to collect their wits about them once again and set about the dreary task of living until the kingdom comes. "He is not here; he is risen." That is not just resurrection morning rhetoric. That is the description of human reality. How do we cope with the "downside" of glory?

"Why stand ye gazing up into heaven?" It is not so much a question as it is a rebuke. Consternation, wonder, and awe are good and holy things; they liberate the imagination, they remind us of the promises, and they make us intimate with the holy and the divine. They are not luxuries in the economy of salvation, they are necessities, but they are not in and of themselves sufficient. Doubtless the apostles would gladly have gone up into the clouds with the Lord. Given the choice of returning to the mundanities of Galilee or of partaking of the glories of heaven, who wouldn't? It was not and is not yet to be. We, like they, are called to love life, in Auden's phrase, "for the time being." We are not permitted the luxury of gazing at Jesus' feet. No, we must get on with Jesus' work, and so it is our vision of the world that is to be that calls us to service in the world that is: a world without Christ, a world that is impoverished in spirit, and that daily devises more means to make life increasingly nasty, brutish, and short. We cannot remain on the mountaintop; we must go back into the cities and countryside to witness, wait, and work for glory. "Why stand ye gazing up into heaven? He will come even as ye saw him go." So, get on with it; but how, we ask, how?

"I will not leave you comfortless," says Jesus. "I will not leave you without assistance." On the Feast of Pentecost we celebrate the coming of that assistance in the gift of the Holy Spirit, that is, in the present tense of God, a new Emmanuel, God with us. Despite the tremendous odds and every indication to the contrary, we are not alone. God has given us three things with which to carry on until he shall come again. He has given us the Spirit, the comforter who is the remembrance of what was and the sign of what is to be while he aids us in managing what is. The comforter: the one who strengthens and fortifies. That is the gift we celebrate on Pentecost. He has also given us the Church, the body of his fellowship whose sacraments, word, and ministry transcend the boundaries of time and the frailties of the human condition; and, dear friends, he has given us one another, imperfect though we may be, as colleagues in the adventure of faithful living. These are imperishable and rich gifts, and we despise them at our peril.

Until that time, when the upward and the downward dimension shall be no more, who or what shall separate us from the love of Christ? Shall tribulation or distress or famine or nakedness or persecution or peril or the sword? No, in all these things we are more than conquerors through him who loves us. "For I am persuaded that neither death, nor life, nor angels, nor principalities, nor things present, nor things to come, nor powers, nor height, nor depth, nor anything else in all creation will be able to separate us from the love of God in Christ Jesus our Lord." Thank God, it is true!

The Gift of Understanding

❖

Text: "... we hear them telling in our own tongues the mighty works of God." *Acts 2:11*

There are many images that leap from the page in the account of that first Pentecost from the book of Acts. There is, first of all, the chaotic sense of the crowd, all those people from all of those places: "Jews, devout men from every nation under heaven," as the text puts it. "Parthians, and Medes, and Elamites, and residents of Mesopotamia, Judea, and Cappadocia, Pontus and Asia, Phrygia and Pamphylia, Egypt, and the parts of Libya belonging to Cyrene, and visitors from Rome, both Jews and proselytes, Cretans, and Arabians." What a mixed multitude! Harvard Square on a warm and busy Saturday afternoon, the streets of New York, or the streets of Calcutta. People everywhere from everywhere come to celebrate the great Jewish festival fifty days after Passover. There is the sense of the crowd, and for many of us that is unattractive, unappealing, and one of the liabilities of Pentecost. There is the crowd with its bad manners and high spirits, its jostling and bargaining, the bizarre and the bazaar. That is one of the great images of Pentecost.

Yet there is another image, one that fascinates us as much as the other assaults us, and that is the image of the esoteric, the fantastic, and the ecstatic that comes in the form of the tongues of heavenly fire and the mighty wind. These are the phenomena of Pentecost: fire and wind, power, and life.

> When the day of Pentecost had come, they were all together in one place. And suddenly a sound came from heaven like the rush of a mighty wind, and it filled all the house where they were sitting. And there appeared to them tongues as of fire, distributed and resting on each one of them.

Medieval artists loved to paint Pentecostal paintings with great gusts of wind filling up Gothic chambers, and flames of fire hovering above the apostolic heads like little gas jets. It is a scene that is bound to attract attention and there is no other like it in all of Holy Scripture: a room invaded by the phenomenon of the divine, a secret space made holy and transformed.

There is a third image, perhaps the most forceful and memorable of all, for it is this image that supplies our notion of the very term "Pentecostal." This is, of course, that ecstatic conversation in tongues, the utterance thought to be inspired, whereby the mute are given speech. We have our images, reinforced by various vivid religious practices of our own day, in which ecstatic utterance overtakes an otherwise quite rational and lucid man or woman and they are given over to a physical and psychic phenomenon in which expression rather than communication is the object of the exercise. From my childhood I can remember attending the testimonial meetings in our little A.M.E. Church in Plymouth, where my eminently respectable elders would, as we used to say, "get happy," and shake and dance and wave, making worship with their bodies and making clear with them what their tongues could not say. It was, and still is, both frightening and fascinating.

A careful reading of the lesson in Acts reminds us that there is more to Pentecost than an eclectic crowd engaged in esoterics and ecstacy.

Indeed, the reality of Pentecost is in none of these, significant as they all are, but the gift of Pentecost, that which the Spirit itself brought to that memorable company, is the gift of understanding. It was possible not only to be entranced, engaged, and even overcome by powerful events at hand, but—and this is the wonder of wonders, the miracle of miracles—it was possible for the particular to become the universal. It was the gift of Pentecost that these many and diverse peoples should understand one another. "And at this sound," the text tells us, "the multitude came together, and they were bewildered, because each one heard them speaking in his own language. And they were amazed and wondered, saying, 'Are not all these who are speaking Galileans? And how is it that we hear, each of us in his own native language? . . . We hear them telling in our own tongues, the mighty works of God.' "

The gift of Pentecost overcame the curse of Babel. At Babel, you will recall, there occurred the confusion of tongues as a result of earthly ambition and pride to build a proud tower unto heaven in the plain of Shinar. Our unity to frustrate the divine purpose and will was destroyed, and we were made the parochial captives of our own languages, divided by our inability to hear or to be heard, to understand or be understood. The diversity we celebrate so frequently and loudly was not a blessing but a curse, and it has served to do little in this world but maintain the differences and erect a wall of ethnocentricism behind which we can hide and from which we can protect ourselves against others. At Pentecost, diversity was overcome by a power that transcended it, the power to understand, to hear in one's own language, one's own accent, regional dialect, patois, the wonderful works of God. The gift of understanding did not diminish the diversity of that great crowd; the people did not cease to be Medes, Persians, and Elamites. They were not reduced to some vague generality without past or place. No, they did not become less than they were, they became more than they had been, for they became at one with all of those who heard and understood that God was alive and active in this world and eager that they, all of them, should participate in his purposes. It is the reality of the particular that makes the universal so powerful and appealing.

The unity of Christ's Holy, Catholic, and Apostolic Church, a unity that is celebrated worldwide today, is a unity that is based upon an understanding of who and what God is and has done, is doing, and will do. The understanding that united the faithful is an understanding of the mighty works of God, but there is another form of understanding at work as well, and that is our understanding that others hear of the same mighty works of God in their own tongues and in their own accents—tongues and accents different from our own. The gospel is not "our" gospel that is to be translated from our language and experience to others for their benefit; the gospel is the good news of Jesus Christ that all of us are privileged to hear, and the unity of what we hear overcomes the diversity of who we are.

We should remember, you and I, that we are members of a fellowship that exceeds our capacity to define it. Since the sixteenth century we Protestants have boasted of what we are not and to whom we do not belong. A religion of protest is essentially a negative, denying religion. Having cut ourselves off from anything beyond our own circle, we have been tempted to make our own circle the object of our worship. It is a dangerous, heretical, even sinful elevation of the particular to the universal, and it is further a denial of the explicit will of God as expressed in Jesus that we should all be one. Pentecost reminds us that the gift of understanding, that gift that transcends logic and diversity, is the gift of the spirit of unity: union with God and his most perfect will, union with our sisters and brothers everywhere, in all places, and at all times, with whom we share and hear in our own tongues the mighty works of God. Such a spirit as this gave birth to our Holy Church and yet sustains it. Such a spirit is its only true and godly hope, and such a spirit, the spirit of understanding, fellowship, and grace, is what we seek to express and share as we gather around the Lord's Holy Table.

At Pentecost the Holy Spirit descended, and with a mighty wind and cloven tongues of fire for a moment overcame human differences and united that diverse and dispirited company by the gift of understanding. They heard the good news as they were, where they were, and they were never the same again. Pentecost is many things—fire, wind, ecstacy, and renewal—but more than all that it is the Spirit whose gift is that of understanding, of knowing who and whose we are. We celebrate today once again that gift to them and to us, and we pray that what transformed them may transform us, and with us the world for God and Christ.

The Big Picture

❧

Text: **After this I looked, and lo, in heaven an open door!**

Revelation 4:1

Today I wish to take up with you the not unweighty subject of the Trinity because, in the universal Christian calendar by which our worship is governed, this is Trinity Sunday, the first Sunday after Pentecost, and the feast day devoted to this central doctrine of the Christian faith. The logic is inescapable. On Christmas we talk about the birth of Jesus; on Easter we talk about the resurrection; on Pentecost we talk about the Holy Spirit; and on Trinity we talk about the Trinity.

Now, in addition to the fact that this is Trinity Sunday and hence a sermon on this subject seems in order, there are several other reasons why I want to offer the Trinity to you. One of the reasons has to do with the fact that the Trinity is a doctrine, and I want to remind all of you, Christians and others among you, that doctrine is an essential expression of a believer's faith. It is very easy to think of the Christian faith as a lovely story about Jesus, or as a historical phenomenon involving

God, or as a series of ethical and social precepts, or even as an aesthetic and cultural experience. All of this is in part true and part of the whole truth, but none of it can or must be used to avoid the fact that there is content, form, and substance to the Christian faith, a content that does not depend upon our assent for its validity, and without which our "assent," whatever that may be, means very little. I think the chief reason I want to talk about the Trinity is to invite you to think about the Christian faith as having a content that forces you not simply to act, which is easy, nor to feel, which is even easier, but to think; that is to say, to open your minds and use your imaginations and wrestle with the implications of what you find as you think about the nature of God, as you imagine for yourselves the largest possible canvas, indeed, the big picture.

The text doesn't speak of the doctrine of the Trinity. I suggest you open your Bibles to Revelation, chapter 4, and make certain you haven't missed something. The text does not mention the word *Trinity*, as many of our non-Trinitarian friends will hasten to point out. The text, perhaps even more enigmatic than the Trinity itself, says, "After this I looked, and lo, in heaven an open door!" We are taken by Saint John the Divine on a guided tour of the spiritual imagination; we are given insight into a visionary's vision; the glimpse through the open door into the wonders of heaven allows us with Saint John to leave the level of debate and argument and enter the realm of the imagination, where wondrous and strange things point to the wonder of all things. This text, like Revelation of which it is a part, is an invitation to extend the consciousness of the mind, to push beyond our petty realities, and to see the things that were, that are, and that are to be. John invites us to a new form of seeing, and like the novice guided to "see" a painting once thought familiar, by a discerning guide and critic, one begins to see new and different and wonderful things.

It is very much like the little girl who could have been a pupil in our Sunday school. She was busily drawing with all of her crayons and all of her might when her teacher asked her what she was drawing. "I am drawing a picture of God," she said. Her teacher replied, "But, my dear, nobody knows what God looks like." To which the little girl replied without stopping her strokes, "They will when I am finished." Such is the purpose and confidence of Saint John, to draw us a picture of God that we will recognize when he is finished.

What are the images that emerge from the labor of his strokes? Don't waste your efforts trying to make sense of all of that wonderful symbolism, trying to figure out what the twenty-four thrones mean, the seven flaming torches, the sea of crystal, and all of that. Look at the passage and see the great white throne in the middle, and the peals of thunder, and the lightning. If it sounds familiar it may be because you, with me, have watched *The Wizard of Oz* many times, and know by heart the scene where Dorothy and her companions finally reach Oz and have their first audience with the Wizard. Frank Baum, the author of *The Wizard of Oz*, is said to have got his sense of the place and its effect from having read this lesson from Revelation.

In reading the Book of Revelation, especially this chapter, one must not be distracted by details, one must always look for the big picture, keep in sight the object of all this frenetic activity and exquisite detail. What is the center of it all? The one who sits on the throne, who lives for ever and ever. That is what verse nine says, and all of this energy and imagination is directed to the worship of one who was, and is, and is to be, who rules—that is, who sits upon the throne—and who lives forever. It is to the one who sits upon the throne that these glorious creatures full of wings and eyes sing without pausing for breath, "Holy, Holy, Holy is God the Sovereign Lord of all, who was, and is, and is to be." What kind of sovereign is he who can command such ceaseless praise? He is described at verse eleven as "Thou art worthy, O Lord, our God, to receive glory and honor and power, because thou didst create all things; by thy will they were created, and have their being."

The picture of God is of one who is the creator, and by whose will all things that are, are. It is what we acknowledge when in the paraphrase of Psalm 100, which we sing to the tune Old Hundredth, we say, "Know that the Lord is God indeed; without our aid he did us make. . . ." Why did he do this? Well, the hymn goes on to tell us:

> For why? The Lord our God is good,
>   His mercy is forever sure;
> His truth at all times firmly stood,
>   And shall from age to age endure.

We have here caught a glimpse through that open door into heaven, and we have seen a God who is worthy to be worshiped because he is the good creator of us all, who himself will last forever, for he is forever. The character of God is good and ultimately enduring, and the fruit, the expression of his goodness, is ourselves and the creation of which we are a part. We are reminded of this when in the Genesis story of creation God is described as calling his own handiwork good, and as being pleased and satisfied with it. That means that goodness is a part of God's intention, and as the creator, like the little girl and her drawing, always puts part of himself into what he creates, we participate in goodness because God is goodness, and we and God therefore share that which is good.

God is not simply good, however, and if that is all that we see in this picture painted for us by Saint John, we have missed the big picture, for the point that gives goodness its validity and makes of it a hopeful enterprise is that God is eternal, that is, forever, the sovereign Lord of all that was, that is, and that is to be. That is the big picture, the biggest picture possible. When we think about God, some may be impressed by the majesty and the glory, some by the raw and naked power, the thunder and the lightning; for others it may be the goodness and benevolence that impresses, but for me and I suspect for most, it is the utter timelessness of God that impresses, the endurance before and beyond our imagination. As Isaac Watts reminds us:

> Before the hills in order stood,
>   Or earth received her frame,
> From everlasting thou art God,
>   Through endless years the same.

Such a big picture of God nearly defies imagination, but it is only imagination that will allow us to grow and be able to see something of that picture. We must remember that the object of Christian theology is not to reduce incomprehensibilities to our small size but rather to make us grow up in some small degree to the capacity of the subject. Saint John gives us his wonderful vision, seen as through a crack into heaven, and the church has described that same vision in its efforts to describe God in the doctrine of the Trinity—that which was, that which is, and is to be—time past: creation; time present: redemption; and time future: the ultimate justice of God. The Trinity is the attempt of the church to paint that big picture of God and to understand it in ways that extend and expand the ordinary consciousness. She baptizes her faithful in the name of the Trinity, she blesses the living and the dead in the undivided name of the Trinity, and the sign of the cross is Trinitarian in form and in expression.

Why does the church cling to the Trinity in the face of the claims of the modern need for tidy, useful thoughts? The church is bound to the Trinity because it works to explain the unexplainable and it helps to draw for us the big picture, it satisfies our need to engage and stretch and stimulate our imagination, it enlivens our worship, it stimulates our debate, and it gives us cause to wait out the impatient adversities of this fallen and falling world. The Trinity is the expression of our ultimate optimism in the face of our provisional pessimism. The Trinity allows us to imagine, experience, anticipate, and celebrate the wholeness and unity of God, and the only appropriate response to all of that is to worship him with those who fall down before him saying, "Thou art worthy, O Lord our God, to receive glory and honor and power, because thou didst create all things; by thy will they were created and have their being." Such is to experience the fullness, the wholeness, the unity of God: the one who was, and is, and is to be; and that's the big picture!

Part Two

THEMES

❀

The Purpose of Freedom

❋

**Text: For freedom Christ has set us free; stand fast therefore, and do
not submit again to a yoke of slavery.** *Galatians 5:4*

Some years ago, I found myself in London celebrating with many of my
English friends the glorious Jubilee Summer of 1977, commemorating
the twenty-five years on the throne of Queen Elizabeth II. On July 4, a
Monday, I was on my unwilling way to the airport in a taxi, and as we
passed Green Park I heard one of those big brassy British military bands
playing "The Star-Spangled Banner." What a strange sound to hear in
London! Then I realized what day it was, and I said with some excitement to the taximan, "Why, it's the Fourth of July!" He replied with
accurate disinterest, "That's right, mate; yesterday was the third and
tomorrow's the fifth." He hadn't a clue, and that made that private
moment all the more precious.

We Americans know, however, that the Fourth means a holiday of
massive proportions and the beginning of summer, and we celebrate it

with flags and bunting, parades and speeches, family gatherings, and food burned to a crisp on an outside grill. We listen to band music and we close the day out with a display of fireworks as large as our municipal budgets or private philanthropy will allow. The only incongruity of our American celebration is the ever-increasing popularity of the 1812 Overture as the climax of the day. I will never understand why we should use a Russian celebration of an 1812 victory over our late French allies, unless it is reduced simply to the fact that we Americans like noise no matter who produces it: bells, cannon, and drums. There is at least one tune in the 1812 Overture we can all hum, and it is coordinated to fireworks. Maybe that is why we like it—a rock show with artillery for the American proletariat, most of whom think it was written to advertise Quaker Oats. This cynicism aside, most of us retire to our beds wearily content that the Republic has survived yet one more celebration of itself.

There is more to the Fourth of July and the celebrating of citizenship than fetes and feasting and noise—at least there ought to be. Citizens who take both their country and their faith seriously should be encouraged to think about the purpose of freedom. Justice Thurgood Marshall of the Supreme Court once uttered an unutterable heresy, and that is that the Constitution of the United States was a flawed document at its inception because it accepted the universal and unacceptable reality of slavery, thus postponing what it would take much blood and many years to address if not resolve. That makes us stop and think on the Fourth.

Thurgood Marshall was joined in this odd sentiment by an even odder ally. When George Wallace was asked what he thought was the greatest thing that could have been achieved by the framers of the Constitution, he replied that he wished that they had resolved the issue of slavery back in 1787, so that the trauma of the Civil War and all of the difficulties and traumas that have ensued could have been avoided, and all the vast energies of our Republic used for other and better purposes. When Thurgood Marshall and George Wallace agree on an issue of constitutional significance, it means that most of us ought to begin to pay attention to it.

The critics of Mr. Justice Marshall focused upon his criticism of the founders when his main point was that the virtues of the Constitution were imposed upon it by the ever-increasing conscience of the nation. In other words, it is the people and not the founders who deserve the credit for the ingenuity of the Constitution; it is time passing and present, not times past that need to be celebrated in this enterprise. Like the founders themselves, Marshall was a pragmatic man. The Constitution is a means, not an end; it is not what the framers intended, he would say, it is what the framers would allow. The credit should go to those who used that freedom, that permission, wisely and well. Mr. Justice Marshall reminded us that freedom is not some abstract eighteenth-century ideal enshrined on vellum and worshiped in the National Archives. Freedom, then, to those pragmatic eighteenth-century souls, was as ambiguous as it is now. It is not a once-and-for-all enterprise. It is the constant renewal, reformation, and extension of freedom carried out by many people over many years under many circumstances that is really to be celebrated and contemplated, with the end and purpose of freedom in mind—in the words of the framers, "the enjoyment of domestic tranquillity."

Under the federal Constitution, which we so easily admire, Mr. Justice Marshall's ancestors and mine had no votes, no legal rights that white people were required to acknowledge, and for purely political purposes we were counted as three-fifths of a white person for the benefit of the economical and political interests of the very South that enslaved us. Under that same instrument women had a higher station but no more legal rights. That such is not the case today, two hundred years later, is not to criticize the founders for not living in the enlightened twentieth century, but rather it is to acknowledge that freedom is a slowly evolving process, not always discernible and not always achievable but always to be pursued, always to be cherished and celebrated when found, and always to be used for its ultimate purpose, its ultimate ends.

In the eighteenth and nineteenth centuries this text from Galatians was a popular text for patriotic preachers around the Fourth of July. The freedom here was always tangible and was achieved by the late-won Revolution. It was freedom from the alleged tyranny of George III. Our cause was won by that great American patriot Jesus Christ himself, and we should be careful lest we come under foreign influence again, and that is why we fought the War of 1812.

Saint Paul, however, was not anticipating the American Revolution or the Republic that emerged from it, despite some of the fatuous exegesis of our public leaders and many of our even more public preachers. Saint Paul was far more of a revolutionary than George Washington or John Adams or any of that lot. He was far more revolutionary than those cautious pragmatic philosopher-kings of Philadelphia two hundred years ago. Saint Paul was interested in a real revolution, a substantial revolution. Saint Paul was interested in real freedom to pursue the reality of the Kingdom of God, a place ruled by the fruits of the spirit, which could be achieved only by the constant exercise of the gifts of the spirit. This was the revolutionary aspect of Saint Paul's invitation to freedom and that to which freedom leads. Walk by the spirit, he warns, in the midst of the most materialistic nation that had yet existed. Walk by the spirit, he warns, do not be like your grumbling, groaning, murmuring ancestors in the wilderness, complaining about what God has done for them, and expecting him to do more every day and every hour. Take responsibility for your freedom to pursue that toward which freedom leads: fellowship with self, fellowship with God, fellowship with neighbor against which there is no law. That is the divine injunction to Christian citizens, and it is on the basis, the authority, of that invitation that Christians indeed can become better citizens in this earthly Republic.

"For you are called to freedom, brethren, only do not use your freedom as an opportunity for the flesh, but through love, be servants of one another." How are we to do this? By living in the spirit, the apostle says. How does one do that? By showing the fruits of the spirit. What are they? You all memorized them: love, joy, peace, patience, kindness, faithfulness, gentleness, self-control—all of those virtues that surround us on every hand by which our families, our schools, our corporations, and our nations have been governed for so long, forgive a bit of irony. Against such as these, says Saint Paul, there is no law. None of these are forbidden, none of these are fattening, none of these are illegal. Perhaps that is just the problem with them; we take them for granted even when they are not in evidence. Perhaps if Saint Paul had said, "The following are

absolutely forbidden on pain of death: love, joy, peace, patience, kindness, goodness, faithfulness, gentleness, self-control"; perhaps if we discovered that these were on some political, moral, and health index, then
we might take them seriously.

The fruits of the spirit, like the virtues of our federal Constitution, or
the sanctity of our marriage vows, or the holiness of our baptismal vows,
do not describe us or things as they are. They describe an end, a purpose,
a destination, an ideal that has been won for us by the grace of God and
the blood of those before us, which is not yet ours to possess, or to take
lightly, or to store up as an investment.

Freedom is not the same thing as these nor is freedom an acceptable
substitute. Freedom's only virtue is that it enables us to pursue that
which God desires for us and which we, in our heart of hearts, desire for
ourselves. That is freedom's only virtue, but it is the only virtue that one
needs if one exercises it and follows it fully. Spiritual freedom, like political freedom, is never sufficient unto itself. Spiritual freedom, like political freedom, exists only to allow us the pursuit of what freedom
allows: fellowship, respect for self, regard for neighbor, love for God, a
community and fellowship and enterprise against which there is no law,
and without which there cannot be any law worth having. For freedom
Christ has set us free; stand fast, therefore, and do not submit again to
a yoke of slavery.

The Beatitudes

❋

Text: Let your light so shine before men, that they may see your good
works, and glorify your Father which is in heaven.

Matthew 5:16 (KJV)

In our conventional reading of the Beatitudes we frequently yield to two
temptations. The first is to regard them as a set of principles, a collection
of rules or aphorisms. They are, in this sense, thought of as a happier
and much improved version of that earlier set of rules and ethics known
as the Ten Commendments. Human progress is indicated here, we are
told, for rather than being forbidden by a stern succession of "thou shalt
nots," we are encouraged, indeed, even rewarded, with a state of beati-
tude, happiness, if we do the right thing. "Carrot" theology rather than
"stick" theology, we might say, and it has proven attractive. Usually
compared with the tortuous theology of Paul and the rigidities of Jewish
law, the Beatitudes of Jesus are the spiritual ancestors of Dale Carnegie,
Dr. Peale, and Dr. Schuller, for they tell us not only how to win friends

and influence people but how to gain eternal happiness in the bargain. These ethical rules are so popular and useful that they acquire a life beyond that of their teachers, and in certain understandings of the Beatitudes as rules for ethical living, Jesus himself is quite superfluous. We have patented the formula for making people good, and we no longer require the services of the inventor. The Pythagorean theorem works quite well without the interfering personality of Pythagoras.

We humans require and respect the stability of principles, the security of rules, laws, and theorems. We may not obey or understand them but it gives us enormous comfort to know that they are there. The most erratic of modern musicians and artists honor the conventional rules of harmony and color, for it gives them all the more joy and power when they ignore them, and in some sense is this not the appeal and mystery of science, at least to the nonscientist? That there are dependabilities and immutabilities, and if we discover them, control them, and codify them we shall have peace, power, and perfection? Principles and rules are important to us whether or not we obey them, and I suspect it is for that reason, among others, that we like the Beatitudes, for here is a recipe for virtue, and if we read it right, use the right ingredients and in the right proportions, we can all cook like Julia Child, and who will then need Julia Child? Here's the rub, however. We have all been invited to dinner parties prepared by people who were tutored over the television by Julia Child but somehow, we admit in our heart of hearts, despite all of the creamery butter, the leeks, and that French copper paraphernalia, the meal is not quite the same without Julia in the kitchen. Once all is said and done, there is more personality than principle to cooking; and there is more personality than principle in the Beatitudes.

What makes the Beatitudes worthy of notice is not their abstract virtue, their essential correctness; on the face of it they make no sense at all. The thought of the meek inheriting the earth is as ludicrous now as it was then, and there is little happiness in mourning or joy in persecution. No, as in cookery, the power of the teaching is in the magic between teacher and taught. The "personality" of the Beatitudes, and hence their so-called authority, rests in the person, the life of Jesus, and in the persons and lives of those people who hear, believe, and act. These principles without the person of their author and the persons to whom they are addressed mean nothing at all. As one commentary notes: "It is not the Christian ethic which makes Christian men and women, it is Christian men and women who can live the Christian life"; and, we might add, they cannot do so without Christ. So the first step in our effort to rehabilitate the Beatitudes is to remember that they are concerned with ordinary people, and not simply with abstract principles.

I have said that there are two temptations to which we are inclined concerning the Beatitudes, and the second is that we postpone them into the future; the good part always comes later. When I was a child I was always told to eat all of my carrots for they would improve my eyesight, and to eat all of my beets for they would make my hair curly. I suppose one out of two is not a bad average, but every child knows he is expected to eat awful vegetables now for some postponed future happiness, and since most of us don't believe it, we neither eat our carrots nor have our sight improved. The radical power of Jesus' extraordinary message to his ordinary hearers is that now, in this moment, in your mourning you have happiness, and in your persecution you have joy. Now, as you eat your carrots, you see.

The various English translations of the New Testament Greek do not do justice to this meaning, for the Beatitudes are rendered as statements: "Blessed are the poor in spirit, for theirs in the kingdom of heaven," but the Greek states them as exclamations, ecstatic utterances of present reality, literally: "Now happiness and the kingdom of heaven for those poor in spirit!" "Now mercy for those who are merciful!"

Do you see what has happened? Tomorrow has become today, the kingdom that is to come is already here; that which we seek, we have, that which we would be, we are! This is not to say, as many do, that this is all there is, or "What you see is what you get." It is, rather, to say that in some real sense those who live in the expectation of faith live the experience of faith. The happiness of the gospel is not hope deferred but the consequence of hope experienced here and now by you and by me, and the wonder of it all is that this extraordinary message is for us ordinary people, who of ourselves can accomplish nothing, but who with Christ can indeed overcome the world. Is that not something for which to be grateful? Is that not sufficient reason to shine and glow and give glory to God in all that we say and do? Does not this add zest to life, and light to those who sit in darkness? That is what the fifth chaper of Matthew is all about, and the New Testament with it, and that is why we are here.

Perhaps some of you remember Ronald Blythe's classic of English sociology, *Akenfield*, published many years ago. It is the study of English village life made not by a survey of the acts of the county council nor of dry statistical data, and not in terms of the epochal world events that swirled about this sleepy country place, but rather by the careful study and analysis of the ordinary lives of ordinary people doing ordinary things in both ordinary and extraordinary times. This is what makes it readable, instructive, humane, and delightful; this is the stuff of history and epic— the ordinary called beyond itself! This, too, is the stuff of the New Testament. True freedom in the land of the extraordinary is freedom to be what we are, quite ordinary sorts in need of good news in bad times; and not only does the gospel apply to the likes of us, but of even more significance, it depends upon the likes of us to be made real in the world. If there is to be light, we are it, so shine as best you can.

Let me illustrate. Whenever I have visitors to my house in Plymouth I inflict upon them a tour of the Pilgrim burial ground, and I point out to them one of my favorite stones, one erected in 1748 to the memory of Mrs. Experience Lothrop, godly and pious woman of the town. What a wonderful name, Experience Lothrop. Today if a girl was known as Experience, it might suggest more than it was supposed to and she would not be grateful to her parents, but in the eighteenth century the name Experience was intended to suggest that this child would have a daily living experience of God in her life, and that those who knew her would have the same experience. The Pilgrims loved to give the names of virtues to their children: Elder Brewster named his two sons Love and Wrestling, and even in our time we have known perhaps a Faith, a Hope, a Grace, a Prudence, or even a Thankful.

To be so named was to be virtually a walking commercial for God, and their light was to shine before men. It is not quite the same with the Karens, Kims, and Tiffanys of this world but the obligation is still there; even though our Christian names do not necessarily represent Christian virtues anymore, our Christian lives are still meant to shine before the world, and our good works to give glory to our Father who is in heaven.

How then may we do this, if we want to? What must we do to let our light shine, we ordinary people? Well, in the first place, it is not what we do but who we are that counts; it is not in doing but in being, and that is a hard lesson for such achievement-oriented souls as we. Phillips Brooks reminded us that preaching is "truth through personality," and that means that what a person is speaks so loudly that we cannot hear what the person says. "Being" comes from within; the light shines out, not in. When Saul went down among the sons of Jesse to find a new king for Israel he was first attracted to Eliab, who was handsome and comely, and Samuel thought, "Surely, the Lord's anointed is before him." The Lord, however, said to Saul, "Do not look on his appearance or on the height of his stature, because I have rejected him; for the Lord sees not as man sees: man looks on the outward appearance, but the Lord looks on the heart." So the search continued until David was found, whose heart was pleasing to God. What David did in his life was not always pleasing to God but who he was, his being, always was, and that is why, flaws and all, he is counted the greatest among the sons of God, for who he was was greater than what he did, and in his best moments he made his name a blessing among the nations.

All of us have had in our time light shed upon our path, and not necessarily by the famous or the powerful or those who get their names in the paper. A teacher here, a friend there, and sometimes by someone who will never be aware of the extent of his influence for good upon us but who at the right time and the right place was the bearer of light in a dark or difficult time. What is always amazing to me is that these bearers of light are almost always ordinary people, men and women like you and me, with no special claim upon the world but upon whom God has placed a claim which by his grace he shares with the world and with us. My mother, known to some of you, was always suspicious of saints; anybody who had that much time just to be good probably wasn't doing what needed to be done, she thought. She would not want to be thought of as a saint, and she wasn't one, thank God. She was more than that for me and for countless others known and unknown to me, a vehicle by which God's grace shone in the world. In that ordinary life God shone with extraordinary brightness, and for that I thank God.

The philosopher William James, on the underestimated power of the ordinary, modest, and simple, said:

> I am done with great things and big things, great institutions and big success; and am for those tiny, invisible molecular moral forces that work from individual to individual through the crannies of the world, like so many rootlets, or like the capillary oozing of water, yet which, if you give them time, will rend the hardest moments of man's pride.

So, what is this all about? The gospel of Jesus Christ comes down to a rather simple proposition for ordinary people like you and like me: If God is to be known, that knowledge will be in the lives of the ordinary people who are redeemed by his extraordinary message of love. What the world knows of God it will know through us; for better or for worse we are the good news, the gospel; we are the light of the world. You don't need to finish your Ph.D. or your A.B., or even the Sunday *Times* to let your light shine. We do not have to postpone the blessedness of Christ into some ever-retreating future, and we dare not wait for more qualified Christians, better prayers, or better rules to come along and do our shining for us. No, the work of God awaits our hands, the love of God awaits our hearts, and the people of God await our fellowship here and now, ordinary and imperfect though we may be. Therefore, undergraduates, graduates, townfolk and gownfolk, brothers and sisters, strong and weak, let your light so shine in the world that all may see your good works, and give glory to your Father which is in heaven.

Identity Crisis

❖

Text: . . . we who first hoped in Christ have been destined and appointed to live for the praise of his glory. *Ephesians 1:12*

Who are you?

There are some questions that when asked are not meant to be answered. You know what they are, and I think that first in the category of this sort of question is "How are you?" We ask it of everyone every day, and we would be horrified if anyone took the trouble to answer it fully and completely.

The question "How are you?" is a means to an end, and not an end in itself. It is meant to get us into a conversation, and is not a census or audit of our present condition, circumstances, or feelings, for there is nothing more tedious than a sincere answer to an insincere question. At least in the West we understand this convention, and when we say to one another—at the door, or at the coffee hour, or in the street, or over lunch—"How are you?" we mean to hear an innocuous reply and move on from there either to a more interesting subject or to a more interesting person, whichever appears first.

This question that I have asked of you, however, is of quite another sort. By its very nature the question "Who are you?" demands an answer, requires an explanation, expects, perhaps, even a defense or an apology, and few of us find ourselves unchallenged when it is put to us. It could be seen as an innocent inquiry into one's identity, and we could suggest that it is only the paranoid, the guilty, or the imposter who has anything to fear from such a question, but anybody who believes that is likely to believe anything at all.

Who are you? Remember that wonderfully intimidating scene in *Alice in Wonderland*—or is it in *Through the Looking Glass*? I can never remember which occurs where—where the precocious and quite self-contained Alice, the soul of rationality, a sensible, well-put-together young girl, is confronted by the caterpillar on his toadstool and asked by this irrational, fantastic creature of wind, smoke, and myth, in tones of cool condescension, "Who are you?"

The problem with the question put that way is that we suspect that the questioner already knows the answer and doesn't like it or doesn't believe it. The questioner knows that we are not who we say we are; the questioner knows that we are not even who we think we are, or who we would like to be. We are imposters, and it is the job of the questioner to unmask us and reveal us for the frauds, fakes, and phonies that we really are; and since all of us are possessed of doubts about our true selves, and all of us have problems with that part of ourselves that we believe to be real, if unpleasant, we all stand indicted by the question no matter what its motive, and we would prefer to be asked, quite frankly, "How are you?" instead. At least we can deal with that question as it deserves to be dealt with.

Every two or three years at the midyear examination time, *The Crimson* reprints a series of examination horror stories, and one of their favorites, and mine, is of the student who sat for an exam and refused to stop writing when the proctor called time—a capital crime in the examination business. Finally, the proctor, losing all patience, demanded that the student come forward and present his blue book *now*. The student came forward, drew himself up to his full dignity, and said to the proctor, "Do you know who I am?" The proctor, a democratic graduate-student type, offended by the implications of the question and its social assumptions, said, "I most certainly do not, and I don't care who you are." The student then replied with a grin, "Good," and threw his book into the large pile of examination books where its anonymity would pro-tect him from censure and punishment.

Who are you? There is a tombstone in Vermont upon which is written "John Brown: born a man, died a grocer." You and I know lots of people who think that they are what they do. In Boston I once spoke to a gathering of chief executive officers of American companies, a whole slew of these *Fortune* 500 types who were in town for a convention. One did not really need to ask any of them who they were, for they had their names, their companies, and their positions on name cards on their left breasts: President and Chief Executive Officer of this, Chairman and Managing Director of that, Chief of Operations for this, President of that, and so on. It was clear that while they were more than their jobs, that they probably had families, hobbies, habits good and bad, and in-terests, they nevertheless took the major part of their identity from their work, and their work was defined by that little title on their left breast.

They were what they did, and more to the point, they were in some measure what others thought they did, or expected them to do. One of the recurring nightmares or dilemmas for people who define themselves in this way, by what they do, is what happens when they no longer do what defines them. For these CEOs, for example, the specter of retire-ment or of being leveraged out is worse than the fear of death, for at least in death, presumably, you aren't around to worry about the way things used to be, you don't have to find something else to do, and more important, you don't have to watch someone else do what you once did.

This fear of being deprived of one's role, and thereby of one's identity, is not confined to those folks approaching sixty-five and the golden hand-shake, or the yellow parachute, as the case may be. I recall a graduating senior saying to me that being a student was the only job he had had or known for sixteen of his twenty-two years. He wasn't prepared for the loss of identity that graduation would impose upon him. "If I'm not a student, the only thing I am conscious of being and doing, then who am I?" It is the best case for student tenure that I know.

Who are you? There is another form of response to that question. We know perfectly well who we are; the problem is, do others?

Who are you? Jesse Jackson has identified the greatest cause of social decay in America today, and it is not racism, it is not poverty, it is not drugs, it is not war, nor is it violence. Those are all symptoms and consequences, but they are not the root cause of the greatest social decay in our America today. The cause is a lack of self-worth, a lack of an identity worth respecting, a lack of self-respect and self-dignity, and that comes from not knowing who we really are.

You see the circumstances surrounding your life, the things by which others define you, and in which seemingly you have little say. You are a pregnant, unwed teenager in Chicago, a corporate executive about to be fired from a stock brokerage firm on Wall Street, a senior dreading graduation, an unemployed intellectual, a professor trapped in a passionless job or a hopeless marriage; you are fearful of too much work or of too little work. All of you, all of us, if we are defined by our circumstances alone, by those things so easily described and measured good, bad, or indifferent, then we are indeed trapped and there is no way out. We are who that person is, described by those horrid, dreadful, unavoidable circumstances.

That is what hell is. Not fire and brimstone and eternal torment, as the medievalists loved to paint it for us, but rather hell is being defined by your circumstances, and believing that definition. That is what hell is all about, and to that condition, the cause of low self-worth, of low self-esteem, of no identity beyond one's own set of particular circumstances, to thousands of teenagers across the country caught in that depressing self-definition, Jesse Jackson's mantra begins to make sense and open eyes, when he calls for them to repeat, "I am somebody." He urges them to continue, "I affirm, I affirm that I am more than what others make me. I affirm that I am more than what others expect or do not expect of me. I affirm that I am more than the sum total of my circumstances and my history." Or, as I would say it, I am not a child of my experience. I am a child of expectation.

That is the beginning of the work of redemption. That's the good news, that's the gospel, that is the liberating intelligence for difficult times and depressed people. The redemptive answer to the hostile question is not to be found in experience, it is to be found in expectation. We are not, you and I, defined exclusively and determinably by where we have been, nor are we defined even by where we are, but rather by where we are going. To what do we aspire, what and where are our expectations to be found?

Who are you? The Christian answers that question with the phrase, "I am a follower of Jesus Christ." I am in process, I am a pilgrim, I am on the journey, on the way, on the road. The purpose of my life is the purpose and praise of God: I live in expectation of great and good things. "We who first hoped in Christ have been destined and appointed to live for the praise of his glory."

Who are you? Surely I am what I do, in part, and I am where I come from, in part, and I am what others see and expect of me, in part. I am a part of all of that and all of that is a part of me. It is true for me, it is true for you, but the good news, the gospel, is that there is more to it and therefore more to you and to me than that. I am more than that. I am somebody of worth because I am made in the image of God who makes nothing bad. I come from somewhere! I am somebody because I come from somebody, and I am what I aspire to be; I am the child of expectation, I am not bound or limited by experience. I am the creature of great expectations, which means, as a follower of Jesus Christ, a Christian. I aspire to fullness and wholeness of joy, a life lived for the praise of his glory. I aspire to a life in which all of the disparate, conflicting and confusing, competing parts and pieces nevertheless conduce to something that is greater than the sum of its parts.

If, then, I am made a person of worth because of the work of God before the beginning of time in God's creation of me, and if it is true that I am shaped by my expectations of a future worth living in because of Christ who has gone to prepare that future for me; if the past and the future are in order, what can possibly happen to me in the present, surrounded as I am on every hand by these signs of providence and these signs of promise?

Who are you? Let me suggest that you are

> Formed by God,
> Nourished by his love,
> Preserved by his mercy,
> Open to his promises,
> Expectant of his future,
> You are the human expression of the Divine hope.
> You are God's best and last chance in the world,
> You are the means for hope and for love in the world.
> Who are you?
> That is who you are.
> You are all of that, and more.
> And for that, we praise God.

Getting to Yes

✤

Text: "What do you think?"   *Matthew 21:28*

There was a man who had two sons. He went to the first and said, "O my son, go and work today in the vineyard." "I will, sir," the boy replied, but he did not go. The father came to the second and said the same. "I will not," he replied. But afterwards he changed his mind and he went. Which of the two did what his father wanted? "The second," they replied. Then Jesus said, "Truly I tell you, tax collectors and prostitutes are entering the kingdom of God ahead of you. For when John came to show you the right way to live you did not believe him. But the tax collectors and prostitutes did. Even when you had seen that, you did not change your minds and believe him."

It should be clear what has happened here. The first has become second, and the second has become first. It ought to get your attention.

Now leave the text and get to the title, which, as most of you know, is by far the more interesting part of preaching. The title, I confess, is a rip-off pure and simple; I stole it. I took it from Roger Fisher's bestselling and now classic little book on negotiation called *Getting to Yes: Negotiating Agreement Without Giving In*. "Every day," says the author in the Preface, "families, neighbors, couples, employees, bosses, businesses, consumers, salesmen, lawyers and nations face this same dilemma of how to get to yes without going to war."

Jesus himself invites our attention and response to the question of those two sons, the first of whom offers a ready yes and does nothing, the second of whom offers a ready no but manages to get to yes. Now we all know that first son, that first child, that first daughter; they are ancestor to us all for they are the ancestors of the people of good intentions, of good and ready will, the people who hear the question, who understand the question, and respond willingly and readily, "Yes." There is something very appealing about this. It is simple, it is direct, and it is uncomplicated. It is not lawyerly or legal: What field do you have in mind, Father? What part of the day would you like me to go there? Would you like me to go immediately or later on? Would you like me to spend all day or part of the day? No, it's simple and clear: "Go." "Yes." Military people like this kind of dialogue. Parents like this kind of dialogue. Church people like this kind of dialogue, and politically correct people insist upon this kind of dialogue. "Go into the vineyard." "I will, sir." This dialogue is the fulfillment of expectation, that is to say, "You ask of me and I promise to deliver." Then the son does not. No explanation, no analysis, no excuse; he simply does not deliver. "I will, sir" is the reply, but nothing is the result.

"But he did not go" is Jesus' very spare narration, not a wasted word. The second son is asked to go, he says no, but then he goes. This is the son to whom Jesus directs the attention of his listeners, and we are drawn to him because we know we are meant to be drawn to him, and we would like to know how he got from no to yes in the space of only one verse.

How does number-two son get to yes rather than stay with no? What do you think? Why does number-one son say yes and not go? What do you think? The text tells us almost nothing of these matters and all that we need to know. It tells us in the first case that yes turned into no and in the second case it tells us that no turned into yes, and to explain the second case all Jesus says is this: "But afterwards he changed his mind and went."

The history of the world is the history of good ideas gone bad, not of bad ideas triumphant, and that is why people like Jesus' listeners, and people like you and me, well-intentioned people, need to hear this lesson, for it is addressed to us. The church, your church, any religious community, is full of people who are willing to say yes to all of the right things. Of course we want peace; of course we want justice and righteousness and of course we want to feed the hungry and clothe the naked; of course we want to see the bars of oppression taken down. Yes, virtue is an easy thing, we see it all the time, but what happens when we cannot deliver? Or, rather, what happens when what we aspire to have delivered doesn't arrive? What happens when what we aspire to cannot be achieved? What happens when your "yes" turns to "no," or your "yes, perhaps" to "maybe," or your "maybe" to "perhaps"? What do you think?

Before you get too depressed or too annoyed, wait a minute: Jesus does not tell this tale of two sons as a simple moral fable, and that's why it's hard to listen to, because you and I are interested and seduced by simple moral fables. Do you remember when as children we read *Aesop's Fables*, there on the left-hand side of the page was the illustration, there on the right-hand side in the middle of the page was the fable, and down at the bottom was the moral. What you did first, if you were like me, you looked at the picture on the left and then you looked down at the moral at the bottom. Then, if you had time, you read the fable, and that's the way most of you read the Bible and that's the way most preachers preach on the Bible. Well, it's simply wrong because it's too simple. Jesus does not tell the tale of those two sons as a simple moral tale between right and wrong, between the good and the bad, between yes and no, between the kind of simplistic editorial morality of the daily newspapers. This story is not about obedience nor is it about consistency as much as it is about the unparalleled virtue of hearing the gospel and changing one's mind, and the grace that allows us to do so. This is a story about grace.

Jesus, in this story, is not interested in the quick-willed "yes," the ready obedience of "I will go, sir." Nor does he spend much time in this story raking over the motivations. He doesn't tell us anything about the character or the circumstances. In fact he gives no insight into the dilemma of the first son at all, but of the second son he simply says, "but afterwards he changed his mind." He doesn't say, "That was good." He doesn't say, "Therefore go and do thou likewise." He doesn't say, "This is the great moral exemplar; this is how it goes." He just says, "Afterwards he changed his mind," because the sons are not the point of the story. Here comes the point of the story, the telling part:

> Truly I tell you, tax collectors and prostitutes are entering the kingdom of God ahead of you. For when John came to show you the right way to live you did not believe him. But the tax collectors and prostitutes did. Even when you had seen that, you did not change your minds and believe him.

Jesus says that if "you"—that is "we," who say yes to the politically correct view at all times, we good church people, we orthodox liberals, we who are ruled by what Emerson once called "a foolish consistency," that "hobgoblin of little minds"—really want to know what the kingdom of heaven is like, if we really want to know what the world would be like if it responded to my preaching, look to those who have feared to change neither their minds nor their behavior. Look to those who have been willing to abandon the security of their consistent actions and behavior. Look at those who say no to God and then see how they get to yes.

Let me pose three new examples that will be as problematic and as offensive to you as those surely were to the listeners of Jesus' circle. These will represent as odd a cast of characters to you as the prostitutes and tax collectors did to Jesus. Fasten your seat belts, here we go.

Richard M. Nixon: Now there are some of you with gray hair who never expected to hear me mention the name of Richard M. Nixon from this pulpit, but Richard M. Nixon changed his mind, and he changed ours. If you can remember back that far, he reestablished relations with China, now a very hot property in the world. Our present troubles with

China notwithstanding, we owe it to Mr. Nixon that we are able even to discuss our present troubles with China and our hopes and ambitions for the Chinese, let alone try to nudge China along into the realism of a democratic society. We owe that possibility to the man we still love to hate even though he is safely dead, the man whose no, at least on that matter, got to yes, and whose yes, in light of his earlier no, makes him intriguing and interesting for all time. Think about Richard M. Nixon in that company of tax collectors, prostitutes, and saints.

The second I shall nominate will perhaps be given a more ready reception among you, and that is Mikhail Gorbachev, often more popular in our country than in his own, and at all times more popular than our own president. Mikhail Gorbachev got to his popularity how? By changing his mind. It doesn't matter entirely why he changed his mind, but the fact of the matter is that he did change his mind and that you and I live now amid the incredible consequences of that movement from no to yes. The old Soviet Union is no more because Mr. Gorbachev changed his mind and went from no to yes.

For many years, as some of you may know, I was president of the International Fund for Defense and Aid in Southern Africa, which had the unenviable and unromantic task of raising money to support the legal procedures of those who were tried under the apartheid rules of that place, and never in my long association did I expect to see with such clarity or such swiftness the events of liberation in South Africa when Nelson Mandela was set free and then was elected president of that beloved country by a free vote. We all rejoiced. How beautiful are the feet of those who preach us the gospel of peace.

Number-two son, here, however, is neither Nelson Mandela nor Desmond Tutu. He is rather the unlikely figure of President deKlerk, who said no "but afterwards changed his mind and went." We do not need to know the details to know that because of the change of mind and heart of one man at this moment, many began to find freedom and peace. He said no but afterward changed his mind and said yes.

"Truly I tell you," says Jesus, "tax collectors and prostitutes are entering the kingdom" before us. That kingdom of which Jesus speaks, and for which he was killed by the politically correct people of his day, was a kingdom centered on or entered into only by those who had the courage to change their minds, to hear the gospel, to acknowledge their limits and their necessities, and to get from no to yes. It is easy to say and easy to fail. We live daily with our failed good intentions, and Christ invites us to reconsider our positions, for getting to yes is the full-time vocation of honest men and women. Getting to yes so that we can respond fully and clearly to the invitation Jesus Christ gives to us to join and enter that kingdom along with all of those other people we never thought had a chance of getting in. Saying yes to Jesus' invitation and looking at the circumstances of the world that surrounds us, can we not say how extraordinary a place that kingdom must be, when God can turn these kingdoms and these nations on their heads? God truly moves in mysterious ways.

The journey from no to yes is our journey, and as with most journeys, getting there is half the fun. What do you think? What do you think about that?

The Kindness of Strangers

❖

Text: But he, willing to justify himself, said unto Jesus, "Who is my neighbor?" *Luke 10:29*

All of us know from our own experience that hospitality, whether given or received, is never simple. My mother was a clergyman's daughter, and when she was a child in a large but poor clerical household before the First World War, her father would invariably have a visiting preacher in tow for lunch or for supper. In the spirit of hospitality the visitor was always offered the first choice of the best parts of whatever was to be served, and as most preachers did not know where their next meal would be coming from, the visiting preacher would accept the offered courtesies and would eat his hosts out of house and home. My mother's lifelong distaste for clergymen came, I believe, from watching such visitors take advantage of her father's table.

Hospitality is one of the occupational hazards of my profession. One is required both to extend it and, what is often worse, to receive it. The clergy are not alone, though, for who of us has not suffered the terror of the knock on the door and the arrival of unannounced friends and relatives just as we are settling down to an afternoon or evening of private pleasure, or even of work? We know that they know that we know that something must be done to entertain them, that food and drink must be offered, conversation made, and civilities observed even when we would rather not have been disturbed. There is within us the notion that we ought always be prepared to show hospitality, and that we ought to enjoy it. That is at least part of the problem of the "giving" part, and there is also the problem of the "receiving" end of things.

When I am invited out to preach or to lecture, if given a choice I always prefer to stay in a hotel or in an inn rather than in a private home. If it is the hospitality of good friends, why of course then I accept with delight. It is, as Tennessee Williams has put it, the "kindness of strangers" that is the chore. Booker T. Washington, the great founder of Tuskegee Institute and one of the most traveled lecturers in America, when asked about his lecture fee, invariably replied, "Fifty dollars, and if you entertain me, then one hundred fifty dollars." Hospitality is not simply cookies and punch after church or endless cups of coffee, and neither is it simply neighborliness or friendliness. Hospitality is a hassle because it is fundamentally a relationship, an entering into a form of intimacy with strangers and the unknown. Biblical hospitality has little to do with the entertainment of one's friends and the convivial gathering of folk who are much like ourselves. No, biblical hospitality has to do with the kindness of strangers, and that is just its problem, and its opportunity.

In our text this morning, the person to whom we ought to pay the most attention says not a word, and not the slightest clue is offered as to who he was, or what he did. Jesus simply says, "A man was going down from Jerusalem to Jericho, and he fell among robbers." That is all we know, and that is why most sermons on this text ignore that man and concentrate upon the priest and the Levite, the good Samaritan, and even upon the innkeeper. An inventive preacher with a sense of analogy and typology such as Saint Augustine or Cotton Mather could, perhaps, even preach a sermon on the donkey. People love to discuss the hypocrisy of the priest and the Levite, how doubtless they were on their way to meetings to discuss how to make the highways safer for pedestrian travel, and hence had no time to stop. More knowledgeable exegetes refer to the various laws and hygienic codes that would have to be broken for priests and Levites to engage in roadside rescue work, and then there is the good and proper emphasis upon the Samaritan and his unhesitating and generous hospitality to the wounded man. Jesus uses the Samaritan to illustrate that one who was himself an outcast and one of the wounded of society was more likely than the privileged to show kindness and hospitality, which is what compassion means. He is described by the lawyer to whom Jesus tells this story as "the one who showed mercy," and we are asked to "go and do likewise."

This use of the word *mercy* I have always thought to be curious in this context, for the word *mercy* suggests an unmerited kindness, the gift of something undeserved. When a judge shows mercy in a criminal case he is not responding to the facts, or to what custom or even justice requires. Full in the face of justice he shows mercy, that is, he forbears to do what is expected to someone whom he has in his power, and who has absolutely no claim upon him of any sort, and instead he shows compassion. It is not simply kindness; it is kindness in the face of the opportunity to do otherwise. Mercy is not less than justice done; it is more than justice requires.

The reason the Samaritan is called "good" and is described as "showing mercy" is because as a Samaritan, that is, as a stranger in Israel, a foreigner, he had no obligation to show hospitality to Jews who were his sworn enemies; and, in fact, if strict justice were to be observed, a dead or dying Jew was one less Jew about whom to worry. No Jew would help a Samaritan; it was the law of the jungle, and the god of the jungle helps those who help themselves and not their sworn enemies. The Samaritan acted in the face of universal expectation and against his own particular expectation and his own particular history and interest; he acted contrary to justice, and he showed mercy.

Now, as we have said before, hospitality is an exercise not necessarily of charity but of power. The guest is in the hands of his host. The victim is in the hands of his rescuer. The Samaritan, although he has little in this world, has the power of life or death over this poor soul on the Jericho Road. It is not a relationship of equality, and in fact the social rules are reversed, for although Jesus is vividly vague on the details of the robbed man, we may assume that he was a Jew, otherwise the role of the Samaritan in relationship to his sworn enemy is less compelling. If we peopled this story with Arabs and Jews and called it The Good Arab, or with Republicans and Democrats and called it The Good Republican, we would have a sense of what was going on. In simple language, it is the power of the oppressed to show mercy, not justice, to their oppressors, and that is a new kind of liberation theology not likely to win friends or influence people. There it is: The wretched of the earth against whom injustices accumulate every day—those who have right and justice on their side—when they have power, the ultimate expression of that power is to show mercy—not justice less than done, but more than justice requires.

One of the greatest fears of any repressive regime is the question of what might happen when those whom they oppress obtain power over them. If justice is to be done where justice has been absent, only the worst can be expected for the oppressors in the hands of the oppressed. The laws of segregation and apartheid were established to prevent the exchange of power, for with power came the opportunity, even the necessity, of a terrible vengeance and retribution. The South was filled with talk about black rebellions and the wholesale murder of whites and the rule of anarchy and violence. It is a normal and justifiable fear. Revolutions are feared because of what the oppressed will now have power to do to the oppressors. Justice is simply what the powerful require of the weak, and what the weak demand of the powerful.

If justice is the tool of the powerful, however, mercy is the power of the weak, for herein is the power not simply to change conditions but to change minds and hearts. The power of the civil rights movement was not in its capacity to hold the nation hostage and to exact a just and violent vengeance. Dr. King did not appeal to the nation's fears, he appealed to the nation's ideals and hopes. He took the power to terrify and transformed it into the power to forgive and to love. He was neighbor to the stranger that was America because he showed it the power of mercy, and we were all transformed by it. This country is not the same today as it was thirty-five years ago, either in attitude or in fact; it is not what it ought to be, but thank God, it is not what it was. The power of the weak, mercy, is still alive and working in the world.

So much for the Good Samaritan. He shows mercy when he could have exacted rough justice. He is not stinting or grudging in his hospitality; he, in fact, leaves a blank check with the innkeeper, an act as generous and foolish then as it is now, and he does not ask for credit or thanks but goes on his way, presumably to live as he had lived before. Jesus upholds him as one who, living beyond what the law requires, has a clue as to what righteousness and eternal life are all about; but before I conclude with a flourish and you leave with a warm, mellow glow, we must remember that Jesus tells this story in reply to a lawyerly question: "Who is my neighbor?" Remember that the questions lawyers put are never to be taken at face value, for either they already know the answer to the question and wish to trap you and flatter themselves by their cleverness, or they aren't interested in the answer you give them, for they get more pleasure in questions rather than in answers. The lawyer had asked Jesus what was necessary for eternal life, and he gave the Mosaic summary of the law:

> Thou shalt love the Lord thy God with all thy heart, and with all thy strength, and with all thy soul, and with all thy mind. This is the first and great commandment: and the second is like unto it: thou shalt love thy neighbor as thyself. On these two hang all the law and the prophets.

You have done well, Jesus had said: Do this, and you will live; but the lawyer wished to put a fine point on this question. "Seeking to justify himself," says the text. It was easy to love God because, relatively speaking, he was easy to define, but "my neighbor"? This is an odd reversal of our role in the Harvard Divinity School, where it seems relatively easy to define our neighbor and rather hard to define God. Surely this able Jewish lawyer knew who his neighbors were not. They were not the Hittites, or the Girgashites, Amorites, Canaanites, Perizzites, Hivites, and Jebusites, of whom we read:

... You shall make no covenant with them and show no mercy to them. ... But thus shall you deal with them: you shall break down their altars, and dash in pieces their pillars, and hew down their Asherim, and burn their graven images with fire.

So much for tolerance of diversity! Having excluded nearly all of the known world, the idea of *neighbor* became a rather narrow and parochial one: We like those whom we already know.

Jesus forces this bright young man to expand his horizons, and the model he is given for mercy is that of an outcast, one of the wretched of the earth and despised of the Jews, but—and this is an interesting turn—Jesus does not bid the young Jew to love the Samaritan for what he did; he bids him do what the Samaritan did for love. It is the stranger who is commended to us, the foreigner who has no claim of kinship or other obligation upon us to whom we open our hearts, not simply because it is expected in the way of minimal civil hospitality but because in the new law that Jesus offers the expected is not enough. Simple justice simply will not do. The old definitions of neighbor will not work, even as the old definitions of justice and hospitality will not work. It is a new and radical day that Jesus proclaims. It is not here yet but it will come, and all the sooner if we live as if it were already here and among us. In showing mercy, hospitality, to the strangers among us, we expand the possibilities for God's revelation and presence among us; we expand the circle of God's providential and refreshing love and thereby free ourselves as well as others from the bondage of our own narrow limits.

In the epistle to the Hebrews, the author writes, "Let brotherly love continue. Do not neglect to show hospitality to strangers, for thereby some have entertained angels unawares" (Hebrews 13:1–2). The reference is, of course, to the strangers who appeared at the tent of Abraham and Sarah and told them that she was to bear children in her old age and thus fulfill God's promise to Abraham. Had these strangers been refused or denied, the message would never have been received and God's people never chosen for their destiny to be a light unto the Gentiles. On the other hand, think of that most neglected of all participants in the nativity story, the innkeeper, who refused hospitality to the holy family. His inn is forgotten and his lack of hospitality legendary, and the world harks to a lowly manger and the kindness of strangers in shepherds, animals, and kings. It is the stranger in the story of the Good Samaritan, the anonymous and battered Jew, who is the means of a revelation of the new kingdom that is to enter in Jesus Christ, for the ultimate of hospitality is that host and stranger are one, that unity overcomes the differences that most surely remain. In the exchange of food and drink, of place and time, the giver and the gifted are united and become at one with each other and with God, who is the source of every good and perfect gift. The neighbor is that person with whom we share not simply the cup of water and the crust of bread but the adventure of life itself, given by God and lived to God's glory; and when we discover that, we will discover not only who our neighbor is, but who and whose we are.

What's in a Miracle?
Feeding the Five Thousand

❖

Text: "Whence shall we buy bread that these may eat?"   *John 6:5*

This is another sermon about hospitality. The story from Saint John's gospel is familiar and we know all of the characters from the hungry multitude—the nervous and doubting disciples, the good-hearted little boy, the five barley loaves and two fishes, and the Lord who pulls it all off. There is little left here to surprise us, for we know how the story ends, and as we hear it yet again we ask ourselves the question that is as familiar as the story: "Is it true?" In some sense, depending upon the answer we are prepared to receive, we will either hear or not hear what the story has to say.

The question "Is it true?," while natural, is quite the wrong question to put, for miracles are not arguments or propositions to which there are yes or no answers. The question to be put about a miracle is not "Is it true?" or even "How can this be?" but rather, "What does this say?" At its essence a miracle is a message—an illustration or a demonstration of a message that God chooses to communicate to us. A miracle is God's extraordinary message in the midst of the ordinary; it is an exercise not in the supernatural or in the irregular but in communication. To understand a miracle is therefore to understand something of God. To see a miracle, therefore, is to see something of God.

The people of the Bible may not know what a miracle is, at least in a rational or intellectual sense, but they know one when they see one, like the farmer down Maine who was asked if he believed in infant baptism. "Believe in it?" he said. "Why, I've even seen it." The shepherds did not ask themselves if they "believed" they saw an angel; they went in fear and haste and worshiped at the manger. The blind man who was given his sight did not ask to understand what happened to him; he acknowledged with simple eloquence that he now could see. The five thousand, once hungry and now satisfied, do not appear to ask questions of supply and demand and "How did he do it?" but recognize that something unusual has happened, for they heard and received the message. "When the people saw the sign which he had done, they said, 'This is indeed the prophet who is to come into the world.' " A miracle is a message from God to us.

What, though, is the content of that message, the message of miracles? Often we are fascinated with miracles because they appear to be demonstrations of raw, naked, and unambiguous power. A reversal of the natural order is a demonstration of power, and we are interested in Jesus and his miracles, at least in the first instance, insofar as they demonstrate for us the uses of power. To heal the sick, as with the lame or the blind or the woman with the hemorrhage of blood, demonstrates power to do the right and good thing. The first miracle that Jesus wrought, at the marriage feast of Cana in Galilee, demonstrates a power to bring order out of chaos, but the essence of a miracle is not in its power, nor in its extraordinary capacity, nor in its ability to attract attention and high visibility, but rather in its capacity to meet and to satisfy a need. A miracle is a response to what is most needed; it is, at heart, not a demonstration of power but an answer to prayer. In the feeding of the five thousand the immediate need of the crowd was met and satisfied by the wondrous extension of the loaves and fishes, but that was not the miracle. The miracle was that in this the people saw "the prophet who is to come into the world." Their eyes were opened and they saw Jesus as he was: God's message to the world.

There is always a great temptation to spiritualize this story, to see the loaves and fishes and the feeding of the crowd as mere metaphors for the kind of spiritual refreshment that Jesus offers his people, and there is some warrant for reducing the food services aspect of this story. Jesus himself later on in John's gospel warns the people that they should not go after the bread that perishes and spoils, like the manna of the Exodus, but should seek "the food which endures to eternal life, which the Son of Man will give to you." He goes on to say, in John 6:33, 35:

> . . . for the bread of God is that which comes down from heaven, and gives life to the world. . . . I am the bread of life; he who comes to me shall not hunger, and he who believes in me shall never thirst.

It is not mere satisfaction that Jesus offers, a mere sating of the appetite; it is substance, that "bread of life" which the world can neither give nor take away. What is important to remember is that Jesus does meet the real need; he feeds the hungry not with metaphors but with food, not with resolutions and presidential commissions but with so much bread and fish that there is an abundance left over. He met the physical needs of his hearers in a generous and openhearted way so that, their stomachs being full, the hunger of their hearts could be addressed. The message of this miracle is clear: It is not the will of God that people should go hungry. The gospel is never offered as a substitute for the fundamental needs of human survival, for it is the will of God that those who hunger and thirst should be given food and drink and that they should be provided generously and without stint. The hunger and poverty of this world are not signs of insufficient piety; they are signs that we continue to mismanage the resources that God has given us. The poor rebuke the rich not because the poor are morally superior to the rich, for they are not, but by reminding them that no one is truly rich while anyone is truly poor. Jesus makes it clear that there is a real relationship between the hunger of the body and the hunger of the soul.

The spiritual and the physical are each part of the divine concern and the divine plan. Jesus fed the hungry on the mountainside, but while he did not ignore or make light of their physical hunger, he did not stop when that had been satisfied; he went on to meet the hunger of their souls.

What about the hunger of the satisfied? What about the needs of those who "hunger and thirst after righteousness"? As long as it is possible to define hunger in terms of the absence of loaves and fishes, we can work, pray, and fight to provide enough loaves and fishes for those who need them; but what happens when the satisfied are not satisfied with satisfaction? The miracle of the feeding of the five thousand is that God is willing to provide not only bread but that he is willing to offer the bread of life as well, the food that does not perish but endures to eternal life.

Once again we learn that the fundamental lesson of hospitality is not simply in giving, but in receiving as well that which we most need to have. Jesus offers not simply food to the hungry but himself to us all.

> I am the living bread which came down from heaven; if anyone eats of this bread, he will live forever; and the bread which I shall give for the life of the world is my flesh.

When you are fed at the Holy Communion, remember not only that Jesus fed the hungry on the hillside with loaves and fishes but that by that act of human charity he was revealed to the crowd as God's message of love to the world. To that world he offers not simply sustenance without which our bodies cannot live, but substance without which our souls cannot live. What he offers he gives in himself, and this memorial that we make of his body and blood allows us to become a part of that message, a part of that miracle whereby we, with those who hunger and thirst after righteousness, may yet be filled.

Friendships and Relationships

❧

Text: A faithful friend is an elixir of life, found only by those who fear the Lord. The man who fears the Lord keeps his friendships in repair, for he treats his neighbor as himself.

Ecclesiasticus 6:16–17

Most of us spend most of our time sorting out our personal lives, our little trials, sagas, victories, and defeats. At the end of the day we tote up our score, not for or against the great social or intellectual systems of the world, but in terms of how we stand with the people we value, and perhaps even love. It is easy for religion to pronounce upon the great affairs and events of our time; it can and must do so, but a heavenly religion that cannot help us sort out our daily dose of human experience is of no earthly good.

The first gift given to us at creation is the gift of companionship: "It is not good that man should be alone," says God before he provides Adam with Eve. The motivation is charitable; he does not say that it is not practical or convenient for man to be alone. He says, simply, that it is not good, and he proceeds to remedy the matter and provide for the first relationship, the essence of which is companionship each for the other.

Adam's need is our need; perhaps we inherited it from him. We need to find ourselves somehow connected to someone other than ourselves. Yes, we are connected with God, our creator, we have that ultimate relationship and we bear the mark of the maker, but even God realizes that this is not enough, not good enough; and so what begins with Eve is not so much a license for marriage as a warrant for fellowship and companionship, the most intimate and ultimate form of which is friendship, itself the gift and the grace of God. The ultimate form of this gift, of course, is friendship with God. This is what we get through wisdom when wisdom, passing from generation to generation, makes us "friends of gods and prophets."

Somehow, however, friendship with God is not in itself sufficient for most of us, and this is why God's gift is so sensible and practical in providing us with the incentive and opportunity for human friendships as a prefiguration of the divine: God has given us the gift of intimacy as a sign of the intimacy he shares with us. In the Apocrypha, from which our text is taken, we read: "A faithful friend is a secure shelter; whoever finds one has found a treasure"; and again we read, "A faithful friend is an elixir of life, found only by those who fear the Lord."

We learn that friendship is a treasure. True friendship is hard to find, like treasure, and true friendship comes from God. Maybe this is why we have so much trouble with our friendships; something so valuable, so rare, and so divine seems out of place and out of character with the realities of our friendships in the world. We all know about the great friendships of history: Damon and Pythias, David and Jonathan, the model of Jesus where a friend gives up his life for a friend. We know the rules—to have a friend is to be a friend; a friend in need is a friend indeed—and we pursue these ideals, always looking for that perfect friend who will support us and comfort us and encourage us for ourselves and despite ourselves.

Yet, these ideals notwithstanding, most of us are scarred by the battle of experience over hope. We know, perhaps more than we would like, the truth of that aphorism directed against Winston Churchill which said: "He had no enemies; only his friends thoroughly despised him." Usually when a Mafia corpse is discovered with cement shoes and body ventilation, those questioned reply with shock at the death of their old colleague: "Why, he didn't have an enemy in the world; only a friend could have done this."

Despite all of this, however, friendship continues to be the ultimate model we pursue to combat that loneliness in creation which God himself has said is not good. Babies are drawn to whoever or whatever is drawn to them. Little children like to run in packs. Teenagers look for the "best friend," that person beyond blood who is to share the universe with them; and all of us sort ourselves out in some effort, in some way, to share the gift of the Garden. That is what friendship is, and that is why we pursue it even though it is not easy to achieve. Note that the text speaks about keeping one's friendships "in repair." That implies that they can, and we know that they do, fall apart, and fall into disrepair. While we can take the desire, the necessity for friendship as natural, even divine, we cannot take friendship itself for granted.

It takes work to maintain a friendship, not just contact but work. More often than not, such "work" is to be found in the little things, the ordinary courtesies and kindnesses. Harry Stern, in his little book on ethics drawn from his column in *Esquire*, describes the actress Lynn Fontanne as crediting the success of her half-century collaboration on stage and in life with Alfred Lunt to the fact that they had never been impolite toward each other.

Now such courtesy may be an impossible standard to maintain, and maybe they didn't see very much of each other, but the credit for success is given to small things just as, in the reverse, the blame for failure is also given to small things. In the breakdown of a marriage, for example, how often do we hear, "He stopped courting me," or "She neglected me," or "We took each other for granted and grew too comfortable with each other."

The use of the word *repair* in our text is telling. Any of you who maintain property know how difficult it is to do so on a large scale. It is the little daily, weekly, annual chores that keep the whole going. To try to do everything at once in one grand renovation seldom works, and to put it off—the bankrupt policy of deferred maintenance—doesn't work and only postpones disaster. Thus there is effort here, labor. "The man who fears the Lord," the lesson says, "keeps his friendships in repair." Is it worth the work? We might wonder. Perhaps friendship is too costly, too demanding.

Some years ago, in that era when any effort that did not produce immediate results was not considered worthwhile, friendship as an ideal passed out along with thrift and prudence, and in its place, thanks in large part to Carl Rogers, we got "relationships," the best of which were meant to be "meaningful," or at least, if not full of meaning, then full of promise. Somehow a relationship seemed a little less demanding than a friendship, but the issue was always more confused when you asked John if he was "in a relationship with Mary," and he replied sadly, "No, we're just friends."

Everybody knows what a "relationship" is. It is sex without marriage, or, as the catchy book title reads, it is *Guilt Without Sex*. It is a means of testing ultimate loyalties without ultimate obligations, and for many people this seems as safe and hopeful a way of proceeding as has yet been devised. Despite the secular euphemism of the term, however, the fundamental distinction that ordinary relationships are between things, and friendships between people, ought to be instructive. Somehow the term "relationship," which was meant to suggest purposeful and productive intimacy, more often than not suggests a rather clinical, even antiseptic, process that promises more than it can deliver. If we have learned anything over the last decade, it is that relationships require as much work as friendships, are equally fragile, and when they work, can produce nearly as much joy.

The search for friendship is a defense against an anonymous and indifferent world. It is our chance, our hope, to make something more of our time here than mere survival or existence, and that is why the gift of friendship is so great a gift from God. The risks are worth taking because the prospect of the alternative is too grim even to think about. The ideal friendship is probably that: an ideal locked up somewhere in some great cosmic mystery. I know, and I suspect you are with me here, few Davids and Jonathans, few Damons and Pythiases. Most of us must be content to be less than the best of best friends, and to accept that state in our friendships and relationships. Indeed, while it is the small things that often cause us to part or to fight, we may suffer as well from too great an expectation. In the marriage business I often deal with couples for whom perfection of every order is normal. They expect the best and they get it, in every detail; they are used to it in business, in pleasure, in labor, and in leisure. They expect the same of their relationships: terrific taste, terrific sex, terrific manners, terrific looks, terrific income, and then when they experience their first failure or frustration, their house of cards falls down and the marriage, or the friendship, or the relationship, is lost. They don't learn from it. They decide that "she" or "he" just wasn't quite right, but that Mr. or Ms. Right is out there, waiting to be discovered. That is the curse of too great an expectation.

Christians know, or should know, that their only great expectation is in God, and that for the rest, life comes with no guarantee except the necessity of effort. There are ideals to which we do and must cling: loyalty, trust, truth, love, joy. These are the ideals, but they serve to sustain us in their absence, for that is what ideals are. Thus, the Apocrypha tells us that the best friendship—relationship, if you will—is that which allows the ultimate friendship of God to rule as model, ideal, for our immediate efforts, allowing for failure and forgiveness, for hope arising out of disappointment, and for charity, the lubricant of all relationships worth having.

Friendship is based upon a sense of security and loyalty, a quality of trustworthiness won over the long haul. In the morning of life, the saying goes, we are acquaintances; at noon, lovers; and in the evening, friends. It is the long haul that tests our capacity for friendship, and friendship with God is the ultimate security and loyalty. In the meantime we have much work to do and many joys to experience, much sorrow to know, and great hope to keep in our pilgrimage to friendship.

A faithful friend is an elixir of life, found only by those who fear the Lord. The man who fears the Lord keeps his friendships in repair, for he treats his neighbors as himself.

Mary and Martha

✾

Text: Now, as they went on their way . . .   *Luke 10:38*

Mary and Martha were not twins and yet invariably we think of them together, not unlike Laurel and Hardy, Abbott and Costello, or Flanders and Swann. It is impossible to think of one without the other, and yet one of the points of this remarkable and familiar story about them in Saint Luke's gospel is that they are quite different. It is the difference between them that commends them to our attention, and just as it is difficult for us not to think of the two together, it is equally difficult not to choose between them and take sides, dividing the world, as it were, into the Marys and the Marthas.

We all know the Marthas, those hardworking people without whom any movement or occasion would starve; churches especially thrive on their Marthas. Who will do the coffee hour? Martha. Who will do the washing up? Martha. Who will feed the visiting choir or put up the visiting firemen? Martha. Who will see that child care is provided? Martha. Who will change the flowers? Who will drive the youth group to its diversion, and who will put on the reception or cope in a volunteer capacity when there is no professional around to do the work? Martha, of course. The unsung heroines of any movement, the Marthas are both the advance and the rear guard. The civil rights movement of a generation ago had its headliners in the likes of Dr. King and other clerical leaders. It had its strategists like Andy Young and Jesse Jackson, but it would not have got to first base, let alone to Washington or to the statute books, without that invisible army, composed mostly of women, who cooked the endless meals in dreary church basements, made the coffee, managed the supplies, and provided for the necessities of life. We know the Marthas of the world, and sometimes we admire them. At all times we need them, and on occasion we are among them.

Our natural sympathies are with Martha. We recognize her condition. The text gives a clear picture of her situation, and there is no reason to believe that Jesus was expected when he came to call: "She received him," it says, which may mean little more than that she opened the door to his knock. If that is so, then there was indeed much to be done, for hospitality was expected for any and every guest, and the more unexpected the guest, the more lavish and bountiful the hospitality ought to be. Any fool can put on a good party when he has invited the guests and is prepared to entertain them; it is a special kind of fool who can entertain the unexpected. Such hospitality is the hallmark of the Jewish home, where even at Passover a spare chair is left for Elijah, should he come to call and partake of the family's meal. Hospitality in the East is not a casual affair, it is the ultimate act of civility, and a house that did not show fitting hospitality was ashamed and embarrassed.

Clearly Martha is now put to it, doing what she ought to do, but she is left to do it alone, and hence her annoyance with her sister, Mary, "who sat at the Lord's feet and listened to his teaching." The text is too polite to say so, but I suspect that she was equally annoyed with Jesus, who appears to be unsympathetic to her needs and who in fact rebukes her, saying, in effect, "Tut, tut, calm down, Martha. Mary is doing the right thing and you are not." I too would have been quite cross with Jesus for this abuse of my person and of my hospitality.

What was wrong with Martha? She had good reason to be "distracted with much serving," and to be "anxious and troubled about many things," and that is just the reason she could have used some help from her dreamy sister. Martha is a sympathetic sister for our time because she is in the business of activity and anxiety: the two chief preoccupations of our age.

The Marthas of this world are bright-eyed, practical-minded people who are intent upon doing the right and good thing at the right and good time. They ask the right questions, want the right answers, and are always informed and concerned. You know who they are for you are one of them. We may not be concerned with placing good meals on the table for unexpected guests, but we are distracted by the need to keep our end up socially, intellectually, and morally; and Lord knows there is enough to keep us anxious and distracted.

We are irritated when Jesus says to us, "Relax!" We want to be rewarded for our efforts, or at least we want a little sympathy for all the effort it takes to keep up this level of activity and anxiety. Does he not understand how difficult it is to be a sensible, sincere, and caring adult in these times?

It is important to note in our text that Jesus does not deny the value of what Martha is or of what she is doing. He does not say to her that everything is all right and that there is nothing to do or to worry about. He is not here practicing a gospel of optimism and mind over matter such as is dispensed from too many of the pulpits of America. No, he says to her, in essence, you have your priorities wrong. Your sister knows that she has something to learn from me: don't just do something, stand there, and listen to me.

It is not that work is unimportant, and it is not that Jesus does not appreciate work, for he knows, as do we, that society would fall apart without the activity and anxiety of the Marthas of this world. Here, however, it is a matter of priorities, of first things first, and Jesus is absolutely unambiguous about what comes first here. He said it once before, in that series of remarks we call the Sermon on the Mount, when he warned people about being anxious about what they should eat and wear. Remember, he concluded that remarkably practical address to us

Marthas with the words "Therefore, do not be anxious . . . for the Gentiles seek all these things; and your heavenly father knows you need them all. But seek first his kingdom and his righteousness, and all these things shall be yours as well" (Matthew 6:31–33). I like to think of that as the "good portion" Mary chose, and which will not be taken from her. Mary has her priorities in order; she knows the value of sitting at Jesus' feet.

What was so important about sitting at Jesus' feet? Surely he had been a visitor before to the house of Martha and Mary. He was a great friend of the family, and we know of his love for their brother, Lazarus. The answer to the question comes in the words that introduce the story, the words I have taken as my text: "Now, as they went on their way . . ." It is not even a complete sentence but it is the crucial context in which we understand not only this story but our own story as well, for if we read the chapters before this one we will find that "they," Jesus and his followers, are on their way to Jerusalem and to the cross. It was Jesus' last journey, his final earthly pilgimage, not a day's outing or excursion or Sunday drive but a purposeful procession across the pages of history to the sure and certain death on the cross, and into the future which he would claim for God. Somehow, in some way, Mary had caught on to the fact that Jesus' message on his visit to their house on this afternoon was of such significance, such urgency, that the routine must be interrupted in order to hear it. You see, I cannot imagine that it was her usual custom to entertain visitors while her sister did all the work. I sense that her sister's irritation with her was because she wasn't doing her usual or fair share of the domestic labors. Somehow she sensed or knew that this was not an ordinary visit. The Lord was passing by, and after he went things would not ever be the same again. The visit of Jesus breaks the routine of that house, and it can no longer be "business as usual," or "hospitality as usual." Mary sensed that Jesus was not there to stay or to pass the time of day but was on his way, and the few minutes he had with them were precious and to be savored. She may not have known "where" he was going, and we can claim no prophet status for her. Her claim to fame is that she knew where she was—in the presence of the Master, whose teachings were the staff of her life.

We learn an important lesson from this story in the example of Mary and Martha. We learn how important it is to receive. The mark of hospitality is the capacity to give. Martha was doubtless very good at that, and she was busy about that very work, giving Jesus a pleasant time, providing for his needs and comforts, organizing his stay under her roof. It is hard work and should be rewarded, as it usually is, with appreciation and gratitude; but just as Jesus interrupts the routine of the household in Bethany, he also interrupts the role, for he is not "guest," he is now "host," for he is the Lord, and it is he who gives and others who must now receive.

An ancient custom of hospitality in England holds that when a sovereign comes to your house, for the time in which the king or queen is there, the house is no longer yours but theirs. They are your hosts under your roof. That may be hard for us to understand but it illustrates the point of our story, understood by Mary, that their hospitality was little compared to what Jesus had to give them. The Marthas of this world find it very difficult to be receivers. It is said that it is more blessed to give than to receive, but it is infinitely more difficult to receive than it is to give. It makes one beholden to the giver, it cuts away autonomy, and it makes one, in some sense, dependent. Try to give someone something and they will insist upon returning something to you, not because they like you but because they want things to be even, they don't want to be obligated. Giving is power; receiving implies need and weakness. We give, you and I, not necessarily because we are generous but because it gives us power. The Marthas of the world are so busy doing good and necessary things, so occupied in the giving, that they do not have time to realize how frequently and deeply they themselves stand in need. When Jesus comes he reminds us that we need that grace and peace he has to offer. Rather than be distracted with much service, anxious and troubled about many things, we would do well to stop, look, and listen.

This, then, is a parable about life, about giving and receiving, about doing and being, about the presence of Jesus in the midst of the ordinary that becomes extraordinary. It is a parable about priorities, first things first, and it is a parable about two women who in their lives and attitudes give our Lord and his church an opportunity to teach an enormously important lesson for our time. More to the point, it is a parable of our own worship, for it reminds us that what we do in our churches—our prayer, our praise, our instruction, and our fellowship—are not what we "do" for Jesus, entertaining him and busying ourselves with his amusement, but rather we come here to "sit at Jesus' feet," to offer him worship and praise as he most justly deserves, and this is the most important of all, to receive from him the means of grace and the hope of glory. We worship not because we are the society of the perfect, the whole, and the holy; we worship because, in the words of Samuel Johnson's hymn:

> Father, in thy mysterious presence kneeling,
> Fain would our souls feel all thy kindling love,
> For we are weak, and need some deep revealing
> Of trust and strength and calmness from above.

From this story we may learn one thing: When Jesus comes to call, things aren't at all the way they used to be, and neither should we be.

The View from Pisgah

❀

Text: "...I have let you see it with your eyes, but you shall not go over there." *Deuteronomy 34:4*

It seems unfair, don't you think? Moses had completed all of the course requirements but God didn't let him graduate. The first five books of the Bible and the life of Moses both end with that enigmatic remark of God which is our text: "I have let you see it with your eyes, but you shall not go over there."

The thirty-fourth and last chapter of Deuteronomy opens with a graphic tour of the promised land, that land toward which Moses had led his people through thick and thin for forty years: up from the lowlands of Moab to Mount Nebo, to the top of Pisgah, eastward from Jericho. "And the Lord showed him the whole land: Gilead as far as Dan; the whole of Naphtali, the territory of Ephraim and Manasseh, and all Judah as far as the western sea; the Negeb and the Plain: the valley of Jericho, the Vale of Palm trees, as far as Zoar." This is it, the object of a lifetime, the culmination of a life's work. The view from Pisgah was all that one could desire, all that one deserved. God promised that land to Israel, and he was faithful to his promise: "This is the land which I swore to Abraham, Isaac and Jacob that I would give to their descendants"; and to the leader who had made that promise possible, God said, "I have let you see it with your eyes," but, and this is the biggest "but" in all of Holy Scripture, "but you shall not go over there." Moses does not. He died as the Lord had said, in the land of Moab; he died where he was, not where he was going, and even his burial place is a mystery, with no cenotaph, no shaft of stones, and no memorial tablet to mark his final resting place. He died aged one hundred twenty years, "his sight was not dimmed nor had his vigor failed," he was given thirty days' mourning, and then the people of Israel got on with their business under their new leader, Joshua.

It is a strange end to a mighty epoch and a mighty life, and almost as if he never was—that the great Moses was one of those of whom the book of Ecclesiasticus would say, "And some there be who have no memorial, who are perished as though they had never been." This is not the "immortality" after which we all crave. This is not the everlasting fame and reputation for which we work and which we hope will be preserved after we are gone. No, to our fair-minded world there appears to be something unfair, unjust about all of this. Moses deserved better, we say, and, more to the point, so do we.

Some commentaries are filled with speculation about God's motivation here, and generally suggest that Moses' modest end is a punishment for his hot-tempered ways early in his career. Others suggest that it is another instance of the arbitrariness of God; and most say, quite correctly, that we simply don't know. We do know, however, that "the view from the top" is not all that it is cracked up to be. We struggle to the top only to see a future into which we cannot enter, or, and this is perhaps worse, to see a future that isn't there.

It is possible to look out from Pisgah and see a landscape of denied opportunities, an inheritance that will never be collected, a future that will never be enjoyed, and there are many who, standing upon their own private eminences, see just that, and shrink back. "We are not ready to cross over," they say. "We dare not leave." For such as these, universities have been created and with them tenure, which means a permanent seat on Mount Pisgah with a wonderful view of a future into which one would never want or have to enter. That land into which Moses looked was filled with both promise and peril for his people. Read the book of Joshua and those that follow, and you find that the promise was not easy, the land flowed not only with milk and honey but with obstacles and problems of every sort and shape. There were surprises and disappointments in store for those who entered, and Moses was, in the opinion of some, better off for not having had to trouble with it.

I hear people standing on Pisgah and saying as they look out over what is to be, "Is there any justice in that land, any peace, any joy? Will it be a place in which I can make a living, raise a family, love, work, and play?" There is trouble in Latin America, trouble in the Middle East, trouble in South Africa. The divorce rate is up and landmines threaten. Violence and discord are the rule, not the exception, and people expect less rather than more of life's good things. I remember a time not so long ago when to ask a senior what she was going to do next year was a sign of friendly interest and not a hostile remark, and round about this time of year the air used to be filled with the purple prose of great expectations; the future beckoned to those at the top of the tree. Now, the more cautious message is "We have barely got ours, and we hope you manage to get yours." The mood is perhaps best illustrated in one of the many stories about President Calvin Coolidge. It seems that some friends decided to call upon the Coolidges in their retirement in Plymouth, Vermont, and arrived at the homestead close to the supper hour. They knocked on the door, and Mr. Coolidge answered and said, "Had your supper? We've had ours."

The view from Pisgah is certainly not unmixed, but we must remember that it is not simply the end of Moses, but rather it is the beginning of a whole new adventure for his people, and hence for us. For the future, while it is not without ambiguity, is always the blessing of God. It is in the future where God sets his promise and toward which he sets the hearts of the faithful. The future is God's time, that time in which our partial sight will become complete and we will know fully even as we are fully known. We will see and understand with the eyes of the heart.

Such a future as one sees from Pisgah is not a land of optimism but rather a land of opportunity, in which the view is clouded by the old canard in which the optimist says, "This is the best of all possible worlds," and the pessimist agrees. It is not all rosy and bright, a land of wishful thinking and positive attitudes, but a land of opportunity for God is in it; he goes before us preparing the way and bidding us to join with him in that pilgrimage that takes us from where we are to where we are to be, and the joy of the trip is in the journey. Pisgah reminds us that what you see is not necessarily what you get, but that what you get is the opportunity to see; and that the future in God is so extraordinary that it exceeds our imagination, and only the rhapsodies of the book of Revelation can begin to describe it: "Eye hath not seen nor ear heard the things prepared for them that love God."

The view from Pisgah is as nothing compared to the vision that awaits the sons and daughters of God, that new heaven and new earth where every tear is wiped away and there shall be an end to death and to mourning and crying and pain; for the old order has passed away. "Behold: I am making all things new . . . I am the alpha and the omega: the beginning and the end." The vision that extends from Pisgah to the great and encompassing Revelation of Saint John is the insight given to all those who would see as God gives light: to see in what is what can and ought to be. Any fool can see what is there and be encouraged or terrified by the sight, but it takes a special kind of fool, a fool for God, to see the things that must be and be sustained by that vision in the midst of what we see. The Bible ends, as did Moses, with a vision, a revelation of the things that are to be.

It was such a vision that guided and sustained Moses, and it was that vision that brought him to the mountaintop. In some real sense he had already seen what it was that God showed him from Mount Pisgah. He was already there, for, like the pilgrim who has in his heart the vision of his destination before he ever reaches it, so too Moses had what no other son of Israel could ever have. He saw with his own eyes the fulfillment of the promises of God, and knew that what he had worked for others could now enjoy. In that knowledge was that peace which this world can neither give nor take away. The ultimate hero, the supreme prophet, is not one who makes a place for himself, who has the supreme pleasure of saying, "I told you so," but rather one whose satisfaction rests in the hope, if not the knowledge, that he has helped to make a way for others, a way so well and so thoroughly built that it will be thought always to have been there, and the name of the builder need not be known.

With very few exceptions the names of the architects and builders of the great cathedrals of Europe are unknown. We cannot say who built Chartres or Salisbury or Amiens or Durham, and no one builder ever saw his masterpiece completed, for the work of a cathedral is the work of many lives and many lifetimes; and yet somebody did the work and there was a time when they were not. The builders and masons and carvers are dead and gone. They never saw the results of what they had begun, yet their vision lives and we who never saw them are sustained by what they saw and by what we see.

Do you remember the last sermon that Martin Luther King ever preached? It was about going to the mountaintop. He had a premonition about his own death and he was not sorrowful but was ready to go, for like Moses he had seen the promised land; he was sustained by a vision of the things that are to be, and although he would not live to see them, he knew they would be. He never got to enjoy the fruits of his labors. Neither did Moses. None of us really does. The justice of God is not that we are allowed to complete what we have begun, but the grace of God is that we are allowed to participate in what God has begun.

Few of us can orchestrate the conclusions of our lives, and all of us will die with our work yet undone, our dreams yet unachieved. If that is unfair, then life is unfair. We may not be able to make an end but by God's grace we are enabled to make a beginning, and that is no small thing. The nature of faith is life lived in its incompleteness, and what each of us has the opportunity to begin right now is that holy pilgrimage that takes us from the crest of Pisgah into the valleys, the highways, and the byways of our longest journey until we reach our rest, which is the perfect will of God.

The Question at the Mouth of the Cave

❃

Text: And behold, there came a voice to him, and said, "What are you doing here, Elijah?"   *I Kings 19:13*

One of the portraits we look at today is of Elijah, and his sojourn at the mouth of the cave. Today we find him not at his most attractive moment but at that terrible point of inward fear and doubt, when, despite the formidable accomplishments of his career, Elijah is alone, defeated, fearful, and faithless. He reminds us of a lesson that all of us in this achievement-oriented, results-oriented world need to know—that failure is not the opposite of success; it is often the result of success.

That Elijah had been "successful" is not open to doubt. He had done what every prophet would like to do. He predicted a drought, and it was painfully dry for three years. He challenged the priests of Baal to battle, and he won. He prayed for rain to do away with drought, and the rain came in torrents. He got A+ in prophecy, and the added pleasure of calling Queen Jezebel to her face a witch with a capital B. He should have been happy and pleased with himself, content to retire and write his memoirs, but we see him not at the height of those powers nor in the midst of his strength but at his lowest point where fear, self-pity, and self-doubt overwhelm him to the point that he desires death to any more of the same. He is at the cave because he is in flight, first from Jezebel and her promise that she would have him killed, and then in flight from himself. He went into hiding in—in words of our time—a state of deep depression, for that is what a cave is, a depression in un-yielding rock that gives, for a while, apparent security and protection.

Now, let us first say a good word about depression. Sometimes it is good to be depressed, and we enjoy it, and I don't care what the shrinks and therapists say, there are times when it is good to feel bad. For that moment the only pleasure we have is in the recalling of our woes, and the capacity to name our fears and to feel them indicates to us that at least we are not as far gone as we might appear to others. There is nothing worse than a friend or a colleague who wants to help us out of our pit before we are ready to be helped, and in some perverse sense the frustration of their efforts adds to our little pleasure. It is said that Abraham Lincoln was at his best when in the midst of his frequent depressions, and the genius of Martin Luther is that he was both de-pressed and constipated. The black moods of genius have given much beauty, power, and purpose to the world. It is possible to think of de-pression, at least in its primary stage, as one of the few places of auton-omy and self-preservation for one on whom the world appears to be closing in, and like pain it can from time to time be redemptive.

So, Elijah was depressed, literally in his cave, and psychically in his spirit, and he had good reason to be, for all of his incredible success had turned to ashes. It is the classic case of the public man's success in the public eye being of very little worth to him in the privacy of his own soul. The conflict between expectation and experience is tough enough, but what happens when your sense of success yields only to the notion of a great fall yet to come? It is just the opposite of our expectations. It ought to be that small successes lead to larger successes and to the largest successes possible, onward and upward forever—the sort of the-ology of optimism that once flourished in America—but we know the truth that the more we have the more we stand to lose, and the more we accomplish the greater will even small failure appear to be. Athletes, businessmen, and scholars all know that each success is an opportunity for an even greater failure, and so we are victims of burnout at thirty-five. The price of success is often the fear of failure, and it is with this bill in hand that Elijah, the prophet of the Lord, hides himself in the cave. No one can get to him there, but neither can he go. No one can get to him there, that is, except the Lord, who is always lurking about and interrupting the privacy of his prophets.

It is the Lord who puts the question at the mouth of the cave: "What doest thou here, Elijah?" Of course, God knows exactly what Elijah is doing in the cave. He is feeling very sorry for himself. "I have been very jealous for the Lord, the God of hosts; for the people of Israel have forsaken thy covenant, thrown down thy altars, and slain thy prophets with the sword; and I, even I, only am left, and they seek my life to take it away." He had done all the right things and had succeeded in them, and is that not the irony here? It is not that he tried and failed, or didn't know what to do and therefore did not try at all. No, he knew what he was supposed to do, he did it, and he succeeded—the American dream—and yet where was the victory, the glory, the happiness, the sense of vindication? Elijah was tired, very tired of success and tired of the fear of failure. He was exhausted by all of his days.

"What are you doing here, Elijah?" asks the Lord. "Nothing at all." Here the prophet of Israel learns his second lesson, for if the first lesson is that failure is often the price of success, the second is that "being in God" rather than "doing for God" is the ultimate sign of faithfulness. He who had done so much, and done it all well, was now incapable of doing anything. He was to be done unto, and God sends him to stand at the mouth of the cave where the doing is done by God. The mighty wind, the earthquake, the tempest, the fire; and yet the Lord was not in any of these. Now, what can this mean? After all, God was and is the God of nature, and the most primitive and the most sophisticated agree that the forces of nature in the fury of these phenomena reduce human beings to insignificant proportions and testify to the mighty immutabilities of nature, to a force beyond human explanation or control. Such things are still called, by those most secular of corporations that sell insurance in Hartford, Connecticut, "Acts of God," against which there is no insurance coverage.

The question at the mouth of the cave has not yet been answered and is put again to Elijah: "What doest thou here?" Elijah repeated his story, but this time the Lord said to him, "Go, return upon thy way to the wilderness of Damascus, and there you shall do a number of things, among which is the anointing of your successor. Go, for there are still things for you to do, and you cannot do them here."

One cannot stay in church all day. One cannot remain on one's knees in constant prayer. Life finally must be lived, work done, efforts made. It is true for prophets of the Lord, it is true for students and teachers, it is true for citizens of the world. This is not, however, simply a call to work as before, as if nothing had happened. Elijah returned to his work, learning, perhaps for the first time in a long while, that it was God's work and not his that he was about. He learned that you cannot "do" unless you can "be," and that "doing" depends upon "being." He was made strong in his humiliation, not because he found some new inner strength but because he found anew the strength of God, and it was that discovery that made it possible for him to go on.

In some sense Elijah and his cave is a parable for worship. People most frequently worship or come to church—not always the same thing— because they are in need of some healing, some hope. We are the wounded, the hurt, the needy, we repair to church as to a yielding spot in an otherwise unyielding surface of life, and here we confess and we feel good about feeling bad. We learn also that we cannot stay here all day and that we must go out and get on with it but that we are able to do so only when we have come to the full knowledge that what we hope to find here is not our better self, or a prescription for survival, nor even a spiritual form of courage, but really the strength and power and love of God.

In the expectation that allows us to hear the voice of God, not in the thunder and lightning but in the heart, we will hear his words that ask us, "What are you doing here? Get on with it, go, and my grace will go with you; for my grace is sufficient to your needs." We worship not the

God of the mountains nor of the fire nor of the forest but the God who is nearer than breathing, closer than hands and feet, that God whose name is love, and who, if we will listen with the expectant silence of the heart, will speak to us and send us on our way rejoicing in the power of the spirit.

Redeeming the Time

❋

Text: And who knows whether you have not come to the kingdom for such a time as this? *Esther 4:14*

The hero of the story is neither youthful nor rich. Surely he isn't powerful and, unlike Robert Redford or such other hero as our age has provided for us, he probably isn't handsome. He is an old Jew named Mordecai. "Now there was a Jew in Susa, the capital, whose name was Mordecai, the son of Jair, son of Shimei, son of Kish, a Benjaminite, who had been carried away from Jerusalem among the captives with Jeconiah, King of Judah, whom Nebuchadnezzar, King of Babylon, had carried away. He had brought up Esther, the daughter of his uncle, for she had neither father nor mother; the maiden was beautiful and lovely, and when her father and her mother died, Mordecai adopted her as his own daughter." Mordecai is important to our story not only because of his kinship to Esther but because he represents the continuity between the Israel that was before captivity, and the present age. His life transcends the transition between what was and what is, and in his person is that living continuity.

Now, in the Hebrew festival of Purim, which the Jews keep in February or March and which commemorates the story of Esther, comes one of the Bible's most convincing villains, Haman the Agagite. Haman was a descendant of the ancestral enemies of the Jews, and a local boy who made good. He made so good that the King, Xerxes, promoted him to Grand Vizier, a sort of press secretary plus, and required that all do honor to him. Now you know how little people with a little power and a little prestige like a lot of show. Haman had made it, he had it made, and he wanted all to be conscious of his new place in society, and on the matter of his unsatisfied pride literally hangs our story.

There is one more minor character, a fulcrum figure, as it were, and that is Queen Vashti. She was very beautiful and, one might presume, as the wife of the King of Persia, a woman of some influence. On the night when the king was giving his grand banquet, after consuming a lot of liquor he determined that the queen, giving a dinner for the women of the court in another place, should be summoned to him to be displayed to his drunken and probably lecherous old guests. The chamberlains scurried off to deliver the royal decree to the queen, and she did what was then unheard of, she refused to come. She declined to be the after-dinner cordial for her husband's menu, and he and all his court were astonished. "What should be done with such a woman, for surely if nothing is done her willfulness will encourage every Persian woman to similar disobedience"; and right they were. Queen Vashti's dignity, or perhaps from the court's point of view, her disobedience, caused consternation. Wise men were consulted, and concluded that she should be deposed and that another should take her place. This was done, and the king conducted a beauty contest throughout his kingdom, looking for a Miss Persia to succeed his recalcitrant Queen Vashti.

It is thus the dignity and deposition of Queen Vashti that made possible the appearance of our heroine, Hadassah, or Esther, soon to be Queen Esther, for, as we all know, she was beautiful and fair to look upon. When Esther was paraded before the king he took to her and had her placed in his harem, where she was soon to rise to his exclusive favor and to win the title of queen. She did not reveal the fact that she was a Jew. Now the king liked Esther not only because she was comely and young but because through her cousin Mordecai she had given him information about a plot on his life. He had uncovered the plot, executed the villain, and established a strict security squad about his person, headed by our friend Haman. Now, at the point of our text, Haman is aggrieved because of Mordecai's refusal to pay him sufficient homage, and is resolved to take revenge not only upon Mordecai but upon all Jews in Persia on the grounds that they were unwilling to be assimilated into the culture.

The rest of the story is perhaps familiar to all of you: how Haman sent his goon squads out to round up and destroy the Jews and how Mordecai, fearing for his people's survival, urged Esther to intercede with the king for their preservation. This is of course where the story's tension builds, for it is an unbreakable law of the Medes and the Persians that the queen does not appear before the king unless she is summoned by name, and the king hadn't summoned Esther in some time. To enter the court is a dangerous presumption, and also the king is unaware that Esther, his favorite, is a Jew. Worst of all, Esther is herself totally unaware of what is going on because she is hidden in the perfumed recesses of the harem quite apart from the political intrigue of her husband and his court, and from the dangers to her people. It is her raggedy old cousin and guardian Mordecai who through eunuch messengers informs her of the dangers to her people and of their need for her intercession with King Xerxes.

Esther had a great deal to lose: her position and security as queen, her very life as a newly discovered Jew, and besides, what king bent upon his will would listen to the political advice of his queen, beautiful and talented though she might be? Not only did Esther need to be informed of the plight of her people, but she had to be persuaded of her duty in that plight. She explained her inability to act but Mordecai, unconvinced, reminded her that her security was precarious at best. "Think not that in the king's palace you will escape any more than all the other Jews. For if you keep silence at such a time as this, relief and deliverance will rise for the Jews from another quarter, but you and your father's house will perish. And who knows whether you have not come to the kingdom for such a time as this?" It is a telling argument, persuasive on many fronts, and as we know, Esther was persuaded. "Go, gather all the Jews to be found in Susa," she said, "and hold a fast on my behalf, and neither eat nor drink for three days, night or day. I and my maids will fast also as you do. Then I will go to the king, though it is against the law; and if I perish, I perish."

Esther did not perish. Through courageous wit and wisdom she won the confidence of the king, entrapped Haman and his family upon his own gallows, preserved her people from slaughter, and saw her cousin Mordecai elevated in rank next to the king himself. To this day the Jews keep Purim as a festival in which they commemorate these events of their deliverance, and celebrate Mordecai and their inimitable Queen Esther.

The point of the story of Esther is lost upon us, however, if we are simply turned on by one more of God's "dirty tricks," one more account of militant preservation. The story of Esther is an intimate story about personal opportunity, and the victory worth celebrating is the victory that Esther makes over herself when she confronts that opportunity and accepts it to her own possible detriment, and yet to the possible salvation of her people. I like to think that it was a struggle. I like to think that between verses fourteen and fifteen in the fourth chapter of Esther is a drama of inner passionate conflict between the security of the moment and the risks of the future. Surely she, like her ancestor Moses when confronted with a similar opportunity, might have said, "Who, me? Why, what can I do? I can't speak, send someone else." Opportunity is the season here, and it is a season of great distress.

Opportunity is also crude and rude; it comes and either you seize it or it passes you by. Opportunity does not admit of too much debate, and because we can never be prepared for opportunity it requires a response written in faithful resignation. Isaiah seized his opportunity in the midst of the smoky temple with the words, "Here am I, send me." Esther, confronted with her opportunity in the message from her guardian, said, "I will go to the king, though it is against the law; and if I perish, I perish." Jesus, after his agony in the garden, resolved, "Not my will but thine be done."

The text, is it not a text about opportunity itself? "And who knoweth whether thou art come to the kingdom for such a time as this?" Surely to the mind of a good Jew like Mordecai, a Jew who had known God's providence not alone to himself but to his fathers as well, opportunity was no capricious accident. Opportunity was the means by which God operated with his children. We might not understand every step and every detail, but somehow the purpose is there, to be revealed at the right time. So must Mordecai have thought. His ward, a good Jew, a concubine in the heathen Persian's court—surely this is what it is all about? Surely, "Who knoweth whether thou art come to the kingdom for such a time as this?"

I have told you before about the ancient lady in Plymouth who upon reaching her ninetieth birthday was asked the familiar and by now inane question "To what do you owe your many years?" "To time," she said. Time indeed, for it is all that we have. Miss Minnie observed, "The Lord has kept me around for a mighty long time; I guess he still has something for me to do, so I'll keep on trying to find out what it is." I am convinced, like Miss Minnie, that God has indeed set us here to redeem the time and effect his will. We are here and not in the eighteenth or nineteenth century. We are here and not in second-century Bibleland. We are here because we, like the men and women of their day, have both a place and a purpose.

The civil rights movement, the antiwar movement, the ecology movement, the women's movement, the movements for ethnic freedom and dignity, the movement in search of meaning and values—these movements are not accidents of sociology upon our neutral landscape; they are the legitimate movements of our time, movements through which God can and does speak to us of our opportunities for redemption and hope. Idealism has always been out of fashion, especially in a place where cynicism is a cheap substitute for wisdom, but it is the energy of the ideal, which in seeking its redemptive opportunity has made and can make the children of God more than passive spectators of passing time. Such idealism requires an interior strength with which to meet our godly opportunity. Maltbie Davenport Babcock wrote of this in his rousing poem:

Be strong!
We are not here to play, to dream, to drift,
We have hard work to do and loads to lift.
Shun not the struggle, face it, 'tis God's gift.

Be strong!
Say not the days are evil—who's to blame?
And fold the hands and acquiesce—O shame.
Stand up, speak out, and bravely, in God's name.

Be strong!
It matters not how deep-entrenched the wrong,
How hard the battle goes, the day how long;
Faint not, fight on! Tomorrow comes the song.

"And who knoweth whether thou art come to the kingdom for such a time as this?"

Acts of Reconciliation

❋

Text: So we are ambassadors for Christ, God making his appeal through us. We beseech you on behalf of Christ, be reconciled to God.

II Corinthians 5:20

Saint Paul wishes to remind us that the sum of the gospel, the whole action from creation to the final resurrection, is contained in one word, *reconciliation:* the bringing back together of that which has been broken, separated, and estranged. It is God's will that we be reconciled to himself; in Augustine's words, "Thou hast made us for thyself, and our hearts are restless till they find their rest in thee." It is the restlessness of God and humankind that calls for reconciliation, and this is what Christ does for us in that supreme act of reconciliation whereby God becomes one of us that we might become one with him. That is what the church teaches.

A picture is worth a thousand words, but it is those few words from the book of Genesis about the sacrifice of Isaac at the hands of his father,

Abraham, that have provided a thousand pictures: The narrative paints, and we see the father about to slay his son in obedience to the will of God, and it is not a pretty picture. Piety tells us that we must admire the faithfulness of Abraham, who always does as he is told and therefore always does well. God tells him to leave his family and kindred, and he does. God tells him to marry Sarah, and he does. God tells him to produce a son, and he does. God tells him to kill his son, and he is prepared to do so and nearly does. Sarah at least laughed at God when he asked impossible things of her, but Abraham, a congenital overachiever, does what he is told; he does his duty, and what a sad and sorry duty it is. What kind of God can ask such a thing of those who put their trust in him? What kind of father is it who can contemplate the sacrifice of his son upon the altar of obedience? By the time of the dramatic rescue and the appearance of the ram in the thicket we have long since ceased to admire either God or Abraham, and the happy ending is not sufficient to overcome our feeling that something is terribly wrong with a story that paints a picture of such a God and of such a man.

Henry Fielding's eighteenth-century novel *Joseph Andrews* has his parson take the point of this story as that "love should be subservient to duty." In the rivalry betwen human affection and divine duty God will not take second place, and so, like Job so many years later, a righteous man is tested by God, for righteousness in the absence of adversity is convenience and not conviction. So Abraham, for his faithfulness to God even to the point of the sacrifice of his son, was rewarded not only with his son's life but with the promise of many sons and daughters, descendants as the stars of heaven and as the sand which is on the seashore. Here indeed ends the lesson and for some the point, but the point of this story seems to me not Abraham's obedience and God's generosity but rather that, after this dreadful ordeal whose pain and humiliation we can only imagine, Abraham and God are reconciled. They become at one with each other, and the duty that was forced to prove love becomes the means to a greater love that mends rather than destroys. It is God who doubts and Abraham who proves faithful. Abraham calls the place where this all happened "The Lord will provide": On the mount of the Lord it shall be provided.

This is the most unpopular story in all of the Bible, and neither God nor Abraham comes out of it in a very appealing way. If we imagine Abraham entering upon this duty with no inner struggle, no wrestling over what is right, we have no respect for him, a mere "good citizen." If he does struggle, he sounds not unlike the parent who says, "This hurts me more than it hurts you," and we don't believe him. If we begin to see in this story more than simply a struggle between duty and love, the aberrations of a jealous God and a moral cipher, we might just see that the miracle, the good news, is not so much in the thicket but in the new relationship that is established between man and God, and we can begin to see the potential sacrifice of Isaac as an act of reconciliation, a reunion between creature and creator, and indeed between love and duty, faithfulness and grace.

I think that something of this sort may have been in the mind of sculptor George Segal, who, in response to a commission to sculpt a memorial to that most horrible of our domestic sacrifices, the Kent State shootings of 1970, cast in bronze an almost erotic life-size depiction of *The Sacrifice of Isaac*, in which the son submits to the father as the father submits to God. So overwhelming is the impact of the scene that we must look beyond it, hoping that what the Lord provides is sufficient to reconcile our feelings of hurt and disappointment. The monument, located at Princeton University, succeeds because we are forced to look beyond and forward; we are anxious to resolve the suspended chord, the dissonance, and get on with it. Surely we are reminded of the pain, the sorrow, the alienation, and the estrangement of our children shooting each other, and yet it is the reconciliation, yes, the redemption of that conflict, both physical and spiritual, toward which we are driven. In such a world as this acts of reconciliation are not luxuries, the happy endings to bad stories, but necessities if our bad stories are to be redeemed.

Perhaps some of you have stood as I did some years ago in the Chapel of Reconciliation that is the bombed-out shell of Coventry Cathedral in England. Looking at that unreconstructed ruin reminds us of the enmity between the nations that produced it and its counterparts in Dresden and other bombed cities of the last war. It is so constructed that it is impossible to enter the new and gloriously uplifting cathedral without passing through the ruins, monuments not to hate or revenge or sorrow unappeased, but reminders that the ministry of reconciliation is to heal the broken and to reunite the separated and estranged. Nothing will be right until we acknowledge that something is quite wrong, but we need not go to England or to Germany to see an act of reconciliation. We need look only to the most eloquent memorial in all of The Memorial Church:

Harvard University has not forgotten her sons who under opposite standards gave their lives for their country, 1914–1918.

It was the Board of Preachers who insisted upon that plaque, and led by my predecessor, Dean Willard L. Sperry, they paid for it and had it installed. It was an earnest good end to a bad story; it was and is an act of reconciliation.

I offer you a third image of reconciliation, this one somewhat farther afield, in Italy where Elie Wiesel once produced a play called *The Trial of God*. It is a play about a Jew whose horrible experiences in the concentration camps of Germany make him rail at the cruel God who can allow such things, and the Christian Church which, in the name of that cruel God, does such things. It is a play that asks and gives no quarter. It asks the question that every Jew since 1945 must ask: If God is God, how could he permit the horror of the Holocaust, and above all to his chosen and faithful people? In a reversal of the Job story it is God who is put on trial and who must hear his three accusers. Anyone who has ever heard Elie Wiesel knows that he is not easy listening for either Jew or Christian, and this play was no exception; and yet it was sponsored by the Roman Catholic Church and given favorable reviews by *L'Osservatore romano*, the Vatican's newspaper. In his speech at the opening, Wiesel said, "The cross that for you symbolizes charity and love, for me as a Jew rooted in tradition symbolizes fear, but you have me before you and I shall be with you; and I offer you my memories to share."

If *reconciliation* means what the Oxford English Dictionary says, in three pages, that it means: "to bring a person again into friendly relations to or with oneself or another after an estrangement; to restore to purity, absolve, or cleanse," then this too, the artistic harvest of bitterness and despair, is an act of reconciliation by which we may be cleansed.

Courage in the face of creation. The modern aphorism for indifference and inaction is "If it isn't broke, don't fix it." Saint Paul, never willing to avoid a problem if he could help it, acknowledges that only that which is broken can be fixed. This time it is God, the same God who asked so much of Abraham, who offers his own son in behalf of those who doubt him, and thus, by Christ, he reconciles us to him and to one another. By what is broken, sacrificed, and fractured we are healed and made whole; and not simply are we mended but, as Saint Paul says, "If any one is in Christ, he is a new creation; the old has passed away, behold, the new has come." It is God who repents of his awful testing of Abraham and who, as an act of reconciliation, offers us himself in Jesus Christ in the feast of his passion, death, and resurrection. Saint Paul invites us to be reconciled to God, to restore the brokenness in our lives and in our world. In Christ God has made the first move toward us; he now invites us to respond, to accept what he offers and who he is. This is an act of reconciliation that we can, and now must, make our own.

Acts of God

❁

**Text: For God so loved the world, that he gave his only begotten
son.**   *John 3:16 (KJV)*

At the close of his Sermon on the Mount, Jesus concludes by saying
that the wise people who hear and understand his words will be like
the wise or the smart man who built his house upon a rock. We know
the story, and a few of us know the Sunday school song that told it so
graphically when we were children: The rains came down and the
floods came up, at least three times, and the house on the rock stood
firm. We also know about that other builder and that other house:
The foolish man and his house built upon the sand, and how the rains
came down and the floods came up, again three times, and the house
on the sand went *smash!* I remember the glee with which we sang that
song with its vivid gestures, and it was an unholy glee for we took our
pleasure, I suspect, not in the security of the wise man's house upon
the rock but in the total and assured destruction of the house of the

foolish man, built upon sand. Like the House of Usher, "great was the fall of it."

Now I know that the point of the story is the need to build soundly and well upon the principles of the new life that Christ offers, and that those principles are the basis of a firm foundation against which the gates of hell cannot prevail. We know that it is wise to build against the evil day. Under fair skies and balmy weather the two builders appear to be equally useful and successful in their efforts to build houses, but when the time of testing comes, only the house that has foundations will survive. We know all of that, we know the ancient secular version of the same in the fable of the ant and the grasshopper, but neither the truth of the story in its biblical or secular version, nor its familiarity as a favorite of preachers and moralists down the ages, is sufficient to relieve most of us of the anxiety, secret or otherwise, that we are more likely to be grasshoppers than ants, and that, if we can get away with it, we would prefer to build our houses on the sand because to do so is so much easier and less expensive.

In that perversity that comes to all of us from time to time in the reading of the scriptures, I wonder if you are one with me in asking whatever happened to that poor foolish man who built his house upon the sand. Was he swept away in the flood? Did he have enough time before he perished, if he perished, to wonder at the foolishness of his enterprise? Did he envy his neighbor's well-built house, and did he hate God and himself? Who knows? In our understanding of God, the same God who preserved and spared the house of the wise man is the God who destroyed the house of the foolish man, and indeed, if the foolish man lived in civilized North America and had neglected to take out a special form of hurricane and flood damage insurance he would have lost everything, for the action visited upon his house is described, not in theological but in insurance parlance, as an "Act of God."

When our ancestors in the times of ancient Israel thought of acts of God, they thought, at least in the first instance, of terrible demonstrations of raw, naked power. The God who was to be taken seriously was the God who could turn nature on its head: floods and earthquakes, mighty winds and heaving seas. The awesomeness of God is the awe that the creature feels and his sense of helplessness and terror in the face of an extraordinary force. The small boat and the vast sea. To look upon God was to look upon the possibility of one's own destruction: Moses did not avert his eyes from the holy one out of modesty or respect or reverence; he did it out of fear, terror, lest he be destroyed by one who was capable of making fire where there was none, among many other wonders.

In the Divinity School reading lists of my day, one of the most important books was *The God Who Acts* by the late Parkman Professor of Divinity George Ernest Wright, my teacher of Old Testament. We read that book avidly and listened with even more enthusiasm to the energetic lecturing of Professor Wright on the subject of the acts of God in the Old Testament. Professor Wright wanted us to understand that the God who was capable of commanding the loyalty of so fractious a bunch as the children of Israel, and by indirection ourselves, was no namby-pamby inert benevolent force. This was a God of activity who did things and got things done, a God who confronted and confused nature, who opened up the seas to swallow all of Pharaoh's army so that there was not one of them left; the same God who sent fire from heaven on behalf of Elijah, and rain as well; who also stopped the mouths of the lions for the well-being of Daniel, and who was capable of anything that suited his will and purpose.

The God who acts in history, as Professor Wright so titled him, was an appealing God, for in some sense, lightning, hailstorms, and earthquakes notwithstanding, such a God appeared at least to have an interest in what was going on in his creation. If there is anything we can understand about God it is his capacity for power, arbitrary though it may appear to be, and even the most godless among us would be impressed if the God who acted in Israel's history would once again act in ours by smiting hip and thigh, for example, those who do wickedness to the innocent and helpless, by demonstrating in a powerful and uncontestable way that God is not mocked in his creation, and hence punishing polluters and those who impoverish our spirits.

However, this God who acts appears to act, if he does at all, in a very curious way; we would rather not have an act of God if it is a mere exercise in divine ego and results in the horrible deaths of victims of earthquake, mud slide, and other "natural" disasters. We don't need that kind of God or that kind of action. It is not worthy of worship but of contempt, and when we do want God to act, as in Bosnia, for example, or in the jungles of Latin America, or in the hearts of men and of women, where is he? We can worship the gods of power and action in our world; we know what the ancients felt when they gave divinity to the power of the sea, the thunder of the sky, and the eruptions of the mountain. We can admire the prudent man who protects himself from the consequences of natural and unpredicated assaults made upon him, but where do prudence and power leave us? Is the answer simply that man must be prudent because God is powerful?

Our text, so familiar as to be often dismissed as one of the Christian clichés, tells us two things about the acts of God. We learn that God's immediate and ultimate relationship to the world is one not of power or of indifference but of affection: For God so loved the world. God's power is subordinate to his love. The world is subordinate to his love. The world is a place that is beloved of God. Like creation it is good, although terrible things happen in it for it is not perfect, it is not without pain, and the price of our freedom is to learn to cope with a world of ambiguity and danger, pain, joy, and opportunity. Through all of that God relates to us out of his love for us. The action of God, the act that counts, is love.

The second thing we learn is that God loves us so much that the ultimate expression of his love, his act of love toward us, is to send us himself in the form of his son. His love is a participating love such that he engages with us and in our behalf in the work and labor of the world. This is no God content simply to intimidate or ignore; this action of God dignifies the whole creation by becoming a part of it so that we might participate with him in the making of a new creation. The God who acts in Jesus Christ does so in such a way as to stir us up to action wherever we can and with whatever we have, so that the love of God can be translated into human form and human effort.

That God should show his love, that God should take his ultimate action in the form of a creature, a man, means that all creation, and all men and women, have somehow been elevated to participate in that ultimate act of God, and that the character of that action, both divine and human, must be out of love and compassion and not out of prudence or power.

God's love is God's ultimate action and it is given human form in Jesus Christ, and if God can invest himself and his love in the unlikely form of a man born of a woman, who suffered as we suffer and died as we shall die, dare we invest less in humanity than God? Dare we invest less in ourselves and in our world than God? Ought we not to take the sign of God's love for us in Christ as a sign that we are lovable and the world is worth loving? If that is so, can there be any possible limit to what we can attempt as God's representatives in the world?

I do not believe that God moves in thunderstorms or speaks in the accents of natural disasters. I do not believe that God interferes in the often tragic course of the world's activity; I do not believe that God is a great puppeteer who somehow pulls the strings for good or for bad, depending upon his temper or ours. Rather, I believe that God has made the world and loves it so much that he has given himself into our hands and thus made his work our opportunity. God has chosen not to act in the form of phenomena; he has chosen now to act in the form of men and women who know him, love him, and serve him. By God's love for us in Jesus Christ we are become in ourselves, in our own persons, in our daily work acts of God, evidence, living proof that the God who acted in the lives of the prophets, the martyrs, and the saints still acts in the likes and the lives of us.

We become then, you and I, not simply the objects of a benevolent, a wrathful, or an indifferent God, pieces of furniture to be arranged at will, but rather we are licensed, as it were, by the incarnation to be the action, the activity of God in the world, for it is through us, our patience, our labor, and our love in a world easily content without God, that God will be known and served; indeed, the Acts of God become the actions of the men and women who know and love him, and who seek to serve him.

The Trouble with Perfection

❖

Text: You, therefore, must be perfect, as your heavenly Father is perfect.   *Matthew 5:48*

At the Second Vatican Council the story was told that the late Pope John XXIII could not tell one American cardinal from another at the conclave, and frequently mixed up Richard Cardinal Cushing of Boston with Francis Cardinal Spellman of New York. Finally, after doing this to the two prelates yet another time, he found himself greatly embarrassed and made profuse apologies to the Americans. To set the pope at his ease, Cardinal Cushing said in his wonderful Boston tones, "That is all right, Holy Father; no one's infallible." No one is perfect, and that is the charm, is it not? of Richard Cardinal Cushing, Pope John XXIII, your wife, your husband, your roommate, or your friend? Perfection can be annoying. The vast expanse of country club lawn makes one long for a heroic dandelion; the cook whose soufflés never fall, the spouse whose checkbook is always balanced, the conversationalist who is always right—

these people do not encourage us to pursue perfection in our own chaos-filled lives; rather, they cause us secretly to wish public disaster to fall upon them. Perhaps the ambiguity of perfection is that it is more fun wishing for it than having it. Mae West once said, "I was pure as the driven snow until I drifted"; and who would have it any other way?

Yet the Bible spends some time in conversation about perfection, and toward the close of his most significant body of teaching, the Sermon on the Mount, Jesus says in our text: "You, therefore, must be perfect, as your heavenly Father is perfect." There would appear to be nothing ambiguous about that. That would appear to be the ideal condition, the state of grace and bliss in which the creature seeks to imitate the creator; and Jesus tells his followers how they might begin the process, for obedience to the old law is not enough. Fidelity to the commandments and the body of practice accumulated around them is no longer sufficient. In the lesson from Saint Matthew he has a series of remarks that begin, "You have heard that it was said, 'You shall not commit adultery . . .' 'You shall not swear falsely . . .' 'You shall love your neighbor . . .'" He gives the summary of the morality of Israel, the counsels of perfection, as it were, from Moses onward. The keeping of these laws is what made a person good, but Jesus then says that "good" is not "good enough." After each of these ascriptions he says, "But I say to you that everyone who looks at a woman lustfully has already committed adultery with her in his heart. . . ." "Do not swear by anything, but say simply 'Yes' or 'No.'" "If you are struck on one cheek, turn the other . . . and not simply love your neighbor, but love your enemy as well."

It is a new law with a radical new dimension of attitude that Jesus introduces. Where there is an admonition he requires an encouragement; where there is a restraint he demands a prohibition. It is a new and strange order that he introduces, and he suggests that it represents the will and conduct of God and the reign of God: "Be ye therefore perfect as your heavenly Father is perfect. Be ye like God." Now the last time we heard that "we should be as gods" was when the serpent told our foreparents Adam and Eve that it was all right to eat of the forbidden fruit, for in so doing we would gain all knowledge and power and we would be as gods. That was dangerous advice, and the sad consequences of it are with us still, but Jesus tells us that we should emulate the perfection of God, not for our own pleasure or personal satisfaction but because the effort must perfectly represent the will of God. Perfection, then, is not intended to create a superhuman being, a form of bionic moral being, but rather, it is intended to reflect the perfected glory of the Father; it is not for goodness' sake, but for God's.

Now, we should be quick to note in the text that these counsels of perfection offered by Jesus assume that the world will continue in its own imperfect and wicked course. Jesus is no utopian idealist here, no architect of a perfect and moral society. His injunctions assume that murder will continue despite the commandment and his injunction that even anger is contrary to the spirit of the commandment. When he talks about lustful looking, he doesn't assume that adultery is going to disappear. When he tells us to turn the other cheek, to go the extra mile, to love those who hate us, he assumes the continued existence of the evils and the violence these injunctions are intended to overcome. If you want to know what the real world is really like, see what it is that Jesus asks us to do or not to do. If you love those who love you, if you are good when it is easy to be good, what reward have you? "Do not even the Gentiles do the same? You, therefore, must be perfect, as your heavenly Father is perfect."

There is only one man in the Bible who has became a byword for perfection, and that, of course, is Job. "There was a man in the land of Uz whose name was Job, and that man was blameless and upright, one who feared God and turned away from evil." Or, as the Authorized Version puts it, "That man was perfect and upright, and one that feared God and eschewed evil" (Job 1:1).

What happened to Job? He became a human experiment in a test of wills between God and Satan. His uprightness was the cause of his troubles. His friends in their many speeches, unaware of the true circumstances of his dilemma, assume that trouble naturally follows sin; it is punishment, and therefore whatever happened to Job he deserved. It was not imperfection that placed him on the griddle, however, but perfection; the ultimate wisdom of Job is that his blessings came not from his merit but from the mercy of God, and his curses not from his own fault but from the power of God. The test for Job is whether he can be righteous not only in the absence of reward but in the face of adversity. The steadfastness of Job has to do not with his own perfection, but in his unwavering faith in the perfection, the perfect nature of God, to whom he would be revealed in the latter day. This is what Job means when he says, "I know that my redeemer liveth, and that he shall stand at the latter day. And though worms destroy this body, yet in my flesh shall I see God." Job is a study in faithfulness, in steadfastness, in the hope of glory in the face of despair; but he is also a study, a portrait, of the ambiguity of perfection and the reality of life lived in the midst of imperfection.

The world of Job makes much more sense to most of us than the world of Jesus. We are, by now, used to living with imperfection. We find ourselves daily surrounded by the inexplicable, and we are always being given advice. Perhaps some of you have read the long-running bestseller by Rabbi Harold Kushner, *When Bad Things Happen to Good People*. It is a Jobian world of which he writes, and people acknowledge it as real and are willing to pay good money to read about it. We are surrounded by the little imperfections—paper bags that are not as strong as they used to be, lightbulbs that don't last as long as they used to, fabrics that don't wear as well as they once did. The human body is a procession of imperfections. We are given maximum resources in order, it seems, to watch them slowly or quickly deplete themselves until we are once again dust and ashes. Parents once could help their children with their math; now the children have to help the parents understand how computers work. Then there are the great imperfections to the secular being, the greatest imperfection of which is death. What a silly waste of all this machinery and potential. Then there is poverty, violence, sickness, disease, corruption, and war. We have refined the means of human existence, but not the end, and yet we think it unreasonable that the world should not be a reasonable place.

Any fool can live in paradise; it ought to be easy: no right or wrong, no sin, no error, no mixed motives, no compromising opportunities. But this is not paradise, and we fools are called to make our way here, making the most out of less than the best. There are men and women who are discouraged because peace is not yet achievable as an item of national policy; there are students who are upset because their vision of a just society with peace is not upheld in Bosnia or experienced in South America or experienced by them here at home. The counsels of perfection are not necessarily the counsels of despair. Jesus reminds us that the perfection we are encouraged to imitate will not reward us with a perfect world for our efforts, but the virtue for the faithful, even if they achieve no other virtue, is that they seek and serve virtue because in so doing they fulfill, they perfect, they make complete the will and the work of God. That work is never done, and that is why we must ever be about doing it.

Wisdom and the Wise

❖

Text: The multitude of the wise is the welfare of the world.

Wisdom 6:24

Late last spring I found myself in a line of traffic held up by the fact that the traffic light on the southern end of the Lars-Anderson Bridge leading across the Charles River to Cambridge was frozen at red. It wasn't a flashing or a blinking red light, it was a broken red light. Now this did not mean, of course, that cars stopped or refused to go through it, despite the fact that cars with a frozen green light on the other side were whizzing by with impunity. This was, after all, still Boston, where driving is a contact sport and traffic lights are merely a handicap to see how well one can do. Despite that, one proceeded through that dead red light with more than usual care and caution before breaking out and running away, and as I paused for my turn I looked at the gatepost of the Anderson Bridge. I'd never paused before to notice the ornate decoration and the filigree upon it, nor had I had time before to read the inscription, but that day in the traffic I saw these words: "The multitude of the wise is the welfare of the world." I paused just one second longer to note the citation, but I couldn't follow it very closely because all of the cars behind me began to honk and I had to move along. Later I looked it up in my concordance and noticed that it was in the Apocrypha and not regularly preached upon. There and then I decided that here was something I could use.

Now, a traffic jam is a wonderfully fit place to contemplate the soundness, the appropriateness, the usefulness, and even the relevance of this text—there amid honking cars and aggressive, angry, frustrated drivers, in the midst of arrogant, indifferent pedestrians, and surrounded by the frontier logic and ethic that it is everyone for himself as fast as possible. One does not have a very high opinion of the multitude. They certainly do not appear to be wise, and if the world depends upon them, those other drivers and those pedestrians, for its welfare, then the world is in an even worse state than it appears. No, the sentiment on that bridge at that moment would be amended by any of us sitting there in a car to read: "Get this bloody multitude out of the way and let me pass, now!"

The multitude is much with us, too much with us late and soon, and most of us pride ourselves in not being a part of the multitude. The traffic jam is a vivid illustration of this, perfected by the automobile. There we all are, thousands upon thousands of us, isolated in our little machines, a great concourse of people on our mobile parking lots called streets and highways, and who in those circumstances ever thinks of himself as part of that crowd? No, if the truth be known, our thought at such an hour is more like this: "All of these people are in my way. They are impeding my progress." Our car, our truck, even our bus or our plane places us in the multitude, but not of the multitude. No wonder people are driven by this odd proximity of the public and the autonomous to such acts of insanity as the gunfights on the freeways of California or the tremendous aggression toward all humankind that one feels after a taxi ride to or from the airport. The multitude is not wise, nor is it good, and thank God, we all say, we are not a part of it.

The text, however, does not say that the multitude is wise. This is not a biblical attempt to celebrate or to make popular a conventional wisdom. We have done and do that all by ourselves and all the time. Autonomous, self-starting, self-maintained, rugged individualists that we all pride ourselves on being, even we find ourselves caught up sometimes, even unawares, in the conventional wisdom, in the prevailing view, whose chief consolation is not that it is intrinsically correct and therefore I hold it, but rather that it is intrinsically correct because so many others hold it and therefore so must and so do I.

Let me illustrate. Some of you may recall with horror or delight that in January of 1985 I took part in the inaugural exercises of President Reagan at the start of his second term. This was an honor no citizen could refuse, in my view, and besides, I thought it would be fun. What a bully pulpit is the east front of the United States Capitol or, as it happened, under the dome of the rotunda. So off I went and it was fun indeed, but one of the people I met in Washington said to me as the ceremonies were coming to a close and I shortly would make my way back to Cambridge, "What will your friends in the People's Republic of Cambridge think about all of this?" Well, I soon found out. I was at dinner, at a fashionable table, in a fashionable house, in a fashionable street, hard by this fashionable church, filled with people who pay others to feed the hungry and clothe the naked, and one lady said to me after the soup and after she had exhausted the limited supply of small talk, in sheer exasperation, "How *could* you?" It was not really a question, don't you see? When I replied that Mr. Lincoln freed the slaves and I felt I owed a debt to the Republican party, she, like Queen Victoria, was not amused. For her and all of her friends and for so many of my parishoners and colleagues, the convential wisdom was clear and unspoken, and in front of fifty million people, I had gone against it. It wasn't that it was right or wrong, it just wasn't the conventional wisdom.

Those who dissent from one conventional wisdom simply to embrace another run the risk of the condemnation of the prophet Isaiah, who warned the multitude of the would-be wise and righteous people of Israel: "Woe to those who are wise in their own eyes, and shrewd in their sight." One might say that such wisdom is its own reward and a small one at that. So, my friends, let the land of the would-be wise, those of you who would number yourselves among the multitude of the wise, be warned. The two worst, the two most perverse constructions one could give to this morning's text, both of which are popular and possible in places such as this, are these:

1. The multitude is wise, because it is the multitude.
2. The multitude would be wise or wiser if everyone in it agreed with me.

The text, however, is saying neither of these but something quite different. The text says that the world will benefit from the increase of those who are truly wise, who know what wisdom is and who therefore pursue it even though they may not achieve it, and that is a fit sentiment to be engraved upon a gate that leads into a great university, and a fit sentiment to apply to ourselves. The first word that we should hear is a word of encouragement, a word of courage as we undertake that pursuit of wisdom. Do not be discouraged as you undertake that pursuit.

Now, one might ask, "What good does it all do?" So many pious sentiments on so many pious gates, and so many pious sermons in the hopes of so many pious and flawed people. What good does it all do? We have been seeking truth, justice, wisdom, virtue, and mercy in this spot for more than three hundred fifty years, and are we, or the world, any better off for it? Every June we graduate yet another class of the best and the brightest, but the problems their bright promises are designed to resolve continue and increase. Someone last year suggested that all the colleges and universities in America should hold a moratorium on commencement for just one year, stop the flood for one year, and see if things got any better, and if they did it would save us all a tremendous amount of effort and work.

My colleague Professor Mason Hammond has been a member of the daily Morning Prayers congregation more or less regularly since 1921. Once he said to me for no particular reason and out of the blue that he was growing rather weary of saying the Lord's Prayer every day as he had done for over eighty years, for he hadn't seen many results of the effort over all of those years and wondered if it was worth continuing. Now he was, of course, being facetious at least in part, but it is easy to grow hard over the short supply of wisdom's fruits, especially if we are reminded annually both of what they could be and of what they are not. A simple survey of our needs and a simple survey of what is possible to achieve always leaves us in a state of spiritual deficit, and there is a discouraging frustration in the familiarity and sameness of it all. So to people like us, the word we need to hear as we apply once again this business of wisdom and the welfare of the world to ourselves is a word of courage. Don't give up, it isn't over yet, and your turn, our turn, has just arrived.

The search for wisdom then requires in the first instance not brains but courage and the willingness to carry on despite the evidence on the one hand and the absence of evidence on the other; and that truly is an unconventional bit of wisdom, an unconventional view. Those who form the multitude of the wise and who add to the welfare of the world are those people who love truth even more than their own possession of it. They are unwilling to give it all up as a lost cause when there is no instant gratification of their highest desires. I prayed for peace all week last week and there's still war in the world. I prayed for the hungry and there are still people going without. I prayed for this and the problem isn't resolved. I shall give it all up.

The welfare of the world does not depend on such people. The welfare of the world is managed not by those who impose an impossible standard and an improbable timetable, but by those whose impossible standards, hopes, and prayers are maintained against all of the conventional wisdoms to the contrary.

Another thing that this text reminds us by its very construction, its very syntax, is that wisdom is not a private possession; it is not an individual goal or quality. It is not one of the things that one gets for oneself, a little dose of self-improvement. Wisdom is both purposeful and public; in other words, wisdom, particularly the wisdom that is talked about in this text, is civic; wisdom is corporate: "The multitude of the wise is the welfare of the world." The connection rests in what you do with what you know and the place where you do what you know, and the combination of sound knowledge and right action is what is called, in all places, in all times, and in all languages, virtue. That's the equation, the moral and civic equation: Sound knowledge and right action equal virtue, or for you math types: K + A = V, to the second power if you want. Now, American morality has made virtue, especially in relation to sex, what you don't do, thereby giving a relatively negative idea of what virtue is all about, but real virtue is in fact a combination of who you are, what you know, what you do, and where you do it. The careful, ceaseless, creative search for this kind of virtue indeed assures the welfare of the world, and among that multitude we would all hope to be numbered. Lest you think we already have it, we do not.

Not only do we not have it now, but we have never had it. Therefore, those of you who think that now is the moment that we celebrate need only look around you to see what remains to be done, and those of you antiquarians who think it was back there somewhere and we've lost it, that we have only to go back and find it again, you too don't understand that what we seek is something that we have never yet had, which is why we continue to seek it. We're not recovering anything, we're hoping to discover something, and that is why virtue and wisdom are necessary ingredients in the ongoing renewal of our public, civic life together. We're not just singing somebody else's song. We're not just celebrating somebody else's achievements or victories. We are celebrating the possibility of what remains ahead for us, and indeed all of that past, all of that history, all of that achievement, and all of the present distresses and opportunities are simply that: opportunity, privileged opportunity for us.

This is where you and I come in. Not rehearsing an old scene, not saying old lines, but saying lines that are as applicable to ourselves and our posterity and future as they ever were to those who said and sang and hoped and worked for them before us. Wisdom remains the means to that ever elusive goal, the welfare of the world, and thus we continue to do what we do, not discouraged by the lack of immediate result but living truly as a learning community, a community of faith looking ahead, not resting, not recollecting, not reminiscing, but looking ahead to that which has yet to be achieved.

God grant that we indeed may be added to that nameless, faceless multitude of people who contribute to the welfare of the world by the grace of God and by the courage and imagination of our own spirits. Indeed, may it be so that the multitude of the wise is the welfare of the world.

In the Midst of Life . . .

❧

Text: Lord, make me to know mine end . . . that I may know how frail
I am.   *Psalm 39: 4 (KJV)*

"In the midst of life," reads the Burial Office from the Book of Common
Prayer, "we are in death." That is a rather grim thought to those of us
who possess an existential but untested notion of immortality, for to be
reminded in the midst of our lives, in the midst of our busy and well-
organized lives devoted to the building of monuments that will endure,
in our prime, that "in the midst of life we are in death" is almost shock-
ingly rude, very bad form indeed. There is a flippant old World War I
ditty sung by the British Tommies which goes:

> The bells of hell go ting-a-ling a-ling
> For you but not for me;
> O death, where is thy sting-a-ling-a-ling,
> Where grave thy victory?

Though death has been around as long as we have and doubtless will be here after we are gone, and despite this little jingle, we have not yet become comfortable with death. Its actions still defy our powers to add or subtract; its capricious calling of the high and the low, the bright and the dull, the rich and the poor, the good and the bad is about the only thing left in this world to evoke that sense of awe and even primeval fear that links us up with our ancestors of the caves and the trees.

Some years ago, on All Saints' Sunday in The Memorial Church, the choir and members of the congregation illustrated today's sermon title through the presentation of Hugo Distler's *Totentanz* or *Dance of Death*. Perhaps some of you know it: A white-faced Death danced down the aisles of the church, confronting all estates and classes and inviting them to dance with him. Rich man, sailor, bishop, teaching fellow, senior professor—all were called, and all found it hard to believe that the summons was for them but it was. "In the midst of life we are in death."

This is a disturbing sentiment, and when anything disturbs us in the Western world we design an infinitely complex way of isolating it, sterilizing it, and making it very clinical. We speak of death in whispers and try to avoid any encounter at all with its grim realities. Any of you who remember the movie *The Loved One*, with its aberrant cemetery in California, Forest Lawn, can testify to that. In Cambridge, where we do things with infinitely more taste than lesser breeds without the law, we have Mount Auburn, the first garden cemetery in America, where we lay our dead to rest amid Eden-like botanical displays. Many of us have read Jessica Mitford's *The American Way of Death*, and we all know one or two funeral directors né undertakers who make us chilly in conversation. In one of the best books on the subject, Elisabeth Kübler-Ross raises the whole tone of this discussion in her infinitely wise *On Death and Dying*, and it is she who along with a few others is forcing us to take the cosmetics off death and dying, for sentiment and fear have served to deny us hope and dignity in death. Strangely enough, the leadership in new attitudes toward death is not coming from the church but from the social and medical sciences. Christians are yet uncomfortable with death, and churches are the last place you expect to hear about it. We speak of it at Easter, but it is so cloaked in the excitement and aura of the resurrection that we really don't hear; and we perhaps allude to it at funerals, but in our mistaken notion of what comfort is we avoid much mention of death and speak in the more reassuring vocabulary of memory and solace.

When we come right down to it, however, the only point to the Christian gospel, the only authentic and real message that it has to communicate to us, concerns not so much how to live the good life or to deal with the bad life as it concerns a new attitude toward death; for in Christ we see that death is not the end, that death itself is conquered, and that we can share in that promise of newness in life through Christ who conquered death for us. Therefore, rather than avoid death, the Christian confronts it, accepts it, and realizes that death is a comma rather than a period. That is the revolutionary attitude toward death, and it is the essential ingredient of the Christian message. Christ through his resurrection from the dead has overcome that ultimate enemy.

Now, if you had known that this was going to be an Easter sermon, you could have bought some new clothes and done it up properly. How can we presume to speak of such things without the accompaniment of trumpets and lilies and a church full of spiritual voyeurs? There are several reasons, one of which is that we meet on Sunday rather than on the Saturday of the commandments not because we are disobedient but because we celebrate the resurrection every first day of the week. So today has as much claim for an Easter sermon as some Sunday in March or April. For the Christian to ignore death or pretend that it doesn't exist is for the Christian to ignore that unique promise which is ours in Christ and which unites us with men and women of all the ages past and yet to be, for it is not the careful, cautious living of our lives that joins us with the infinite number of the saints, but rather the victorious negation of the fear of death and the tomb that binds us up in one great fellowship of strivers and believers.

"In the midst of life, we are in death." The quality of our living is determined in large measure by the attitude we take toward our dying, and that is why the psalmist's words are such arresting ones to us, for rather than trying to avoid a discussion of an impolite or improvident subject, he asks pleadingly of God, "Lord, make me to know the measure of my days, that I may know how frail I am"; or as it is rendered in the Great Bible, "Lord, let me know the number of my days, that I may be certified as to how long I have to live." What does one want with such grim knowledge? Someone has said that death is nature's way of telling us to slow down, and that may be, but the question of our text is one of confrontation rather than of avoidance. "How long do I have, Lord; let me know so that I can set my affairs in order." If we were to paraphrase the text, we might make it read: "Lord, remind me of my weakness, my frailty, that what I do and get is all temporary, and in the time I have left, let me serve you well."

This, then, is a text about limitations and opportunities, and we must be reminded of our limitations. "For man walketh in a vain shadow and disquieteth himself in vain. He heapeth up riches and cannot tell who shall gather them."

You can't take it with you, we are told, but many have tried. The Egyptians buried their pharaohs together with servants and riches and tools and all the things of this life so that they could carry on without interruption in the next. Somehow, the acquiring of worldly goods deserved a better end than to be left to the state or to undeserving relatives, and yet they provided only fodder for grave robbers. The heaping of riches is a vain show, for as the old saw goes, "The richest man in death needs but two pennies for his eyes." The acquiring of great wealth, great influence, great power, the gifts of this world in profusion—these vanities remain to entice someone else in their acquisition. We need to be reminded by the text of our limitations, that we shall pass away and become but a part of that from which we came. "Ashes to ashes, dust to dust; dust thou art, and to dust thou shalt return." If this were all that the psalmist mentioned, life would be one fatalistic game of Monopoly, and just as sure as you go to Park Place and Boardwalk, you must go to jail. No, the psalmist is reminded of his frailty, his limitations, but such knowledge, rather than intimidating him into a cringing submission to fate and the inevitable, stimulates him to the useful employment of his time: "And now, Lord, what is my hope? My hope is in thee. O spare me a little, that I may recover my strength before I go hence and be no more."

Until death comes to us all we are going to have to live life with that sense of the incomplete, the unready, the ill-prepared, for to wait until we are ready is to wait forever. Graduate students who work on their theses spend years gathering materials, reading the works of other people, conferring with advisers and colleagues. Often they don't dare begin to write a page, for surely someone somewhere has already hit upon their idea or there is more and more evidence to be discovered, or they need to check out just one more series of notes. Preparation is fine, but preparation that inhibits action until one is 100 percent certain means that nothing is ever done, and in the case of the thesis, it never gets written at all, not out of indifference but out of too much preparation. One has to make a start, a stab, and one has to learn to live with the tensions of tentativeness. Only so much rehearsal, and a piece must be sung if it is to live at all. Only so much preparation, and a life must be lived if it is to be life at all. It is not the perfection of our efforts so much as the persistence with which we try again and again that marks the quality of our living. We have to know our limits, but within them the options are ours to contemplate.

It is the fear of death that binds us to an idolatry of life, and it is Christ who liberates us from that bondage through his very triumph over the grave. We, then, the church militant, struggle against the demonic forces of this world, the forces of darkness, doubt, and oppression, but we also fight against an idea of death that denies us joy in this life and hope in the next. John Donne tells us in his tenth holy sonnet: "One short sleep past, we wake eternally, and death shall be no more; death, thou shalt die."

We live and labor and love with Christ who sets us free from the fear and corruption of death, and through that cosmic encounter of Christ with death we are brought together with his saints into newness of life. As Saint Peter says, "Blessed be the God and Father of our Lord, Jesus Christ. By his great mercy we have been born anew to a living hope through the resurrection of Jesus Christ from the dead, and to an inheritance which is imperishable, undefiled, and unfading, kept in heaven for you, who by God's power are guarded through faith for salvation ready to be revealed in the last time." We therefore rejoice with those who have run their course, and we pray now for the strength to run our own.

Time, Talent, and Treasure

❄

Text: For to everyone who has will more be given, and he will have
abundance; but from him who has not, even what he has will be
taken away.   *Matthew 25:29*

This is a "hard" text; it paints a picture that we would rather not see;
it speaks a truth we would rather not hear. It implies an injustice and
an inequality that most of us find difficult to accept; it cuts across the
conventional wisdom of what the teachings of Jesus are all about; and
that is just the reason that we should examine this text.

In an age where the rich have more than they could possibly need,
and the poor have considerably less than they need, where is the "good
news" in a gospel that would appear to perpetuate abundance at the
expense of deprivation? Surely this is one of those texts in the Bible that
we can afford to ignore, along with the Ten Commandments, the sacrifice of Isaac, and the more aggressive writings of Saint Paul? In yielding
to this temptation to editorial selectivity, however, and in choosing to

hear only those texts that satisfy our image of ourselves or of Jesus, we run the considerable risk of learning more and more about less and less, which is an agreeable situation for a Harvard graduate student, perhaps, but perilous for the honest inquirer after the Christian faith. I suggest that "the terrible tale of the talents," as we read it in Saint Matthew's gospel, has something essential to say to us, even in our egalitarian age. This may well be called a "hard text for hard times."

The parable is called "The Parable of the Talents," and as a talent was a denomination of ancient money, it would appear that this is a story about money and its use. The master gave sums of money to three of his servants and the text tells us that the money was "entrusted," which means that the master expected to have it back. It was not a gift and not even a loan, for there is no reason to believe that the servants were in need; the money was given to the servants to be held until the master's return. The text suggests that there was an expectation as to the management of the money, for it says that he gave the sums to each "according to his ability"; so not only were they not given equal sums but their capacity to manage the sums given them was also unequal. Each did not start with either the same sum or with the same ability.

We know what they did with the money and how their ability was put to work, and when the master returned to settle his accounts, we know that the first servant had invested his five talents and got two more, thus giving seven back to his master. The second servant had done likewise with his two with the same rate of return, and returned to his master four talents. Thus far, the master has made four talents on the deal. The third servant, however, fearing his master and being a cautious soul, did not risk his talent and returned exactly what he had been given, one talent; and we sympathize with this third prudent servant, for clearly he did know his master. He thought that his master had more confidence in the others than in him and hence the small initial investment in his abilities, and he shared his master's lack of confidence in himself. Fearing to lose what little he had, "He went and dug in the ground and hid his master's money."

Now, if we were to rewrite this story according to our image of what a good master should do, assuming, of course, that the master is God, we would have the master say to the now terrified servant, "There, there;

I understand your fear and your ambitions. I know you have a learning disability as far as figures are concerned and I know that you wanted to do what was right. It could be worse; you could have lost all of the money in some foolish investment. As it is, you did the best you could; I appreciate your concern for protecting my money. You can keep what you have. You could have made more, but at least you haven't lost out completely." This then would have been a tale about the cautious servant and the forgiving master.

That, however, is not what the text says. The poor servant is harangued for his caution and deprived of the little money he has preserved by that caution, and the moral of the tale is that he who has will get more, and he who hasn't will get to hell, where such men weep and gnash their teeth—not a pretty sight. This tale so affected Karl Marx that he reversed its implications and came up with his classical theory of socialism: "From each according to his ability; to each according to his needs." Of this text, and particularly of the fate of the poor third servant, Krister Stendahl likes to tell the tale of the old Swedish Lutheran pastor who preached on the text to his elderly congregation of literalists, one of whom was worried about the fate of people similar to this servant who, like himself, no longer had any teeth to gnash. The pastor, not willing to undermine faith, replied, "Teeth will be provided." More than teeth will have to be provided for us, however, if we are to take this text as more than a vengeful fable of capitalist economics.

As a first step toward the rehabilitation of this text, I suggest that despite the popular title attached to it, "The Parable of the Talents," the story is not about money at all but about time, and not just about any time but about the time in which we find ourselves, the time between the beginning and the end, the "time being," as W. H. Auden would put it. This story is told by Saint Matthew between the story of the wise and foolish virgins and the story of the last judgment. It is the second of the three final stories that Jesus tells just before he is delivered up to his captivity and death on the cross. The very next chapter marks the beginning of the end, and so this parable is among those most significant last sayings of Jesus, concerning the end both of his ministry and of the age of which his ministry was a sure and certain sign. The story places a premium not on how to use and spend money but on how to use and spend time, especially as there was not very much of it left to go around.

Jesus was always warning his followers that the end of the age would come like a thief in the night, with great suddenness, without warning or preparation, and therefore the faithful were encouraged to be watchful, and some were so anxious to be watchful that all they did was watch. They gave up the responsibilities of their normal lives, and the rules of the world no longer applied, for they were waiting for the rapture, waiting for the end, waiting to be delivered, and they neglected the affairs entrusted to them. Why feed the hungry or even bury the dead? Jesus is coming soon. Why plant crops and weed the fields? Why worry about the harvest? The end is in sight. Why should we marry or have babies? Why should we start a new generation, when Jesus is on the way and the end in sight?

In his parables about time Jesus warns that what counts is not so much how we anticipate the future but how we use what time we have, what resources we are given, and how we redeem the present. The parable of the talents has nothing to do with investment and everything to do with engagement, of what we do with what we have where we are. When the master in our parable went away he did not tell his servants how long he would be or when he would return. He left them with a splendid sense of insecurity, what the late Dean Samuel Howard Miller of Harvard Divinity School used to call "creative insecurity." The test was to see how, living in that insecurity, which then as now was normal, one would manage, each according to his ability. The burden of the text is not "What do we do when he returns?" but rather "What is to be done in the meantime?"

We get a hint of what Jesus expects to be done until he returns when, in the verses following our story in Matthew, he talks about those who are welcomed into heaven because "I was hungry and you gave me food; I was thirsty and you gave me drink; I was a stranger and you welcomed me; I was naked and you clothed me, sick and you visited me, in prison and you came unto me." These were the things that were done for Christ, to the surprise of those who did them, since, as Jesus said, "because they were done to the least of my brethren, you did them unto me." Jesus' meaning is unmistakable: We are not simply to wait, mark time, until he comes, or until it all ends; and as it is true for Jesus, it is true for his followers: "We must do the works of him who sent us" and "We must not grow weary in well-doing."

The third man, the subject of the parable of the talents, suffers from what we may well call a loss of nerve. He is given an opportunity and he finds himself in a state of paralysis. Filled with fear of God and fear of himself, fearful that he will not succeed and fearful of the master, he plays the safest game possible: no risk, no fault. "If I don't try great things, I get credit if I don't lose great things. Who can ask for more than that? I will give back what I was given." It seems so simple, so sensible an arrangement, and it appeals to us cautious Yankees. When in doubt, don't. What might have been an example of prudence, a virtue most esteemed in the Bible, becomes in fact an example of cowardice and selfishness, for rather than try to enhance what has been entrusted to him, the servant is more interested in protecting himself, and thus his is a denial of the trust that has been given him. In the modern sense, he refused to use his talent, a word that no longer means money but means rather the God-given combination of ability and opportunity. It is important to realize that such talent—ability and opportunity—is understood to be the gift of God, and hence the talent does not really belong to the talented but to God, who gives it.

This is not the first time that Jesus uses money, the coin of the realm, to make a clear point about the use of that which belongs to God. Remember the tricky question about Caesar's coin. Jesus asks, "Whose face is on it?" "Caesar's" comes back the answer from his questioners. "Then render to Caesar what is his, and to God what is his," responds Jesus. Since we ourselves are created in the image of God, imprinted with his likeness even as the coin was imprinted with Caesar's, so do we belong to God and must give ourselves and what we are and have to God, who gave them to us. Talent belongs to God; God gives us ability and opportunity that we might better do the work he has given into our hands, and in not using his talents to the fullest of his limited ability, the servant of our story cheated God by not giving full value. God requires that our ability and opportunity be put to use, and that nearly always means put at risk. If a talent is to grow it must be put to use.

The most gifted and profound talent, unpracticed, unemployed, never put at risk, is as good as nothing.

The great Arthur Rubenstein was once asked why he practiced the piano so much. He replied, "If I don't practice one day, I know it; if I don't practice two days, the critics know it; and if I don't practice three days, everybody knows it."

A great talent or a modest talent, if it is to have the chance to do good things on behalf of the one who grants it, must be practiced, used, and employed; and if the talent given by God is not used, if the gift is not practiced, it will be lost. As is said of privileges and athletic skill: "Use it or lose it." This is the saddest and hardest part of the terrible tale of the talents: The unimproved, unused talent is taken from the cautious servant, and the one who risked the most is given the most, and what remains for the cautious when even caution is removed? Not very much. This is not an example of taking food from the mouths of those who have not to fill the stomachs of those who have. It is rather to say that those who dream no dreams shall have no vision; this poverty is not virtue; this poverty is the worst kind of impoverishment—the lack and fear of imagination. The cautious servant trusted neither himself nor his master, and in the end, like a criminal who is not allowed to profit from his ill-gotten gains, the servant is not allowed to profit from his lack of faith and action. He fails the course and is required to withdraw.

Now, a clever exegete and a cleverer preacher can put our minds to rest about the terrible tale of the talents. We understand this to be an eschatological tale about the end of the age and an encouragement to good works as venture capital. The simple maxim, simply put, is "no risk, no gain." It is an extreme story told in extreme times and we may now better understand it, but what on earth does it have to do with us?

This is a story about time, about the right and good uses of time, and about the time in which we are found: in the time being, or now. It is a story as well about talent, not about money but about the ability and the opportunity that God gives us to use our time to his glory and the help of his people here and everywhere. When we consider that our time and our talent are the greatest gifts that we have, we understand them rightly to be our treasure, that precious cargo we are privileged to bear in this world. Je-

sus tells this story near the end of his own time in order to warn that we
will be judged not on how much we have, or even on how much we get or
give, but on how wisely and well we use what we have in the time that we
have. God has great expectations; so too must we.

This then is a parable about stewardship, and so is this sermon. You are
asked in the time that you have to use wisely what you have been given for
the kingdom of God. That means that you must consider not only how you
spend your time but how you spend your money, and how you use your talent as well. The gifts that you have do not belong to you; they are not yours
to possess but rather they are yours to improve, and if you do not, you will
lose them. The parable, and life, are very clear.

We live in lean times; I know that and I know that you know that.
There is a sense of urgency, even of despair, in the air, and we live under
the threat of a cloud. Fear and caution abound, and you and I wonder
what we can do. Life is harsh and unfair, and judgment swift and arbitrary. The rabbis tell us that when a wise man heard that the end of the
world was near he went out into his garden and planted a tree, an act
of courage, audacity, and hope—the only possible response.

Perhaps it is John Wesley to whom we must turn, who, in times not
dissimilar to our own, and on behalf of the cautious to the question "But
what can I do for the kingdom?" replied:

> Do all the good you can,
> By all the means you can,
> In all the ways you can,
> In all the places you can,
> At all the times you can,
> To all the people you can,
> As long as ever you can.

If you give serious consideration to this use of your talent, your time,
and your treasure, then neither your church nor the whole church of
Jesus Christ need ever fear, and for that let the whole church say Amen.

The Bible and the Believer

❊

Text: Thy word is revealed, and all is light; it gives understanding even
to the untaught.   *Psalm 119:130*

A collect used on the Second Sunday in Advent reads:

> Blessed Lord, who hast caused all holy scriptures to be written for
> our learning: grant that we may in such wise hear them, read, mark,
> learn, and inwardly digest them, that by patience and comfort of thy
> holy word we may embrace, and ever hold fast, the blessed hope of
> everlasting life which thou hast given us in our Saviour Jesus Christ.

Protestants are said to be people of one book, the Bible; and years ago
my Baptist church in Plymouth had as its motto, "Preaching from the
Book That the Pilgrims Brought." Oaths continue to be administered
upon it, cornerstones and arches bear inscriptions from it, its stories and
allusions form the common vocabulary of the Western intellectual and

aesthetic experience. These things cannot be denied; the book is very much with us and is an integral part even of our secular, modern world. That the Bible has a cultural and aesthetic influence in the world is quite evident and well attested, but what has the Bible to do with the believer, the church, the community of the faithful who, represented by such as ourselves, are bade "read, mark, learn, and inwardly digest" what is read from these books?

Growing up in the church where they preached from the Book that the Pilgrims brought, the answer was very clear. The principal feature of the sanctuary was its large central pulpit, behind which the minister stood and expounded the word of God. An enormous Bible sat on an open stand on the communion table at the front of the church, and the warrant of what we were to do and were not to do was found there. Children were expected to memorize large portions of the Bible, and since I was good at that sort of thing, I won prizes for consuming vast passages of scripture, a skill that served me in good stead when I came to the Divinity School.

Every evangelist I met owned a dog-eared, red-letter edition of the Bible which fit his left hand like a glove and appeared to open itself to the relevant passages. The inhabitants of this book came to life in their remarkable setting: Adam and Eve, the patriarchs and judges of Israel, the succeeding good and wicked kings, the prophets and the poets; and in the New Testament, Jesus and his adventures, the apostle Paul and the evangelists, the great doctrines of Hebrews, and the extraordinary visions of Revelation. I knew this book because it was filled with living people and living principles, and any and all of them would come to my aid when I needed them. As the compass was to the wandering Boy Scout, and the evening star to the pilot at sea, so was the Bible an infallible guide to the wandering Christian: "read, mark, learn, and inwardly digest." It was as we sing:

> Lord, grant us all a right to learn
> The wisdom it imparts,
> And to its heavenly teaching turn,
> With simple, childlike hearts.

When I became a man I put away childish things, and among them was the Bible. How could these things be? What had the Bible to do with the atom bomb? Hadn't Clarence Darrow once and for all destroyed the credibility of a book that flew in the face of scientifically demonstrated evidence? As literature it wasn't bad, but it paled next to Homer and it wasn't half as much fun as some of the Roman classics, the Song of Solomon notwithstanding. The Bible has always had its staunch defenders, men and women who have risen in its service against all the odds of the secular world, and I found them strange and curious; and I am reminded of the story of the Scottish minister and the local agnostic who were arguing about the validity of scripture. The agnostic said to the minister, "Well, brother, how can you read the book and preach from it every Sunday of your life? It is filled with utter nonsense." To which the reply was, "Nonsense or not, it is the word of God." So it seemed, but if it was the word of God, God was, albeit colorful, quite inconsistent and probably liable to the charge of nonsense.

Traveling in the twentieth century with the Bible as map and compass was like taking a road journey with a two-thousand-year-old atlas: interesting to read but hardly likely to get you to where you wanted to go. In those days many like me took comfort from the story of the Catholic priest, who, while crossing the Atlantic on one of the first transatlantic flights, heard the horrifying announcement from the captain that the plane was in trouble and likely to crash. Seeking comfort from the scriptures, he opened his New Testament and seized upon the first verse his eye met, which was the twelfth verse of the sixth chapter of Saint John's gospel: "Gather up the fragments that nothing be lost."

Our own text says, "Thy word is revealed, and all is light; it gives understanding even to the untaught"; and in the equally rhapsodic earlier verses of Psalm 119, "Thy word is a lamp unto my feet and a light on my path. . . . Thy instruction is my everlasting inheritance; it is the joy of my heart. I am resolved to fulfill thy statutes; they are a reward that never fails."

In the book of Romans, we are reminded, "Whatsoever things were written aforetime were written for our learning, that we through patience and comfort of the scriptures might have hope." By this I believe that the apostle Paul and the fathers of the church want to remind us that the scriptures are a means to God's sublime end of redemption, a means that we cannot afford to ignore, but a means nevertheless. Contrary to popular opinion, the Bible never was meant to be an object of worship. Such a view would be anathema to any good Jew who knew the commandments, which read, "Thou shalt have no other gods before me," and "Thou shalt not bow down to images and idols." What is holy about this book that we call holy is that it directs by precept and example the mind and spirit toward the mind and spirit of God. In other words, one's devotion begins when one closes the Bible. The faith becomes the lively word when it becomes rooted in the hearts and lives of the believers, and by such means secures us in the hope that the promises made and the guidance offered are trustworthy and true.

Now what does all this say to the vexing problems of the modern age of biblical criticism, where some of the faithful feel it necessary to defend the Bible from the hands of the literary and textual critics, and many of these same critics seem bent upon destroying any shred of authority that the Bible still might have? Many Christians whose lives are a light in our times believe that to apply secular canons of criticism to the Bible is to reduce its stature; and many other Christians, equally pious, believe that a mature Christian faith has outgrown the mythological needs of the Bible. It is important to note here that the scriptures have never been unexamined. Rabbinic scholarship for centuries has been based upon the principle of interpretation: What does it mean and how came it to be so? If the scriptures were always self-evident and without need of interpretation and understanding, teachers such as Jesus and Moses and Hillel would not have been necessary. Saint Augustine and the fathers of the Western church spent long hours and countless volumes trying to make clear the levels of scriptural meaning, and they, living closer in time to the formation of the sacred canon, would have recoiled at the notion and term of "fundamentalism." Their sense of the scriptures as lively and organic and the agency of God's spirit and our understanding was far more sophisticated than many of our contemporary opponents of biblical criticism, and they were able to do what they did with the scriptures because they had what many of us have lost, a context of the faithful community within which to work, the church, and a firm belief that the Holy Spirit is the means by which our understanding is enlarged and enlightened.

The Bible was not for those teachers an isolated set of divine Yellow Pages cataloging God's will and our necessity. It was one of the means by which God had chosen to reveal through human instruments and examples his will for the world, and it was no more or less infallible than the life of which it was composed and toward which it was directed. It was the record of an all-too-human people seeking, finding, losing, and being found of God. The Bible spoke, and speaks, not the last word but the lively word by which we would be kept in remembrance of the things that were, and in hope of the things that are yet to come. Because it is not intended to be a substitute for science or history or politics or even religion, it can neither be made nor destroyed by these agencies for it is at the same time both less and more than all of these. It is, in the whimsical phrase of Krister Stendahl, once dean of Harvard Divinity School, "Not history minus but poetry plus."

The Bible, then, is the church's book; it records in its pages the mystery of God's continuous incarnation through the prophets, the judges, the kings, and, indeed, is the supreme example of his coming to us in the advent of Jesus Christ. As we read in the epistle to the Hebrews on Chrismas Day:

> God, who at sundry times and in diverse manners spake in times past unto our fathers by the prophets hath in these last days spoken unto us by his son, whom he hath appointed heir of all things, by whom also he made the world.

Through this book we hear the history beyond history of our people who have traveled before us the road upon which we now find ourselves, but by that book we are not called to lead our lives as pale imitations, trying to reproduce in our times the circumstances and characters of third-century Bibleland. If that book speaks to us with the same power that spoke to our fathers and to those whose lives are recorded in it, then we are led by that same spirit that says that we too must live our lives in the fearful and faithful search for the will of God who made us and the love of Christ that saved us. With the Bible, then, our work is not done but is just beginning, for in its penetrating light we must now live our lives even as our ancestors lived theirs, working out our salvation in fear and trembling.

The Bible is the beginning of belief, but for the Christian it must never be a substitute for belief. What is written is indeed written for our learning, but as we are reminded by Paul, ". . . written for our learning that we through the patience and comfort of the scriptures might have hope."

Get Out of the Way

❁

Text: We ought not to put fresh difficulties in the way of those who
are turning to God from among the Gentiles.

Acts 15:19 (Moffatt Bible)

The text sounds crisp and different because it is in the translation of
James Moffatt. If some of our texts seem to be from fragments of notes
to himself on Saint Paul's refrigerator door, and to others in passing, this
lesson from Acts is the incomplete notes or the interrupted transcript of
a church council or a church meeting. We find ourselves in the middle
of an argument in progress. We don't know where it begins. We are not
clear what the issues are. It is not certain even who is speaking. We have
some vague idea of resolution. We know that it must be resolution because it is the end of the chapter, but we are not quite clear what is
resolved. The speaker is not even Paul, but James. We are at a loss to
figure out just what is going on, but the words that form our text, James's
words here in his testimony, ring out loud and clear and on their own

without regard to the context, and they capture our attention. They say something that might be worth reflecting upon: "We ought not to put fresh difficulties in the way of those who are turning to God from among the Gentiles." That is Mr. Moffatt's translation. Mine is simply, "Get out of the way."

Now the debate in which James is making this case with Paul and Barnabas and Silas and Judas and all that lot of interesting, contentious disciples has to do with how much of the Jewish law non-Jews should have to keep in order to become Christians. The success of the apostolic preaching was such that non-Jews were being drawn to Christ in great numbers but not by means of the Jewish law which Christ himself, as a Jew, had kept. What did this mean for non-Jews as well as for Jews, Gentiles, and Christians? Now if you really want to know the answer to that question, and if you really insist on having this all sorted out to your satisfaction and clarity, I suggest that you read the Acts of the Apostles first, and then any number of decent and respectable commentaries. They will tell you all that you ever wanted to know and considerably more than you actually need to know about the subject. A clue, however, which will suffice, is given at the eleventh verse where Peter says in response to all of this *contretemps*, "But we believe that we shall be saved through the grace of the Lord Jesus just as they will." It is as simple as that. We believe that we will be saved through the grace of the Lord Jesus and that they will be saved in the same way. We ought not to get in the way of that process of their salvation or of our own. That is all that you need to remember or to know.

What drew me to this text was not the party politics of the early church, interesting though they are. It was not the debate between Christian Jews and Christian Gentiles that draws us to this, interesting as that may be to those who teach the stuff for pay and who study it for credit. What appeals to me and I hope ultimately to you, is admittedly at the surface level: the notion that in behalf of God we often place obstacles in the way of those who seek God and who are sought by God. In a way, we often stand in the way and become obstacles to ourselves in God's transaction with ourselves, and in a nutshell, it is the notion that religious people often get in the way of religion and that religion often gets in the way of God. Good people for good reasons often do silly and even bad things that make it difficult for others and for themselves to come to God.

James tells us quite clearly that we ought not to put fresh difficulties in the way of those who are turning to God from among the Gentiles. That word *fresh* is interesting because it says that there are already enough difficulties in this relationship of allowing God into our lives. There are already enough obstacles in the way that God wants to enter into our lives, and we ought not to be erecting new ones.

Now, of all the complexities of the text, this little fragment of it may seem a rather superficial aspect. Ought we not to be considering the Judaizers and the relationships between Jewish Christians and Gentile Christians, and all of that sort of thing? Sermons are by their nature superficial and so, too, are preachers and so, too, are congregations. Let us not kid one another. Who knows? Perhaps by condescending to consider what we just might understand we might learn something, and in learning something we might be both helped and helpful. So I declaim it at the start as superficial, but superficial is sometimes good for us.

Don't get in the way of those who would turn to God, or of God who would turn to you. Don't get in the way. At first it may seem odd to think of ourselves as in any way obstacles to God's work: "God has no hands but our hands," we used to sing in Sunday school. Among our brethren and sisters we are in some way the means by which God does his work in the world. True, we may not be evangelists in the sense of Paul and Barnabas and Silas and James and the rest of them. We may not see ourselves as evangelists in turning people on to God. That is not our way, but neither are we engaged at our better moments in keeping people out of God's way. We may do no good but we certainly don't do any harm. Like ourselves we let others make their choices and take their chances in their own time and in their own way.

Now there is much to be said for getting out of the way in this particular sense, and we have all said it and we all know it. We know what it is like to be pressed, to be pushed, to be pulled, to be persuaded, and to be manipulated into things that we would rather not do. It is the stock in trade of many branches of the household of faith to do just that, and many of us have been victims of that kind of enterprise.

In the church experience of my youth we often had what was called an "invitation." At the end of the service the preacher would say, "We are now going to throw open the doors of the church." It was an opportunity for people not to leave as you will, through the doors, but to enter into a relationship with Jesus Christ, to join the church and to accept Christ. This meant doing something; it meant standing up and coming forward and being seen by everybody, and then tucked away in a little room off to the side where you wondered what they would do to you. Great was the pressure, I recall, to accept those invitations at the end of the service. Your parents hoped you would and your Sunday school teacher expected that you would. Your friends dared you to do it, and not to do it was to defy all of the efforts of the church; as theologian Harvey Cox likes to say, "Not to choose is to choose." By not choosing God in that invitation, you were choosing someone else. You were choosing Satan. How many souls were forced down that sawdust trail, later to repent of their repentance? I know quite a few. What might have happened to them if we hadn't got in their way and had let them turn to God even as God would turn to them, not on our timetable, not even on their timetable, but on God's timetable?

That is one case for getting out of the way and allowing God to save, not for our church's credit or for our own but for his glory and by his grace. This is what we call nowadays a "destructive religious experience," and it acts as if we don't trust that there is an authentic religious experience that can and does and has and will work by God's grace. Don't get in the way. For many of us it is so difficult, no matter what our tradition or our inclination, to realize that the transaction of faith is one between God and the individual soul and not between the church and society. The church and society have their place and their role, but the ultimate transaction and transformation is between God and the soul. The church ought to be the means of that encounter between the human and the divine, not the end, and not a substitute or an impediment or an obstacle. It is hard not to get in the way because it is in our nature to get in the way.

I remember many years ago an Easter Sunday sunrise service in Plymouth, when we stood looking out to sea from the hill overlooking Plymouth Rock toward the horizon, where it was still cold and gray and dark. We all stood huddled, the minister before us, singing hymns and saying prayers and singing psalms, and waiting for that resurrection sun to come over the dark horizon. If any of you has ever watched a sunrise you know that the sun doesn't rise gradually, it pops up over the horizon. So, we sang our hymns and said our prayers and knew that we were waiting for the first glimpse of resurrection sun, when it would pop up over that dark, straight line far out at sea; and just at the crucial moment the minister leading the service turned toward the sun and said, "Christ has risen!" and held out his hands—and blocked the view of that rising sun until it had risen and we had all missed it. He had enjoyed that glorious instant of resurrection sun, but he had got in the way and the rest of us couldn't share the instant because of him. We didn't see the resurrection sun until it was up there shining and round as if it had been there all the time.

Christians, in our desire to witness for Christ, are tempted to get in the way, and this is perhaps for us the first temptation: not that we believe so much in ourselves but that we appear to believe so little in God's ability to know and to do the right thing at the right time. God needs all the help that he can get, indeed, but all the help that we can give to God is not always helpful to God. We profess to be people of faith, yet most of our time is spent in proving how faithful we are. A witness, however, is one who sees, who tells, and who is. The witness has something to see, something of which she can speak with authority, as the woman at the tomb said, "I saw the Lord." She witnessed this with her own eyes. As Isaiah says, "I saw the Lord high and lifted up." A witness not only sees, however, a witness tells what is seen. "We have seen; we have heard with our ears, O God." Then a witness must always point beyond herself. A witness is you. You are your testimony. You are what you attest to. You are what you witness to as a landmark, a means, a direction, a signpost. As Saint Paul says, "You are the evidence of which you speak." It is not simply what you see and what you tell, but what you are. Don't get in the way, but be the way by which God enters the world and the lives of his creation.

A colleague and friend in the university and in daily Morning Prayers,

Professor Elliot Forbes, tells the gentle story of how his father and his uncle as very young boys enjoyed a walk through the woods of Naushon Island with their aged grandfather, Ralph Waldo Emerson. He said that the younger of Emerson's grandsons, Professor Forbes's own father, a boy of six, apparently bashful and shy and very much in his own way aware of the greatness in which he stood with old Ralph Waldo Emerson, picked a buttercup from along a roadside in Naushon and approached his grandfather with it, saying, "Look, Grandfather, a buttercup." His older, smarter brother, Cameron, said, "Of course Grandfather knows that that's a buttercup." The intimate, fragile moment between the little boy and the old man was shattered by the rude insistence of what we call truth and reality. El says that his father never quite fully forgave his brother, even though they both lived well into their nineties.

God moves toward us in tender and insistent ways, in love divine, all loves excelling. Despite ourselves we, too, move toward God as plants seek the light and as birds invariably the dawn. I profoundly believe this to be so. There is much in all of this for believers to be and for believers to do, and one of the first things that believers must learn to do is not to get in the way of that transaction. Don't get in the way. Get out of the way. Be the way and allow the light to shine through you and on you and in you. "We ought not to put fresh difficulties in the way of those who are turning to God from among the Gentiles. . . . But we believe that we shall be saved through the grace of the Lord Jesus, just as they will."

The Mystery of Our Religion

❖

Text: Great indeed, we confess, is the mystery of our religion.

> He was manifested in the flesh,
> Vindicated in the Spirit,
>   Seen by angels,
> Preached among the nations,
>   Believed on in the world,
> Taken up in glory.

I Timothy 3:16

Many of you have learned to make sense out of religion. Our Western world and the Protestant reformed version of Christianity have prided themselves on the developed ability to discern and to understand. We have long since rejected superstition and mumbo-jumbo as fit alone for the jungle and the fraternity, and we rejoice in clear minds and sound judgments. Instruction is what we are about, and we would be tutored in matters of religion as in a foreign language until that blissful day when we will know precisely what the Virgin was not, exactly what happened on Easter day, and what was the ultimate plan behind the plan of creation. Once we have discovered these things, then we will be prepared to be perfectly religious. We will then be able to explain to our skeptical friends and our skeptic selves just what it is that we do and do not believe, and why or why not.

In making sense of religion we can join efforts with Thomas Jefferson, who, in his desire to bring the Bible up to date with his own understanding, took scissors and paste and excised all those passages that no longer conformed to the world as he saw it, and rearranged the rest. Needless to say, little was left but the teaching of Jesus and I Corinthians 13.

What Jefferson did with the Bible many of us would do with our religion. "Faith," as the farmer down Maine once said, "is believing what you *know* ain't so." Thus, preaching's task is to make faith understandable and thereby believable. Good sermons, particularly those of Easter and Christmas when most people are around to hear them, are those most likely to make the extraordinary events of those holidays conformable to our capacity and expectation. They tame the wary prey of doctrine, remove the fear of irrationality, and send us on our way with the assurance, to be renewed in the next year, that nothing can happen that we cannot understand.

It is the peculiar task of a university church to make sense out of religion, for a church and religion are in a university on sufferance, and they both must be made worthy of the company. Religion, therefore, must be both reasonable and relevant. By reasonable we mean that it must take its place in the democratic plurality of knowledge, and it must conform to what we learn in physics, mathematics, sociology, psychology, history, and economics. No longer the queen of sciences that it once was, it must be treated as a deposed dowager who was once able to exert profound influence and even power, but who now is tolerated only if she knows enough to know that she no longer knows enough.

If it is reasonable it will also seek to be relevant, for it will now have to justify its place and space in the world. It will recognize that its worth depends upon what it is able to perform for the general good here and now. It should at least be able to feed the hungry, clothe the naked, solace the poor, and soothe the rich. When it can do none of these, it should became a patron of the arts. It should finally be able to identify itself with any movement for human progress and social advancement which chooses to identify with it, and should be grateful for the opportunity.

When we will have been able to make religion both reasonable and relevant, then we will have found it to be a worthy colleague and citizen of university and world. The rough places will have been made plain and the crooked straight. We will have tamed the beast, and we will find that at the end of the string, while we may have something that now makes sense, we will not have Christianity. For at its heart the religion that we profess is neither reasonable nor relevant, and every effort to make it so has proven to be disastrous. Beyond reason and relevance is that central mystery, that ineffable, sublime affirmation seen in Jesus Christ, as we read in I Timothy 3:16:

> He was manifested in the flesh,
> Vindicated in the Spirit,
> Seen by Angels,
> Preached among the nations,
> Believed on in the world,
> Taken up in glory.

We can do nothing less than affirm, and indeed confess, how great is the mystery of our religion.

Mystery is unwelcome because it intimidates many of us, suggesting a limit to our capacity to know and to understand, and hence to control. Few of us are prepared to sacrifice a hard-won intellectual and spiritual autonomy for an awesome encounter with seraphim and cherubim continually crying "Holy, Holy, Holy." Those critical gifts given to us by Newton, Darwin, and Freud have made it possible for us to survive in a hostile and alien world. Why should we suddenly cease to employ them in our own defense, even though they are but capable of telling us less and less about less and less? So we sit, well-armed in our well-lit churches and in the world, ready to swat into oblivion any hint of transcendent mystery that might have managed to survive the eighteenth century. Think of the spiritual thralldom into which the world has been cast by the powers of so-called "mystery." Priestcraft and popery, we are told, transformed the simple ethics of Jesus and the community of love into a complicated, irrational jumble of scholastic creeds, formulae, and hocus-pocus designed to keep power in the hands of those who had it. Thus, like the Wizard of Oz, the whole thing was a clever and diabolical scheme of levers and mirrors designed to preserve the fantasies of the little old man behind the green curtain in the Emerald Palace. It is to Dorothy rather than to Luther that we must look for our liberation, for she has seen what we could not bear to see. Mystery, like modesty, is for those who need it; but in a world come of age, mystery simply gets in the way.

The "brave new world" is not so brave, probably because it is not so new, and it is the rediscovery of the power of the mysterious and of our own limitations which is perhaps the most remarkable phenomenon of our collective consciousness these days. For example, we have rediscovered evil and the satanic forces of darkness. Surely we knew that evil existed, but we always thought that it was somehow manageable, and that violence and hatreds were social aberrations which, with a little more money and a little more time, would became extinct. The movie *The Exorcist* put in tabloid form only what the American people were prepared to accept, and the reality of sin, malevolence, and wickedness is now difficult to avoid. The "rip-off" culture is with us, and all the sociologists and psychologists and government bureaucrats cannot explain away the phenomenon or our incapacity to deal with it, and so we have had to come to terms with our limitations in the management of life.

Together with our management of evil we have discovered death. Just as many believed that we had come to the point where medical science would discover a cure for death, the ancient mystery of what life is when confronted with death becomes more important than ever before, compelling us to new attention to that mystery which had been banished from our thoughts. Some time ago I was invited to lecture at Emmanuel College in Boston on "The History of Death and the Future of Dying," as part of a sixteen-week series titled "The Life Cycle," and I went and found a lecture hall of nearly three hundred people, most of whom were under twenty-five, and all of whom had paid good tuition money to hear a discourse on death. What brought them there? Fear, curiosity, hope, anger? What brought them there is in many ways what brings us to church—a rising consciousness of the mystery that surrounds us and a need to address that mystery which demands an unaccustomed humbleness at the point of transition where control is no longer our own.

It is at these extreme points in existence and transition that reason and relevance yield to the curious powers of mystery and faith, it is here that mystery affirms itself and moves beyond mere utility and understanding, and it is the central mystery of our faith that Saint Paul calls upon when, in the face of both evil and death, he affirms:

> No, in all these things we are more than conquerors through him who loved us. For I am sure that neither death, nor life, nor angels, nor principalities, nor things present, nor things to come, nor powers, nor depth, nor height, nor anything else in all creation will be able to separate us from the love of God in Christ Jesus our Lord.

Dare we say that reason is irrelevant and relevance an unreasonable requirement of religion? What about those who are unwilling to write off the last five hundred years as intellectual arrogance, those who with my predecessor George A. Buttrick would say that no church door should be so low that a believer must leave his head outside in order to worship. Must we have all these embarrassing miracles in order to have Jesus? In considering the consequences of mythology, did God say to Moses, "I have for you some good news and some bad news: The good news is that I will permit you to pass unharmed through the Red Sea. The bad news is that you will have to prepare an environmental impact statement"?

To the question "Is the Christian faith reasonable?" the answer must be no. That is not to say that there is no reason in Christianity, which is a different matter, but it is to say that by the measure of reasonable understanding faith is not reasonable, and if that makes you uncomfortable, that is the way it is supposed to be. It reminds us of the lady who heard the Archbishop of Canterbury preach on the end of the world. At the door she said, "Your Grace, I so much enjoyed that sermon," to which he replied, "But Madam, you weren't supposed to enjoy it." What the world calls "wisdom," Paul reminds us, is folly and foolishness to God, and what the world calls foolishness and weakness is the power of God unto salvation. What is reasonable about God made manifest in the flesh, vindicated by the Spirit, seen of Angels, and taken up into Glory? How do we explain those extraordinary phenomena of Christmas, Easter, the Ascension, and Pentecost? We don't. We confront them as emblematic of the central mystery of our faith, and we are driven to our knees in their presence not because we know but because we know only that we can do nothing else. It is true, then, as a clerical colleague suggests, that the university does not need more mastery but rather a greater sense of mystery, that humble awesomeness for which we long, and that is difficult of achievement: "In a world dedicated to the rational and workable," Eleanor McLaughlin writes, "to be as one called to mystery instead of mastery would invite laughter. One could expect to be ignored rather than martyred. Such a tone would not be taken seriously, and an academic career might well be put in jeopardy." Such indeed is the risk of our calling.

Mystery rather than mastery: Is that not a rather strange juxtaposition for our age? Indeed, one of the greatest casualties of our age has been just that loss of the sense of mystery, reverence, and awe which is at heart of any authentic religious experience. In our zest for rationality and intimacy we have made a fetish of desacralization. It was important in April 1969, for example, for the Students for a Democratic Society to seize University Hall, not because of what was in there, which were some files and a few frightened deans, but because that place was the center of the university's myth system; and thus was it necessary for those students to occupy not only the building but the holy of holies, the faculty room. They must sit in the president's chair and desecrate, as it were, the busts and memorabilia of past presidents. Just as the Parisian mobs of 1789 denuded Notre Dame of her sacred vessels, and Oliver Cromwell and his dreary partisans raped the cathedrals of England, so too have we in our zealous reason and relevance sought to level to our degree all that we see, and to destroy all that we do not understand. "God is dead," said those "famous" theologians of the sixties whom nobody remembers, "because he cannot fit into our cozy cosmology any longer." We have lost that sense of wonder, awe, and holiness. Like Adam and Eve we have tasted of the fruit of knowledge, and we have discovered that not only are we naked and can bear the sight neither of each other nor of God, but that we can do very little to hide our nakedness. If any parable is apt to tell us that what we do not need is more knowledge, this is it, and yet we persist in the notion that if we know better what we are doing, we will do it better and be the better for doing it.

One day I smelled incense in this church, so up I came from my office to find out what was going on, and I found myself in the midst of a Russian Orthodox funeral service in Appleton Chapel. Black-bearded and robed priests straight out of *Boris Godunov* were chanting the Burial Office for the Dead, with a large mixed choir singing the service with them. Up and down went the thick smoke of the censer, and I distinctly heard the rumble of generations of Peabodys and other Harvards turning in their tombs at Mount Auburn Cemetery. I was transfixed, and I stayed for the service although I knew neither the deceased nor a word of what was being said or sung. Yet, indeed, I did know what was going on, and I was a part of that worship not because I knew but because I was. Now, you may well say that they knew what was going on, and I trust that they did, but if I understood the essence of that liturgy, they knew that they were standing at the place beyond which knowledge would not take them. They knew that what they were doing, irrelevant to the needs of the world that day, was the most relevant thing possible to their souls and bodies at that moment, and I, ignorant of it all, was yet a part of it.

I fear that many of us feel that we will come nearer to the mystery, nearer to God, by a better translation, a more updated vernacular, a "kiss of peace, and a new and improved liturgy." Such efforts are not without their merit, and the church should never make a virtue of ignorance and antiquarianism, but such efforts are no substitute for that ultimate confrontation between self and Christ which is predicated upon what we do not know and cannot articulate, and cannot demonstrate in the terms that this world finds acceptable.

This is what T. S. Eliot means when he tells us in *Little Gidding*:

You are not here to verify,
Instruct yourself, or inform curiosity
Or carry report. You are here to kneel
Where prayer has been valid. And prayer is more
Than an order of words, the conscious occupation
Of the praying mind, or the sound of the voice praying.
And what the dead had no speech for when living,
They can tell you, being dead: the communication
Of the dead is tongued with fire beyond the language of the living.

We are then, as Paul reminds us in I Corinthians, "servants of Christ and stewards of the mysteries of God." We might wish to be "colleagues with Jesus and masters of the knowledge of God," but we are not, and the more often we are reminded of that, the better. We confront a mystery that confounds the world and our own capacity to understand and contain it: that Christ for our sake should take frail flesh and die, and that in his dying for our sake we might live. Great, great is the mystery of our religion:

He was manifested in the flesh,
Vindicated in the Spirit,
  Seen by angels,
Preached among the nations,
  Believed on in the world,
Taken up in Glory.

The Fellowship of the Incomplete

Text: . . . since God had foreseen something better for us, that apart from us they should not be made perfect.   *Hebrews 11:40*

In the medieval church one of the preacher's tasks was to instruct the faithful concerning the feasts and fasts of the church that would occur on the weekdays between Sundays, reminding them of their duty and of the meaning of the holy days in question. This practice in most Protestant churches is a casualty of the Reformation, and most holy days with it. We are freed, we are told, of such obligations, and the implied notion is that Sunday is sufficient. I have chosen over the years of my ministry to revive this custom from time to time, not so much because I am asked to do so but rather because I am moved to do so for your sake as well as for my own.

First, we must observe that All Saints' Day has as much to do with us as it does with the commemoration of those now long gone; it has as much to do with how we live our lives now as it ever had to do with how they lived their lives then. It has not so much to do with an esoteric community in the sky as it has to do with how we define and experience our community on earth, with how we engage in what can be called the search for fellowship.

Now, fellowship has a bad ring to it for many of us. Fellowship suggests a rather enforced camaraderie, which suggests that in church, at least, people become nicer over cookies and coffee. Some years ago a religion writer for a large midwestern daily decided to review Sunday church services in the exact same fashion as his colleagues reviewed plays and concerts. He would take himself each Sunday to a different church, and on Monday would publish in his column his findings, to the instruction of all and the irritation of many. He gave fair evaluation of the music, the sermon, and the aesthetics of the place, but what frequently received the most considered discussion was what we might call the fellowship aspect of the church, leading the writer to conclude, along with many others, that there can be nothing lonelier than a church's coffee hour. Fellowship, in our Protestant sense of that word, suggests a form of social intercourse that my English friends call "hearty," a quality peculiarly American, which in this context means less than sincere.

One could preach on the sociology, even on the theology, of coffee hours and Wednesday teas and the like, but it is fellowship of a far different sort of which I speak, a fellowship that is suggested both by our enigmatic text and the feast day toward which that text points us. Fellowship suggests belonging to, having a share in, being a part of something. A Fellow of an English college is a permanent member of the corporate body; fellowship in even its most colloquial sense implies a degree of participation and relatedness that is more than casual or occasional. When I think of fellowship, however, I think neither of coffee hours nor of corporate bodies but rather of some odd but apt lines from Willa Cather, called to my attention some years ago by my dear friend, the poet David Thompson Watson McCord. In her novel *My Ántonia* Miss Cather has one of her characters say, "That is happiness; to be dissolved into something complete and great." These words are carved upon her tombstone in Jaffrey, New Hampshire, and although an epitaph, the words are yet in some sense cousin to the sentiment of our text. Fellowship, like happiness, transcends the particular and the parochial self; it seeks for union with something worthy of our labor, loyalty, and love. The search for true fellowship is a pilgrimage toward that true belonging into which each of us yearns to enter, a belonging that has to do with what the theologians call "at-one-ment," or being at one; and for the believer and the seeker, the goal of the pilgrimage of life is to be at one with the creature, the creation, and the creator.

It took me a long time to realize that the Christian faith is not the triumph of individuals over evil, or even the solitary accomplishment of good, but rather a community, a fellowship of explicitly shared hopes and experiences, frustrations and failures. How long it has taken me to realize that there is no such thing as a "private" Christian, no such thing as a "personal" faith in the sense of its belonging to me and to no one else. The Bible, not to mention the historic witness of our faith, reminds us that from Genesis to Revelation we are part of God's revealed fellowship, that we belong to God and God belongs to us. At the creation God says that it is not good for man to be alone and so he creates for him a helpmeet, a companion, a woman. Even in the mind of God his creation cannot be fully realized or totally accomplished until there is a community, a fellowship, albeit of two, to receive and to share it.

Throughout the history of Israel and the fellowship of the New Testament church, it is to a community that God most fully reveals himself. Certainly individuals have their heroic and personal encounters with God, but if you think about it, these *tête-à-têtes* are never for the benefit of the individual but rather for the larger community, or the fellowship. "God so loved the world," we are told by Saint John; not just the church, not just Israel, not just you and me, but the world and all that is therein; and when we come to the close of the Bible it is with that book of the cosmic community, Revelation. In symmetry to the first creation it bespeaks a new creation in which the only object is the corporate worship of God by the fellowship of the redeemed. It cannot be escaped, it dare not be avoided. As T. S. Eliot puts it in "Choruses from *The Rock*":

> What life have you if you have not life together?
> There is no life that is not in community,

And no community not lived in praise of God.
Even the anchorite who meditates alone,
For whom days and nights repeat the praise of God
Prays for the church, the body of Christ incarnate.

It is the sense of community, of fellowship in the largest possible sense, toward which the church moves, and its definition of that fellowship is nothing less than the communion of saints expressed in the Festival of the Saints that the church keeps on All Saints' Day. Here it is not just the living and the proximate who are summoned together under the lordship of Christ, it is all who have been and all who ever will be with whom we are joined in that most radical and mystical of claims.

What a thrill it was for me as a young Christian to realize that the whole of God's history in the world belonged to me, and that I, a part of that whole history, belonged to God. It was perhaps from that consciousness that I first refused to allow the denominational map makers to tell me just what part of Christian history was mine and what part was not. Who were they to tell me that Abraham, Isaac, and Jacob belong only to the Jews and not to me as well? Who were they to tell me that I cannot pray on my knees or invoke the blessed Virgin Mary because "Protestants don't do that"? Who were they to say that the Christian faith is no larger than the particular corner of the world or experience in which it first came to be known? I refused to be deprived of the Apostles' Creed, the saints and martyrs, the witnesses and miracles, simply because they are not a part of the truncated tradition handed over to me. Am I not one with all who know the same Lord that I do, who have shared the wonder of that knowledge in all ages and in all times? Am I not a part of that ceaseless circle of praise of which Saint John speaks with such vivid power in his Revelation, whose object is the throne of God and the love of Christ, and from whom, as Saint Paul tells us, nothing can separate us? Indeed I am.

Now, when we celebrate All Saints' Day and read these wonderful accounts in the book of Hebrews, most of us identify with those great heroes and heroines of the faith, those people who did great things for God and who are justly and mightily remembered for those deeds. Of them we sing in the hymn "For All the Saints," "We feebly struggle, they in glory shine . . ." They have attained and we are still contending, but, and this is an enormous but, our text reminds us that the story is not over even for them, for you and I are yet part of the process of redemption and it will not be accomplished without us. God has not created us simply to be onlookers to his great work and to that of his servants, but to be participants in that work; indeed, apart from us these great heroes of the faith cannot be made perfect. We share with them in an unfinished drama; we with them are all part of the plan. As J. B. Phillips puts it in his modern translation:

> All these won a glowing testimony to their faith, but they did not then and there receive the fulfillment of the promise. God had some-thing better planned for our day, and it was not his plan that they should reach perfection without us.

There is an even stronger implication for us in this text. Not only are we involved, but the saints now gone depend in some measure upon us to continue, if not to finish, that for which they lived and died. Not only do we depend upon them, but in a very real sense, the text says, they depend upon us. Their perfection cannot be accomplished until we share with them in the fellowship of God's promise; we cannot rest on their laurels, even as they cannot rest upon ours. It is a community of coop-eration in which the dead, the living, and the yet-to-be-here share in that glory which is the presence of Christ and the perfect will of God. Think of it: Abraham and Sarah, Paul and Silas, Peter and John, Mary and Martha, all depend upon the likes of you and of me—and without us they are incomplete. We need each other.

All Saints' Day reminds us that the Christian faith is not so much the community of recollection as it is the fellowship of participation and anticipation, and we share both with the saints who without us will not be made perfect.

The word *saint* gives us some trouble, for it suggests perfection and the accomplishment of virtue. The saints of the Roman canon are people who have been attested to as holy and to whom miracles and mighty works are attached. They are in stained glass and on marble pedestals. They are not like you and like me. A saint in the early and reformed churches, however, was one who was engaged in a holy struggle, who was identified with the redeemed community, who was not so much perfect as persevering. In this sense Paul speaks of the saints at Corinth, who were naughty indeed; and the Pilgrims of my native Plymouth referred to themselves as the saints, not in the sense of having arrived but as yet on the journey. All who take the name of Jesus seriously and who associate themselves with his work, his will, and his church are saints by calling, and we all are imperfect until all is made perfect in God; all the saints, whether on earth, or in heaven, or yet in the mind of God, engage in the struggle for holiness, and as such we in this puny corner of the universe have fellowship with them. That is what is meant by the old gospel hymn we used to sing, "What a fellowship, what a joy divine, leaning on the everlasting arms . . ."

We then, dear fellow saints, are not alone, for we have the companionship of all of heaven with us and the hope of yet more to come. We share with one another and with those of whom we sing an inestimable fellowship, and in the midst of it all is that fellowship we share in God's revelation of himself in Jesus Christ our Lord. It was indeed the fellowship of his presence and promise that the bewildered apostles expressed in that blessed walk toward Emmaus, a presence in which he was made known to them in the breaking of bread. That was the fellowship for which they had longed, the abiding presence of which they were so anxious to be a part. We share in the fellowship of his presence, and we share in the fellowship of his promise that together with all his faithful ones in that perfect time that is to be we with them may receive the crown of glory that fadeth not away.

Redeeming the Familiar

❊

Text: Though the fig tree do not blossom, nor fruit be on the vines, the produce of the olive fail and the fields yield no food, the flocks be cut off from the fold and there be no herd in the stalls, yet I will rejoice in the Lord. I will joy in the God of my salvation.   *Habbakuk 3:17–18*

A week or so ago when I saw the Christmas lights being strung up across the city streets, and I saw the tinsel and the Santa Clauses in the store windows at Sears, I knew that Thanksgiving could not be far away; and sure enough, it has come and gone. A Plymouthian, I always spend Thanksgiving at home in Plymouth. Down there we claim a certain responsibility for this national festival, and if there were no Pilgrim fathers and mothers to tug at the national heartstrings, the cranberry and the turkey people, not to mention the greeting-card people and the football coaches, would be in the throes of economic and psychic depression. We all know the story so well, perhaps even too well: English immigrants, later to be called Pilgrims, sail rather by accident into Cape Cod harbor and claim the territory that they call New Plymouth. They work hard, fight plague, disease, and disaffection, and produce "The Mayflower Compact" and many children in the meanwhile. After a harvest in 1621, more bounteous than their meager skills at husbandry deserved, they had a harvest festival to which they invited the natives. Grateful to God for keeping them out of the hands of the Indians, their English creditors, and the evils of communism, they ate and drank themselves silly for three days.

In our ritual observance of this familiar story and holiday, however, there has been of recent years a new note: the discordant note of protest. The American Indians, most of whom we thought dwelt on obscure reservations or on even more obscure nickels, suddenly became turned on to the fact that they did not have very much for which to be thankful. In 1970, the 350th anniversary of the landing of the Pilgrims at Plymouth, these Indians conducted a "Day of Mourning," and this event has been repeated with increased pathos and ferocity each succeeding year. Many Plymouth people, and a large proportion of the Thanksgiving tourist population, resent what they feel to be the intrusion of these Indians upon the tranquillity of Thanksgiving Day.

The Indian protests, however, have managed to do what countless sermons and essays have not been able to: They have forced us to reexamine what has become for too many of us too familiar a story. They are, I suggest, a part of that necessary and irritating process that is redeeming the familiar not only for themselves but for us all as well. Now, I will be the last person to snatch one iota of praise and esteem from the Pilgrims of Plymouth, but I must hasten to say that Thanksgiving neither begins nor ends with them. Thanksgiving, if there is to be any at all, must begin and end with God. Once we have been able to liberate Thanksgiving from the clutches of the Pilgrim mystique as well as from the countercultural clutches of the protesters, and once we have been liberated from the "count-your-many-blessings-name-them-one-by-one" routine, we will have made a significant step in that process of redeeming the familiar. An old story can give a new perspective, and we will be able to live in our time just as truly as our foreparents lived in theirs.

I suggest that our text from Habbakuk is one means of redeeming the familiar notion of Thanksgiving for our use. Rather than a litany of all God's goodness to us or of God's wonderful attributes, we find a rather bleak and depressing picture painted for us. Failure rather than success seems to be the order of the day, and yet in the midst of that failure, in the midst of that privation, is that cry of hope and confidence: "I will rejoice in the Lord, I will joy in the God of my salvation." Thanksgiving begins not with our success and not even with ourselves; it begins with God.

One way toward redeeming the familiar in our own too familiar American story of Thanksgiving is to realize that we do not give thanks for the Pilgrims. Rather, we give thanks for that God whom they adored, that God to whom the slaves of Africa rendered praise, that God who caused Habbakuk and Job to rejoice in their misery, that God of all ages past and all ages yet to be. Thanksgiving, then, begins with God.

We are thankful not only for God's constancy and for our place in his plan, but, if we are truly to be a part of the process of redeeming the familiar, we are most thankful that with God we are given a second chance. When we miss our opportunities, when we fail in the few noble efforts that we make, we know that we are the children of a God who is loving and forgiving, who hates the sin but loves the sinner. We are thankful that we are children of the "second chance." It is God's forgiveness of our humanity and our forgiveness of our fellow humans that makes this process work. You know the parable of the unforgiving steward who owed his master a sum of money but was unable to pay it and begged mercy of his master, who forgave him the debt. This same steward had another servant in debt to him for a smaller figure than he himself owed, and he threatened to have his debtor thrown into jail. The incident was reported to the master, and the unjust steward was himself thrown into prison. Jesus concludes the story with this warning: "So also my heavenly Father will do to every one of you, if you do not forgive from your heart." It seems to me that forgiveness between God and man and between man and man is the true context for Thanksgiving. In his supreme act of forgiveness God sent us his Christ in the place of our Adam, and that Christ asked forgiveness for the very ones who put him to death.

Thanksgiving Day is not very far away from Advent and Christmas. That is an accident of the calendar, but it does represent a very important relationship, for it is in Advent and Christmas that we look forward to the coming again of our second chance. In the great expectations of that season, hope is reborn, and with it there is rekindled within each of us the sense that we can perhaps start afresh with a new slate. That is why it is such a welcome time, and that is why it has such a high claim upon the affections of people of great and of little faith. We are not washed up, the book is not closed, the last word has not been spoken or written, and we have cause for thanksgiving that we are privileged to live, as Auden says, "for the time being."

> Let us therefore be contrite but without anxiety,
> For powers and times are not gods but mortal gifts from God;
> Let us acknowledge our defeat but without despair
> For all societies and epochs are transient details,
> Transmitting an everlasting opportunity
> That the kingdom of heaven may come, not in our present
> And not in our future, but in the fullness of time.

God is. We are. In spite of our fumbles and because of God's grace we are not daunted by the troubles of this age, nor are we fearful of what is to come. We do not bless God for our wealth, our health, or for our feeble wisdom. We bless God that God is, that we are, and that his promise and love shall be with us when time itself shall be no more.

Though the fig tree do not blossom, nor fruit be on the vines, the produce of the olive fail and the fields yield no food, the flocks be cut off from the fold and there be no herd in the stalls, yet I will rejoice in the Lord. I will joy in the God of my salvation.